CLIFFS

Entry Level Mathematics
Test Review

by

Jerry Bobrow, Ph.D.

Contributing Author

David Arnold, M.S.

INCORPORATED

LINCOLN, NEBRASKA   68501

ACKNOWLEDGMENTS

I would like to thank my family: my wife, Susan; daughter, Jennifer Lynn; and my sons, Adam Michael and Jonathan Matthew, for their support during the time-consuming writing and editing process.

Jerry Bobrow

ISBN 0-8220-2071-8

SECOND EDITION

© Copyright 1992 by Jerry Bobrow

Previous edition © Copyright 1987 by Jerry Bobrow

PART III: STRATEGIES

Part I: Introduction

Why You Need This Guide

If you are planning to take the

ELM (Entry Level Mathematics) Test

and need an easy-to-use, understandable, well-focused review, this book is for YOU!

Cliffs *ELM Test Review* is designed specifically to review, refresh, and reintroduce many of the skills you need to pass the ELM. The author's nineteen years of teaching and directing test preparation programs at over thirty universities gives this guide a unique focus—a *test-oriented* math review.

Our unique approach combines insights and strategies with basic skills to bring back memories of mathematical rules once learned but since forgotten.

What This Guide Contains

Cliffs *ELM Test Review* provides an excellent and extensive overview of the areas you will encounter on the ELM test:

- Algebra—beginning and intermediate
- Geometry
- Word Problems and Graphs
- Test-taking Strategies

This book also includes a review of arithmetic as a refresher for basic computations.

Each review section includes a diagnostic test, explanations of rules and concepts with examples, practice problems with complete explanations, a review test, and a glossary. Throughout this guide, language will be nontechnical but consistent with the terminology used on most standardized exams.

ELM (Entry Level Mathematics Test)—General Description

The ELM test is designed to measure basic skill levels in algebra and plane geometry. The test's main purpose is to determine class placement for students in college level mathematics.

The test is 75 minutes long and is made up of 65 multiple-choice problems (five of which will be experimental, will not count towards your score, and may be scattered throughout the test). Each exam item is designed primarily to test understanding of mathematical concepts, not merely computational ability or memorization. Competency on the ELM test is considered to be a raw score of 39 or more problems correct out of the 60 that count. There is no penalty for guessing on the test; only right answers are counted.

The approximate number and percentage of problems in the skill areas are as follows:

Skill Area	Approximate Number of Problems	Percent of Problems That Count
Algebra	48	80%
Geometry	12	20%

How to Use This Guide

1. Review the materials regarding the ELM test provided by your local state university. This information is available free of charge and contains a few sample problems.
2. Set up a consistent study schedule. The time might be one to two hours each day or every other day but should be no longer than about two and a half hours at any one study period. This consistent schedule will be conducive to quiet, quality study time.
3. Take the diagnostic test in arithmetic.
4. Check your answers on the diagnostic arithmetic test. If your results warrant extensive arithmetic study, then—
5. Work through the arithmetic review and practice problems.
6. If your results on the arithmetic diagnostic test do not warrant extensive arithmetic review but you still have some weakness in that area, *skip step 5* but concentrate on the review sections

pertinent to your weaknesses. (The diagnostic test answers are keyed to appropriate review pages.)

7. Take the arithmetic review test.
8. Based on your results on the review test, review any sections still requiring improvement.
9. Follow the same procedure (steps 3 through 8) for each review section (algebra, geometry, word problems).
10. Read the introduction to graphs.
11. Notice that the final section of this guide includes strategies for general math problems. This section will help you "fine tune" your ELM review and improve your problem-solving skills.

Note: Since 80 % of the ELM test is devoted to algebra, spend most of your time on the algebra review.

QUESTIONS COMMONLY ASKED ABOUT THE ELM TEST

Q: WHO MUST TAKE THE ELM?
A: All undergraduate students admitted to a California State University are required to take the ELM *unless they qualify for exemption.* Check with your California State University (CSU) Admissions Office to see if you qualify for one of the exemptions.

Q: WHEN SHOULD I TAKE THE ELM?
A: Take the ELM as soon as possible after admission.

Q: HOW DO I REGISTER?
A: If you have not received a copy of the registration form in the mail, you may pick one up at any CSU Admissions Office. The registration form must be mailed to the test office on the campus where you wish to take the test.

Q: WHERE WILL THE TEST BE GIVEN?
A: The ELM will be given at all CSU campuses. You may register to take the test at whichever campus you choose; it does not have to be the campus you plan to attend.

Q: WHEN IS THE ELM GIVEN?
A: The ELM is given about four times a year. Check with your local CSU campus for the test dates.

Q: IS THERE LATE REGISTRATION?
A: Early registration is recommended. Registration is taken on a first-come, first-served basis; therefore, if you register late and the test center is filled, you may have to wait until the next scheduled administration.

Q: IS THERE WALK-IN REGISTRATION?
A: Walk-in registration may be available on a first-come, first-served basis provided that adequate materials and space are available after preregistered students have been admitted. *You should check with your testing office regarding walk-in policies and required materials.*

Q: WHAT MUST I TAKE TO THE TEST?
A: You must take (1) the validated admission ticket, (2) proper personal identification, such as driver's license, student ID, or any other official identification with a photograph (alternate official identification must have the registrant's signature), (3) a check or money order for the test fee (payable to Educational Testing Service) with your name appearing on the face of the check (no admittance without this test fee payment), (4) several number 2 lead pencils with erasers, and (5) a ball-point pen (only if you are taking the EPT—English Placement Test).

Q: WHAT CAN'T I TAKE WITH ME?
A: You may NOT take books, calculators, slide rules, watch calculators, rulers, or papers of any kind into the testing room.

Q: DO I GET SCRATCH PAPER FOR WORKING THE PROBLEMS?
A: No. All of your work will be done in the testing booklet, but you must transfer your answer as you complete each question onto a special answer sheet.

Q: HOW DO I RECEIVE MY TEST SCORES?
A: Your scores will be mailed to the address you provide on the day of the test.

Q: CAN I PREPARE FOR THE ELM TEST?

A: Yes. Reviewing arithmetic (if necessary), elementary and intermediate algebra, and geometry will be very helpful. If you have not taken a math course recently, a thorough review of these topics could improve your scores considerably. Remember, you should focus on algebra. Understanding and practicing test-taking strategies is also helpful.

Q: WHAT IS A PASSING SCORE?

A: 39 or more correct answers out of the 60 problems that count are considered to indicate competence in entry level mathematics.

Q: SHOULD I GUESS ON THE TEST?

A: Yes. Since there is no penalty for guessing, guess if you have to. If possible, first try to eliminate some of the choices to increase your chances of choosing the right answer. But always fill in an answer before you leave a question.

Part II: Basic Skills Review

Each review section includes:

- A diagnostic test to assess your strengths and weaknesses.
- Explanations of rules and concepts to demonstrate important mathematical processes.
- Practice problems with complete explanations to enable you to apply the rules and concepts.
- A review test to help you focus on areas still needing improvement.
- A glossary to assist in your understanding of mathematical terms used in problems and explanations.

Areas covered include:

- Arithmetic
- Algebra—beginning and intermediate
- Geometry
- Word Problems and Graphs

Remember, 80% of the ELM is devoted to algebra, and although a review of arithmetic will strengthen your basic skills, do not spend excessive time on an arithmetic review. You should, however, be familiar with the material on pages 57 through 78.

ARITHMETIC

ARITHMETIC DIAGNOSTIC TEST

Questions

1. Which of the following are integers? $\frac{1}{2}$, -2, 0, 4, 3.2

2. Which of the following are rational numbers?
   5.8, 6, $\frac{1}{4}$, $\sqrt{4}$, $\sqrt{7}$, π

3. Is 37 prime?

4. Which of the following are perfect cubes? 1, 6, 8, 9, 27

5. The commutative property of addition is represented by
   (A) $2 + (3 + 4) = (2 + 3) + 4$
   (B) $2 + (-2) = 0$
   (C) $3 + 5 = 5 + 3$

6. $(6 \times 10^4) + (3 \times 10^2) + (4 \times 10^{-1}) =$

7. Simplify $3[3^2 + 2(4 + 1)]$.

8. Round 4.4584 to the nearest thousandth.

9. $-4 + 8 =$

10. $-12 - 6 =$

11. $(-6)(-8) =$

12. 2,730 is divisible by which of the following? 3, 4, 8

13. Change $5\frac{3}{4}$ to an improper fraction.

14. Change $\frac{32}{6}$ to a mixed number in lowest terms.

15. $\frac{2}{7} + \frac{3}{5} =$

16. $1\frac{3}{8} + 2\frac{5}{6} =$

17. $11 - \frac{2}{3} =$

18. $6\frac{1}{8} - 3\frac{3}{4} =$

19. $-\frac{7}{8} - \frac{5}{9} =$

20. $-\frac{1}{6} \times \frac{1}{3} =$

21. $2\frac{3}{8} \times 1\frac{5}{6} =$

22. $-\frac{1}{4} \div \frac{9}{14} =$

23. $2\frac{3}{7} \div 1\frac{1}{4} =$

24. $\dfrac{1}{3 + \dfrac{2}{1 + \frac{1}{3}}} =$

25. $.08 + 1.3 + .562 =$

26. $.45 - .003 =$

27. $8.001 \times 2.4 =$

28. $.147 \div .7 =$

29. Change $\frac{3}{20}$ to a decimal.

30. Change 7% to a decimal.

31. 79% of 64 =

32. 40% of what is 20?

33. Change $\frac{1}{8}$ to a percent.

34. What is the percent increase of a rise in temperature from 80° to 100°?

35. Express .00000023 in scientific notation.

36. $(3.2 \times 10^3)(2.4 \times 10^8) =$

37. $(5.1 \times 10^6) \div (1.7 \times 10^2) =$

38. $8^3 \times 8^7 =$

39. $9^5 \div 9^2 =$

40. $(5^3)^2 =$

41. Approximate $\sqrt{30}$ to the nearest tenth.

42. Simplify $\sqrt{80}$.

43. $-\sqrt{9} =$

CONTENTS

44. $\sqrt[3]{64}$ =

45. Find the arithmetic mean, mode, median, and range of the following group of numbers: 6, 4, 4, 2, 5, 9

46. If 1 kilometer equals .6 mile, then 25 kilometers equal how many miles?

Answers

Page numbers following each answer refer to the review section applicable to this problem type.

1. $-2, 0, 4$ (p. 15)

2. 5.8, 6, ¼, $\sqrt{4}$ ($\sqrt{4}$ = 2) (p. 15)

3. yes (p. 15)

4. 1, 8, 27 (p. 15)

5. (C) (p. 16)

6. 60,300.4 (p. 19)

7. 57 (p. 20)

8. 4.458 (p. 22)

9. 4 (p. 24)

10. -18 (p. 25)

11. 48 (p. 26)

12. 3 (p. 27)

13. $^{23}/_4$ (p. 30)

14. $5^2/_6 = 5^1/_3$ (p. 30)

15. $^{31}/_{35}$ (p. 36)

16. $4^5/_{24}$ (p. 41)

17. $10^1/_3$ (p. 43)

18. $2^3/_8$ (p. 43)

19. $- ^{103}/_{72} = -1^{31}/_{72}$ (p. 40)

20. $- ^1/_{18}$ (p. 44)

21. $^{209}/_{48} = 4^{17}/_{48}$ (p. 45)

22. $- ^7/_{18}$ (p. 46)

23. $^{68}/_{35} = 1^{33}/_{35}$ (p. 48)

24. $^2/_9$ (p. 49)

25. 1.942 (p. 51)

26. .447 (p. 51)

27. 19.2024 (p. 52)

28. .21 (p. 53)

29. .15 (p. 53)

30. .07 (p. 55)

31. 50.56 (p. 57)

32. 50 (p. 57)

33. 12½% or 12.5% (p. 55)

34. 25% (p. 61)

35. 2.3×10^{-7} (p. 62)

36. 7.68×10^{11} (p. 63)

37. 3×10^4 (p. 64)

38. 8^{10} (p. 67)

39. 9^3 (p. 67)

40. 5^6 (p. 67)

41. 5.5 (p. 69)

42. $4\sqrt{5}$ (p. 71)

43. -3 (p. 68)

44. 4 (p. 68)

45. mean = 5 (p. 72)
    mode = 4 (p. 75)
    median = 4½ or 4.5 (p. 74)
    range = 7 (p. 75)

46. 15 miles (p. 77)

ARITHMETIC REVIEW

You should already be familiar with the fundamentals of addition, subtraction, multiplication, and division of whole numbers (0, 1, 2, 3, . . .). The following is a review of signed numbers, fractions, decimals, and important additional topics from arithmetic.

Preliminaries

Groups of Numbers

● In doing arithmetic and algebra, we work with several groups of numbers.

NATURAL or COUNTING NUMBERS: The numbers 1, 2, 3, 4, . . . are called natural or counting numbers.
WHOLE NUMBERS: The numbers 0, 1, 2, 3, . . . are called whole numbers.
INTEGERS: The numbers . . . -2, -1, 0, 1, 2, . . . are called integers.
NEGATIVE INTEGERS: The numbers . . . -3, -2, -1 are called negative integers.
POSITIVE INTEGERS: The natural numbers are sometimes called the positive integers.
RATIONAL NUMBERS: Fractions, such as $\frac{3}{2}$ or $\frac{7}{8}$, are called rational numbers. Since a number such as 5 may be written as $\frac{5}{1}$, all *integers* are *rational numbers.*
IRRATIONAL NUMBERS: Another type of number is an irrational number. Examples of irrational numbers are $\sqrt{3}$ and π.
REAL NUMBERS: Real numbers consist of all *rational* and *irrational* numbers. Typically most standardized exams use only real numbers, which are the numbers you are used to using.
PRIME NUMBERS: A prime number is a number that can be evenly divided by only itself and 1. For example, 19 is a prime number because it can be evenly divided only by 19 and 1, but 21 is not a prime number because 21 can be evenly divided by other numbers (3 and 7). The only even prime number is 2; thereafter, any even number may be divided evenly by 2. Zero and 1 are *not* prime numbers. The first ten prime numbers are 2, 3, 5, 7, 11, 13, 17, 19, 23, and 29.
ODD NUMBERS: Odd numbers are whole numbers not divisible by 2: 1, 3, 5, 7, . . .

EVEN NUMBERS: Even numbers are numbers divisible by 2: 0, 2, 4, 6, . . .

COMPOSITE NUMBERS: A composite number is a number divisible by more than just 1 and itself: 4, 6, 8, 9, 10, 12, 14, 15, . . .

SQUARES: Squares are the result when numbers are multiplied by themselves: $(2 \cdot 2 = 4)$, $(3 \cdot 3 = 9)$; 1, 4, 9, 16, 25, 36 . . .

CUBES: Cubes are the result when numbers are multiplied by themselves twice: $(2 \cdot 2 \cdot 2 = 8)$, $(3 \cdot 3 \cdot 3 = 27)$; 1, 8, 27 . . .

Ways to Show Multiplication

• There are several ways to show multiplication. They are

$$4 \times 3 = 12 \qquad 4(3) = 12$$
$$4 \cdot 3 = 12 \qquad (4)3 = 12$$
$$(4)(3) = 12$$

Common Math Symbols

• Symbol references:

$=$ is equal to	$\geq$ is greater than or equal to
$\neq$ is not equal to	$\leq$ is less than or equal to
$>$ is greater than	$\parallel$ is parallel to
$<$ is less than	$\perp$ is perpendicular to

Properties of Basic Mathematical Operations

• While the following *terms* are not likely to be tested, understanding the concepts can be helpful.

Some Properties (Axioms) of Addition

• *Closure* is when all answers fall into the original set. If you add two even numbers, the answer is still an even number; therefore the set of even numbers *is closed* under addition (has closure). $(2 + 4 = 6)$ If you add two odd numbers, the answer is not an odd number; therefore the set of odd numbers is *not closed* under addition (no closure). $(3 + 5 = 8)$

• *Commutative* means that the *order* does not make any difference.

$$2 + 3 = 3 + 2$$
$$a + b = b + a$$

Note: Commutative does *not* hold for subtraction.

$$3 - 1 \neq 1 - 3$$
$$a - b \neq b - a$$

- *Associative* means that the *grouping* does not make any difference.

$$(2 + 3) + 4 = 2 + (3 + 4)$$
$$(a + b) + c = a + (b + c)$$

The grouping has changed (parentheses moved), but the sides are still equal.
Note: Associative does *not* hold for subtraction.

$$4 - (3 - 1) \neq (4 - 3) - 1$$
$$a - (b - c) \neq (a - b) - c$$

- The *identity element* for addition is 0. Any number added to 0 gives the original number

$$3 + 0 = 3$$
$$a + 0 = a$$

- The *additive inverse* is the opposite (negative) of the number. Any number plus its additive inverse equals 0 (the identity).

$$3 + (-3) = 0; \text{ therefore 3 and } -3 \text{ are inverses}$$
$$-2 + 2 = 0; \text{ therefore } -2 \text{ and 2 are inverses}$$
$$a + (-a) = 0; \text{ therefore a and } -a \text{ are inverses}$$

Some Properties (Axioms) of Multiplication

- *Closure* is when all answers fall into the original set. If you multiply two even numbers, the answer is still an even number; therefore the set of even numbers *is closed* under multiplication (has closure). ($2 \times 4 = 8$). If you multiply two odd numbers, the answer is an odd number; therefore the set of odd numbers *is closed* under multiplication (has closure). ($3 \times 5 = 15$)

• *Commutative* means that the *order* does not make any difference.

$$2 \times 3 = 3 \times 2$$
$$a \times b = b \times a$$

Note: Commutative does *not* hold for division.

$$2 \div 4 \neq 4 \div 2$$

• *Associative* means that the *grouping* does not make any difference.

$$(2 \times 3) \times 4 = 2 \times (3 \times 4)$$
$$(a \times b) \times c = a \times (b \times c)$$

The grouping has changed (parentheses moved) but the sides are still equal.
Note: Associative does *not* hold for division.

$$(8 \div 4) \div 2 \neq 8 \div (4 \div 2)$$

• The *identity element* for multiplication is 1. Any number multiplied by 1 gives the original number.

$$3 \times 1 = 3$$
$$a \times 1 = a$$

• The *multiplicative inverse* is the reciprocal of the number. Any number multiplied by its reciprocal equals 1.

$$2 \times \frac{1}{2} = 1; \text{ therefore 2 and } \frac{1}{2} \text{ are inverses}$$
$$a \times \frac{1}{a} = 1; \text{ therefore a and } \frac{1}{a} \text{ are inverses}$$

A Property of Two Operations

• The *distributive property* is the process of distributing the number on the outside of the parentheses to each term on the inside.

$$2(3 + 4) = 2(3) + 2(4)$$
$$a(b + c) = a(b) + a(c)$$

Note: You cannot use the distributive property with only one operation.

$$3(4 \times 5 \times 6) \neq 3(4) \times 3(5) \times 3(6)$$
$$a(bcd) \neq a(b) \times a(c) \times a(d) \text{ or } (ab)(ac)(ad)$$

Place Value

● Each position in any number has *place value*. For instance, in the number 485, the 4 is in the hundreds place, 8 is in the tens place, and 5 is in the ones place. Thus, place value is as follows:

3 , 0 9 2 , 3 4 5 , 8 7 6 . 4 3 6 2 9 7 0 2

billions — hundred millions — ten millions — millions — hundred thousands — ten thousands — thousands — hundreds — tens — ones — tenths — hundredths — thousandths — ten-thousandths — hundred-thousandths — millionths — ten-millionths — hundred-millionths — etc.

Practice: Place Value Problems

1. Which digit is in the tens place in 483?
2. In 36,548, which digit is in the thousands place?
3. The digit 7 is in which place in 45,328.769?
4. Which digit is in the hundredths place in 25.0671?
5. Which digit is in the ten millions place in 867,451,023.79?

Answers: Place Value Problems

1. 8   2. 6   3. tenths   4. 6   5. 6

Expanded Notation

● Sometimes numbers are written in *expanded notation* to point out the place value of each digit. For example, 345 can be written

$$300 + 40 + 5$$
$$(3 \times 100) + (4 \times 10) + (5 \times 1)$$
$$(3 \times 10^2) + (4 \times 10^1) + (5 \times 10^0)$$

These last two are the more common forms of expanded notation, one with exponents, one without exponents. Notice that in these, the digit is multiplied times its place value—1's, 10's, 100's, etc.

Another example: 43.25 can be written

$$40 + 3 + .2 + .05$$
$$(4 \times 10) + (3 \times 1) + (2 \times \tfrac{1}{10}) + (5 \times \tfrac{1}{100})$$
$$(4 \times 10^1) + (3 \times 10^0) + (2 \times 10^{-1}) + (5 \times 10^{-2})$$

Notice that the tenths place is 10^{-1} and the hundredths place is 10^{-2}, and so on.

Practice: Expanded Notation Problems

Write in expanded notation using exponents.

1. 576   2. 1,489   3. 3.581   4. 302,400

Answers: Expanded Notation Problems

1. $(5 \times 10^2) + (7 \times 10^1) + (6 \times 10^0)$
2. $(1 \times 10^3) + (4 \times 10^2) + (8 \times 10^1) + (9 \times 10^0)$
3. $(3 \times 10^0) + (5 \times 10^{-1}) + (8 \times 10^{-2}) + (1 \times 10^{-3})$
4. $(3 \times 10^5) + (0 \times 10^4) + (2 \times 10^3) + (4 \times 10^2) + (0 \times 10^1) +$
    (0×10^0) *or* $(3 \times 10^5) + (2 \times 10^3) + (4 \times 10^2)$

Grouping Symbols: Parentheses, Brackets, Braces

Parentheses ( )

● *Parentheses* are used to group numbers or variables. Everything inside parentheses must be done before any other operations. *For example:*

$$50(2 + 6) = 50(8) = 400$$

When a parenthesis is preceded by a minus sign, to remove the parentheses, change the sign of each term within the parentheses. *For example:*

$$6 - (-3 + a - 2b + c) =$$
$$6 + 3 - a + 2b - c = 9 - a + 2b - c$$

Brackets [ ] and Braces { }

● *Brackets* and *braces* are also used to group numbers or variables. Technically, they are used after parentheses. Parentheses are to be used first, then brackets, then braces: $\{[()]\}$ Sometimes, instead of brackets or braces, you will see the use of larger parentheses.

$$\left((3 + 4) \cdot 5\right) + 2$$

A number using all three grouping symbols would look like this

$$2\{1 + [4(2 + 1) + 3]\}$$

and simplified as follows (notice that you work from the inside out):

$$2\{1 + [4(2 + 1) + 3]\} =$$
$$2\{1 + [4(3) + 3]\} =$$
$$2\{1 + [12 + 3]\} =$$
$$2\{1 + [15]\} =$$
$$2\{16\} =$$
$$32$$

Order of Operations

● If multiplication, division, powers, addition, parentheses, etc., are all contained in one problem, the *order of operations* is as follows.

1. parentheses
2. powers and square roots
3. multiplication⎫ whichever comes first left to right
4. division⎭
5. addition⎫ whichever comes first left to right
6. subtraction⎭

Examples:

1. $6 + 4 \times 3 =$
   $6 + 12 =$ (multiplication)
   18 (then addition)

2. $10 - 3 \times 6 + 10^2 + (6 + 1) \times 4 =$
   $10 - 3 \times 6 + 10^2 + (7) \times 4 =$ (parentheses first)
   $10 - 3 \times 6 + 100 + (7) \times 4 =$ (powers next)
   $10 - 18 + 100 + 28 =$ (multiplication)
   $-8 + 100 + 28 =$ (addition/subtraction left to right)
   $92 + 28 = 120$

An easy way to remember the order of operations *after parentheses* is: **P**lease **M**y **D**ear **A**unt **S**arah (**P**owers, **M**ultiplication, **D**ivision, **A**ddition, **S**ubtraction).

Practice: Order of Operations Problems

Simplify:

1. $6 + 4 \times 3^2$
2. $3^2 + 6(4 + 1)$
3. $12 - 2(8 + 2) + 5$
4. $8[3(3^2 - 8) + 1]$

5. $6\{4[2(3 + 2) - 8] - 8\}$
6. $6(12 + 8) \div 2 + 1$

Answers: Order of Operations Problems

1. $6 + 4 \times 3^2 =$
   $6 + 4 \times 9 =$
   $6 + 36 =$
   42

2. $3^2 + 6(4 + 1) =$
   $9 + 6(5) =$
   $9 + 30 =$
   39

3. $12 - 2(8 + 2) + 5 =$
   $12 - 2(10) + 5 =$
   $12 - 20 + 5 =$
   $-8 + 5 =$
   -3

4. $8[3(3^2 - 8) + 1] =$
   $8[3(9 - 8) + 1] =$
   $8[3(1) + 1] =$
   $8[3 + 1] =$
   $8[4] =$
   32

5. $6\{4[2(3 + 2) - 8] - 8\} =$
   $6\{4[2(5) - 8] - 8\} =$
   $6\{4[10 - 8] - 8\} =$
   $6\{4[2] - 8\} =$
   $6\{8 - 8\} =$
   $6\{0\} =$
   0

6. $6(12 + 8) \div 2 + 1 =$
   $6(20) \div 2 + 1 =$
   $120 \div 2 + 1 =$
   $60 + 1 =$
   61

Rounding Off

● To *round off* any number:

1. Underline the place value to which you're rounding off.
2. Look to the immediate right (one place) of your underlined place value.
3. Identify the number (the one to the right). If it is 5 or higher,

round your underlined place value up 1. If the number (the one to the right) is 4 or less, leave your underlined place value as it is and change all the other numbers to its right to zeros. *For example:* Round to the nearest thousand:

345,678 becomes 346,000
928,499 becomes 928,000

This works with decimals as well. Round to the nearest hundredth:

3.4678 becomes 3.47
298,435.083 becomes 298,435.08

Notice that the numbers to the right of the rounded digit are dropped when working with decimals.

Practice: Rounding Off Problems

1. Round off 137 to the nearest ten.
2. Round off 4,549 to the nearest hundred.
3. Round off .4758 to the nearest hundredth.
4. Round off 99.483 to the nearest one.
5. Round off 6,278.38512 to the nearest thousandth.

Answers: Rounding Off Problems

1. 140   2. 4,500   3. .48   4. 99   5. 6,278.385

Signed Numbers (Positive Numbers and Negative Numbers)

Number Lines

● On a *number line,* numbers to the right of 0 are positive. Numbers to the left of 0 are negative, as follows.

Given any two numbers on a number line, the one on the right is always larger, regardless of its sign (positive or negative). Note that fractions may also be placed on a number line. *For example:*

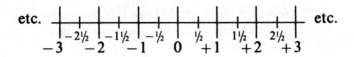

Practice: Number Line Problems

Complete the number line below, and then locate

1. $+2$ 2. -3 3. $+1\frac{1}{2}$ 4. $-\frac{1}{2}$ 5. $+3\frac{1}{4}$

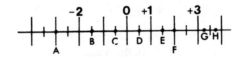

Answers: Number Line Problems

1. F   2. A   3. E   4. C   5. G

Addition of Signed Numbers

● When *adding two numbers with the same sign* (either both positive or both negative), add the numbers and keep the same sign. *For example:*

$$
\begin{array}{r} +5 \\ +\ +7 \\ \hline +12 \end{array}
\qquad
\begin{array}{r} -8 \\ +\ -3 \\ \hline -11 \end{array}
$$

When *adding two numbers with different signs* (one positive and one negative), subtract the numbers and keep the sign from the larger one. *For example:*

$$
\begin{array}{r} +5 \\ +\ -7 \\ \hline -2 \end{array}
\qquad
\begin{array}{r} -59 \\ +\ +72 \\ \hline +13 \end{array}
$$

Signed numbers may also be added "horizontally." *For example:*

$$+9 + 6 = +15$$
$$-12 + 9 = -3$$
$$8 + (-5) = 3$$

Practice: Addition of Signed Numbers Problems

1. $+25 + 8 =$

2. $-10 + 15 =$

3. $\begin{array}{r} -7 \\ + -3 \\ \hline \end{array}$

4. $\begin{array}{r} -82 \\ + +60 \\ \hline \end{array}$

5. $-18 + (+5) =$

Answers: Addition of Signed Numbers Problems

1. $+33$ 2. $+5$ 3. -10 4. -22 5. -13

Subtraction of Signed Numbers

● To *subtract positive and/or negative numbers,* just change the sign of the number being subtracted and then add. *For example:*

$$\begin{array}{r} +12 \\ - +4 \\ \hline \end{array} \qquad \begin{array}{r} -14 \\ - -4 \\ \hline \end{array} \qquad \begin{array}{r} -19 \\ - +6 \\ \hline \end{array} \qquad \begin{array}{r} +20 \\ - -3 \\ \hline \end{array}$$

$$\begin{array}{r} +12 \\ + -4 \\ \hline +8 \end{array} \qquad \begin{array}{r} -14 \\ + +4 \\ \hline -10 \end{array} \qquad \begin{array}{r} -19 \\ + -6 \\ \hline -25 \end{array} \qquad \begin{array}{r} +20 \\ + +3 \\ \hline +23 \end{array}$$

This may also be done "horizontally." *For example:*

$$+12 - (+4) = +12 + (-4) = 8$$
$$+16 - (-6) = +16 + (+6) = 22$$
$$-20 - (+3) = -20 + (-3) = -23$$
$$-5 - (-2) = -5 + (+2) = -3$$

Practice: Subtraction of Signed Numbers Problems

1. $\begin{array}{r} +9 \\ - +3 \\ \hline \end{array}$

2. $\begin{array}{r} +25 \\ - -9 \\ \hline \end{array}$

3. $+36 - (-5) =$

4. $-27 - (+4) =$

5. $-30 - (-2) =$

Answers: Subtraction of Signed Numbers Problems

1. $+6$ 2. $+34$ 3. $+41$ 4. -31 5. -28

Minus Preceding Parenthesis

- If a *minus precedes a parenthesis,* it means everything within the parentheses is to be subtracted. Therefore, using the same rule as in subtraction of signed numbers, simply change every sign within the parentheses to its opposite, and then add.

Examples:

1. $9 - (+3 - 5 + 7 - 6) =$
   $9 + (-3 + 5 - 7 + 6) =$
   $9 + (+1) =$
   10

2. $20 - (+35 - 50 + 100) =$
   $20 + (-35 + 50 - 100) =$
   $20 + (-85) =$
   -65

Practice: Minus Preceding Parenthesis Problems

1. $2 - (+5 - 3) =$
2. $6 - (+8 - 5 + 10) =$
3. $10 - (-12 - 5 + 3) =$
4. $25 - (-4 + 7 - 8 - 5 + 6) =$

Answers: Minus Preceding Parenthesis Problems

1. $2 - (+2) = 2 + (-2) = 0$
2. $6 - (+13) = 6 + (-13) = -7$
3. $10 - (-14) = 10 + (+14) = 24$
4. $25 - (-4) = 25 + (+4) = 29$

Multiplying and Dividing Signed Numbers

- To *multiply or divide signed numbers,* treat them just like regular numbers but remember this rule: An odd number of negative signs will produce a negative answer. An even number of negative signs will produce a positive answer. *For example:*

$$(-3)(+8)(-5)(-1)(-2) = +240$$
$$(-3)(+8)(-1)(-2) = -48$$

$$\frac{-64}{-2} = +32$$

$$\frac{-64}{+2} = -32$$

Practice: Multiplying and Dividing Signed Number Problems

1. $(-3)(+9) =$

2. $-8 \div -2 =$

3. $(-8)(+3)(-2) =$

4. $\dfrac{-10}{+5} =$

5. $\dfrac{(-4)(+2)(-6)}{-12} =$

Answers: Multiplying and Dividing Signed Number Problems

1. -27 2. $+4$ 3. $+48$ 4. -2 5. -4

Multiplying and Dividing Using Zero

- Zero times any number equals zero. *For example:*

$$0 \times 5 = 0$$
$$0 \times (-3) = 0$$
$$8 \times 9 \times 3 \times (-4) \times 0 = 0$$

- Likewise, zero divided by any number is zero. *For example:*

$$0 \div 5 = 0$$

$$\frac{0}{3} = 0$$

$$0 \div (-6) = 0$$

Important Note: Dividing by zero is "undefined" and is not permitted. *For example:*

$$\frac{6}{0} \text{ is not permitted}$$

because there is no such answer. The answer *is not* zero.

Divisibility Rules

- The following set of rules can help you save time in trying to check the divisibility of numbers.

A NUMBER IS DIVISIBLE BY	IF
2	it ends in 0, 2, 4, 6, or 8
3	the total of its digits is divisible by 3
4	the number formed by the last two digits is divisible by 4
5	if it ends in 0 or 5
6	if it is divisible by 2 and 3 (use the rules for both)
7	(no simple rule)
8	the number formed by the last three digits is divisible by 8
9	the total of its digits is divisible by 9

Examples: Divisibility Rules

1. Is 126 divisible by 3? Total of digits = 9. Since 9 is divisible by 3, 126 is divisible by 3.
2. Is 1,648 divisible by 4? Since 48 is divisible by 4, then 1,648 is divisible by 4.
3. Is 186 divisible by 6? Since 186 ends in 6, it is divisible by 2. Total of digits = 15. Since 15 is divisible by 3, 186 is divisible by 3. 186 is divisible by 2 and 3; therefore it is divisible by 6.
4. Is 2,488 divisible by 8? Since 488 is divisible by 8, then 2,488 is divisible by 8.
5. Is 2,853 divisible by 9? Total of digits = 18. Since 18 is divisible by 9, then 2,853 is divisible by 9.

Practice: Divisibility Problems

1. 4,620 is divisible by which of the following numbers?
   2, 3, 4, 5, 6, 7, 8, 9
2. 13,131 is divisible by which of the following numbers?
   2, 3, 4, 5, 6, 7, 8, 9

Answers: Divisibility Problems

1. 2, 3, 4, 5, 6, 7

   2—the number is even
   3—the digits total 12, which is divisible by 3
   4—the number formed by the last two digits, 20, is divisible by 4
   5—the number ends in 0
   6—the number is divisible by 2 and 3
   7—divide 4,620 by 7 and you get 660
   8̸—the number formed by the last three digits, 620, is not divisible by 8
   9̸—the total of the digits is 12, which is not divisible by 9

2. 3, 9

   2̸—the number is not even
   3—the digits total 9, which is divisible by 3
   4̸—the number is not even
   5̸—the number does not end in 0 or 5
   6̸—the number is not even
   7—divide and you will see that there is a remainder
   8̸—the number is not even
   9—the digits total 9, which is divisible by 9

Common Fractions

Numerator and Denominator

● Fractions consist of two numbers: a *numerator* (which is above the line) and a *denominator* (which is below the line).

$$\frac{1 \; numerator}{2 \; denominator} \quad \text{or} \quad numerator \; 1/2 \; denominator$$

The denominator lets us know the number of equal parts into which something is divided. The numerator tells us how many of these equal parts are being considered. Thus, if the fraction is ⅗ of a pie, then the denominator 5 tells us that the pie has been divided into 5 equal parts, of which 3 (numerator) are in the fraction. Sometimes it helps to think of the dividing line (in the middle of a fraction) as meaning "out of." In other words, ⅗ would also mean 3 "out of" 5 equal pieces from the whole pie. All rules for signed numbers also apply to fractions.

Negative Fractions

● Fractions may be *negative* as well as positive. (See number line on p. 22.) However, negative fractions are typically written

$$-\frac{3}{4} \quad \text{not} \quad \frac{-3}{4} \quad \text{or} \quad \frac{3}{-4} \quad \text{(although they are all equal)}$$

$$-\frac{3}{4} = \frac{-3}{4} = \frac{3}{-4}$$

Proper Fractions and Improper Fractions

● A fraction like ⅗, where the numerator is smaller than the denominator, is less than one. This kind of fraction is called a *proper fraction.* But sometimes a fraction may be more than one. This is when the numerator is larger than the denominator.

Thus, ¹²⁄₇ is more than one. This is called an *improper fraction.*

Examples of proper fractions: ⁴⁄₇, ²⁄₅, ¹⁄₉, ¹⁰⁄₁₂

Examples of improper fractions: ⁷⁄₄, ³⁄₂, ¹⁰⁄₃, ¹⁶⁄₁₅

Mixed Numbers

● When a term contains both a whole number (3, 8, 25, etc.) and a fraction (½, ¼, ¾, etc.), it is called a *mixed number.* For instance, 5¼ and 290¾ are both mixed numbers. To change an improper fraction to a mixed number, you divide the denominator into the numerator. *For example:*

$$\frac{18}{5} = 3\tfrac{3}{5} \qquad\qquad 5\overline{)18} \;\; \begin{array}{r} 3 \\ \underline{15} \\ 3 \end{array}$$

To change a mixed number to an improper fraction, you multiply the denominator times the whole number, add in the numerator, and put the total over the original denominator. *For example:*

$$4\tfrac{1}{2} = \tfrac{9}{2} \qquad\qquad 2 \times 4 + 1 = 9$$

Practice: Mixed Number Problems

Change the following improper fractions to mixed numbers.

1. $\frac{3}{2}$ 2. $\frac{7}{4}$ 3. $\frac{10}{3}$ 4. $\frac{16}{5}$ 5. $\frac{23}{4}$

Change the following mixed numbers to improper fractions.

6. $1\frac{3}{4}$ 7. $4\frac{1}{2}$ 8. $5\frac{3}{4}$ 9. $21\frac{3}{4}$ 10. $8\frac{4}{5}$

Answers: Mixed Number Problems

1. $1\frac{1}{2}$ 5. $5\frac{3}{4}$ 9. $\frac{87}{4}$
2. $1\frac{3}{4}$ 6. $\frac{7}{4}$ 10. $\frac{44}{5}$
3. $3\frac{1}{3}$ 7. $\frac{9}{2}$
4. $3\frac{1}{5}$ 8. $\frac{23}{4}$

Equivalent Fractions

Reducing Fractions

● A fraction must be *reduced* to *lowest terms*. This is done by dividing both the numerator and denominator by the largest number that will divide evenly into both. For example, $\frac{10}{25}$ is reduced to $\frac{2}{5}$ by dividing both numerator and denominator by 5. *Other examples:*

$$\frac{30}{50} = \frac{30 \div 10}{50 \div 10} = \frac{3}{5}$$

$$\frac{8}{40} = \frac{8 \div 8}{40 \div 8} = \frac{1}{5}$$

$$\frac{9}{15} = \frac{9 \div 3}{15 \div 3} = \frac{3}{5}$$

Practice: Reducing Fractions Problems

Reduce the following fractions.

1. $\frac{6}{8}$ 2. $\frac{15}{20}$ 3. $\frac{18}{36}$ 4. $\frac{40}{90}$ 5. $\frac{75}{30}$

Answers: Reducing Fractions Problems

1. ¾   2. ¾   3. ½   4. ⁴⁄₉   5. ⁵⁄₂

Enlarging Denominators

● The *denominator* of a fraction may be *enlarged* by multiplying both the numerator and the denominator by the same number. *For example:*

$$\frac{1}{2} = \frac{1 \times 5}{2 \times 5} = \frac{5}{10}$$

$$\frac{3}{4} = \frac{3 \times 10}{4 \times 10} = \frac{30}{40}$$

Practice: Enlarging Denominators Problems

1. Change ⅗ to tenths.
2. Express ¾ as eighths.
3. ⁵⁄₇ = ²⁄₂₁
4. ²⁄₁₅ = ²⁄₄₅
5. Change the fraction ⅜ to an equivalent fraction with a denominator of 24.

Answers: Enlarging Denominators Problems

1. ⁶⁄₁₀   2. ⁶⁄₈   3. ¹⁵⁄₂₁   4. ⁶⁄₄₅   5. ⁹⁄₂₄

Factors

● *Factors* of a number are those whole numbers which when multiplied together yield the number. *For example:* What are the factors of 8?

$$8 = 2 \times 4$$
$$8 = 1 \times 8$$

Therefore, the factors of 8 are 4 and 2 because $4 \times 2 = 8$ and 1 and 8 because $1 \times 8 = 8$.

What are the factors of 24?

$$24 = 1 \times 24$$
$$= 2 \times 12$$
$$= 3 \times 8$$
$$= 4 \times 6$$

Therefore, the factors of 24 are 1, 2, 3, 4, 6, 8, 12, and 24.

Practice: Factor Problems

Find the factors of

1. 6   2. 9   3. 12   4. 48

Answers: Factor Problems

1. 1, 2, 3, and 6   3. 1, 2, 3, 4, 6, and 12
2. 1, 3, and 9   4. 1, 2, 3, 4, 6, 8, 12, 16, 24, and 48

Common Factors

● *Common factors* are those factors which are the same for two or more numbers. For example: What are the common factors of 6 and 8?

6: 1, 2, 3, 6
8: 1, 2, 4, 8

1 and 2 are common factors of 6 and 8. *Note:* Some numbers may have many common factors. *For example:* What are the common factors of 24 and 36?

24: 1, 2, 3, 4, 6, 8, 12, 24
36: 1, 2, 3, 4, 6, 9, 12, 18, 36

Thus the common factors of 24 and 36 are 1, 2, 3, 4, 6, and 12.

Practice: Common Factor Problems

Find the common factors of

1. 10 and 30   3. 6 and 15
2. 12 and 18   4. 70 and 80

Answers: Common Factor Problems

1. 1, 2, 5, and 10   3. 1 and 3
2. 1, 2, 3, and 6   4. 1, 2, 5, and 10

Greatest Common Factor

● The *greatest common factor* is the largest factor common to two or more numbers. *For example:* What is the greatest common factor of 12 and 30?

$$12: ①,②,③, 4,⑥, 12$$

$$30: ①,②,③, 5,⑥, 10, 15, 30$$

Notice that while, 1, 2, 3, and 6 are all common factors of 12 and 30, only 6 is the greatest common factor.

Practice: Greatest Common Factor Problems

Find the greatest common factor of

1. 6 and 12   3. 24 and 60
2. 24 and 40   4. 40 and 100

Answers: Greatest Common Factor Problems

1. 6   2. 8   3. 12   4. 20

Multiples

● *Multiples* of a number are found by multiplying that number by 1, by 2, by 3, by 4, by 5, etc. *For example:*

Multiples of 3 are: 3, 6, 9, 12, 15, 18, 21, etc.
Multiples of 4 are: 4, 8, 12, 16, 20, 24, 28, 32, etc.
Multiples of 7 are: 7, 14, 21, 28, 35, 42, 49, 56, etc.

Practice: Multiples Problems

Name the first seven multiples of

1. 2   2. 5   3. 6   4. 8   5. 10

Answers: Multiples Problems

1. 2, 4, 6, 8, 10, 12, 14
2. 5, 10, 15, 20, 25, 30, 35
3. 6, 12, 18, 24, 30, 36, 42

4. 8, 16, 24, 32, 40, 48, 56
5. 10, 20, 30, 40, 50, 60, 70

Common Multiples

● *Common multiples* are those multiples which are the same for two or more numbers. *For example:* What are the common multiples of 2 and 3?

$$2 \rightarrow 2 \quad 4 \quad \boxed{6} \quad 8 \quad 10 \quad \boxed{12} \quad 14 \quad 16 \quad \boxed{18} \quad \text{etc.}$$
$$3 \rightarrow 3 \quad \boxed{6} \quad 9 \quad \boxed{12} \quad 15 \quad \boxed{18} \quad \text{etc.}$$

Notice that common multiples may go on indefinitely.

Practice: Common Multiples Problems

Find the first three common multiples of

1. 2 and 6   2. 3 and 4   3. 4 and 6

Answers: Common Multiples Problems

1. 6, 12, 18   2. 12, 24, 36   3. 12, 24, 36

Least Common Multiple

● The *least common multiple* is the smallest multiple which is common to two or more numbers. *For example:* What is the least common multiple of 2 and 3?

$$2 \rightarrow 2 \quad 4 \quad \boxed{6} \quad 8 \quad 10 \quad \boxed{12} \quad \text{etc.}$$
$$3 \rightarrow 3 \quad \boxed{6} \quad 9 \quad \boxed{12} \quad \text{etc.}$$

6 is the smallest multiple common to both 2 and 3. *Another example:* What is the least common multiple of 2, 3, and 4?

$$2 \to 2 \quad 4 \quad 6 \quad 8 \quad 10 \quad \boxed{12} \quad \text{etc.}$$
$$3 \to 3 \quad\quad 6 \quad 9 \quad\quad\quad 12 \quad \text{etc.}$$
$$4 \to \quad\quad 4 \quad\quad 8 \quad\quad\quad 12 \quad \text{etc.}$$

12 is the least common multiple of 2, 3, and 4.

Practice: Least Common Multiple Problems

Find the least common multiple of

1. 3 and 4   2. 4 and 6   3. 3, 4, and 5

Answers: Least Common Multiple Problems

1. 12   2. 12   3. 60

Adding and Subtracting Fractions

Adding Fractions

● To *add fractions* you must first change all denominators to their *lowest common denominator* (LCD)—the lowest number that can be divided evenly by all the denominators in the problem. When you have all the denominators the same, you may add fractions by simply adding the numerators (the denominator remains the same). *For example:*

$$
\begin{array}{ll}
\dfrac{3}{8} = \dfrac{3}{8} & \\[2mm]
+\dfrac{1}{2} = \dfrac{4}{8} \leftarrow \left\{ \begin{array}{l}\text{one-half is}\\ \text{changed to}\\ \text{four-eighths}\end{array}\right. \\[4mm]
\hline
\dfrac{7}{8}
\end{array}
\qquad
\begin{array}{l}
\dfrac{1}{4} = \dfrac{3}{12} \\[2mm]
+\dfrac{1}{3} = \dfrac{4}{12} \\[4mm]
\hline
\dfrac{7}{12}
\end{array}
\left\{ \begin{array}{l}\text{change both}\\ \text{fractions to}\\ \text{LCD of 12}\end{array}\right.
$$

In the first example, we changed the $\frac{1}{2}$ to $\frac{4}{8}$ because 8 is the lowest common denominator, and then we added the numerators 3 and 4 to get $\frac{7}{8}$. In the second example, we had to change both fractions to get the lowest common denominator of 12, and then we added the numerators to get $\frac{7}{12}$. Of course, if the denominators are already the same, just add the numerators. *For example:*

$$\frac{6}{11}$$

$$+ \frac{3}{11}$$

$$\frac{9}{11}$$

Note that fractions may be added across, as well. *For example:*

$$\tfrac{1}{2} + \tfrac{1}{3} = \tfrac{3}{6} + \tfrac{2}{6} = \tfrac{5}{6}$$

Practice: Adding Fractions Problems

1. $\frac{1}{4} + \frac{3}{8} =$

2. $\dfrac{1}{2}$
   $+ \dfrac{3}{10}$

3. $\frac{7}{8} + \frac{3}{10}$

4. $\dfrac{4}{15}$
   $+ \dfrac{2}{5}$

Answers: Adding Fractions Problems

1. $\frac{1}{4} + \frac{3}{8} = \frac{2}{8} + \frac{3}{8} = \frac{5}{8}$
2. $\frac{1}{2} + \frac{3}{10} = \frac{5}{10} + \frac{3}{10} = \frac{8}{10} = \frac{4}{5}$
3. $\frac{7}{8} + \frac{3}{10} = \frac{35}{40} + \frac{12}{40} = \frac{47}{40}$ or $1\frac{7}{40}$
4. $\frac{4}{15} + \frac{2}{5} = \frac{4}{15} + \frac{6}{15} = \frac{10}{15} = \frac{2}{3}$

Adding Positive and Negative Fractions

● The rules for signed numbers apply to fractions as well. *For example:*

1. $-\dfrac{1}{2} + \dfrac{1}{3} = -\dfrac{3}{6} + \dfrac{2}{6} = -\dfrac{1}{6}$

2. $+\dfrac{3}{4} = \quad +\dfrac{9}{12}$
   $+ -\dfrac{1}{3} = + -\dfrac{4}{12}$
   $\qquad\qquad +\dfrac{5}{12}$

Practice: Adding Positive and Negative Fractions Problems

1. $+\dfrac{4}{5}$

   $\underline{-\dfrac{1}{10}}$

2. $-\dfrac{9}{10}$

   $\underline{+\dfrac{4}{15}}$

3. $+\dfrac{3}{4} + \left(-\dfrac{1}{2}\right) =$

4. $\left(-\dfrac{3}{4}\right) + \dfrac{1}{3} + \left(-\dfrac{1}{6}\right) =$

Answers: Adding Positive and Negative Fractions Problems

1. $+\dfrac{4}{5} = +\dfrac{8}{10}$

   $\underline{-\dfrac{1}{10} = -\dfrac{1}{10}}$

   $\phantom{-\dfrac{1}{10} = -}\dfrac{7}{10}$

2. $-\dfrac{9}{10} = -\dfrac{27}{30}$

   $\underline{+\dfrac{4}{5} = +\dfrac{8}{30}}$

   $\phantom{+\dfrac{4}{5} = }-\dfrac{19}{30}$

3. $+\dfrac{3}{4} + \left(-\dfrac{1}{2}\right) = +\dfrac{3}{4} + \left(-\dfrac{2}{4}\right) = \dfrac{1}{4}$

4. $\left(-\dfrac{3}{4}\right) + \left(\dfrac{1}{3}\right) + \left(-\dfrac{1}{6}\right) =$

   $\left(-\dfrac{9}{12}\right) + \left(\dfrac{4}{12}\right) + \left(-\dfrac{2}{12}\right) = -\dfrac{7}{12}$

Subtracting Fractions

- To *subtract fractions,* the same rule (find the LCD) given earlier applies, except that you subtract the numerators. *For example:*

$$\frac{7}{8} = \frac{7}{8} \qquad\qquad \frac{3}{4} = \frac{9}{12}$$

$$-\frac{1}{4} = \frac{2}{8} \qquad\qquad -\frac{1}{3} = \frac{4}{12}$$

$$\frac{5}{8} \qquad\qquad\qquad \frac{5}{12}$$

Again, a subtraction problem may be done across, as well as down:

$$+\frac{5}{8} - \left(+\frac{3}{8}\right) = +\frac{2}{8} = +\frac{1}{4}$$

Practice: Subtracting Fractions Problems

1. $\frac{3}{4}$

   $-\frac{1}{2}$

2. $\frac{5}{6}$

   $-\frac{1}{3}$

3. $\frac{3}{8}$

   $-\frac{1}{9}$

4. $\frac{5}{12} - \frac{2}{5} =$

Answers: Subtracting Fractions Problems

1. $\frac{3}{4} = \frac{3}{4}$

   $-\frac{1}{2} = -\frac{2}{4}$

   $\frac{1}{4}$

2. $\frac{5}{6} = \frac{5}{6}$

   $-\frac{1}{3} = -\frac{2}{6}$

   $\frac{3}{6} = \frac{1}{2}$

3. $\dfrac{3}{8} = \dfrac{27}{72}$

$\dfrac{-\dfrac{1}{9}}{} = \dfrac{-\dfrac{8}{72}}{\dfrac{19}{72}}$

4. $\dfrac{5}{12} - \dfrac{2}{5} = \dfrac{25}{60} - \dfrac{24}{60} = \dfrac{1}{60}$

Subtracting Positive and Negative Fractions

● The rule for subtracting signed numbers applies to fractions as well. *For example:*

1. $+\dfrac{9}{10} = \qquad +\dfrac{9}{10} = +\dfrac{9}{10}$

$\dfrac{--\dfrac{1}{5}}{} = + +\dfrac{1}{5} = +\dfrac{2}{10}$

$\qquad\qquad +\dfrac{11}{10} = 1\dfrac{1}{10}$

2. $+\dfrac{2}{3} - \left(-\dfrac{1}{5}\right) = \dfrac{10}{15} - \left(-\dfrac{3}{15}\right) = \dfrac{10}{15} + \dfrac{3}{15} = \dfrac{13}{15}$

3. $+\dfrac{1}{3} - \dfrac{3}{4} = +\dfrac{4}{12} - \dfrac{9}{12} = +\dfrac{4}{12} + \left(-\dfrac{9}{12}\right) = -\dfrac{5}{12}$

Practice: Subtracting Positive and Negative Fractions Problems

1. $+\dfrac{3}{4}$

$\dfrac{-\dfrac{1}{3}}{}$

2. $+\dfrac{1}{6} - \left(-\dfrac{1}{3}\right) =$

3. $-\dfrac{1}{4} - \left(+\dfrac{2}{3}\right) =$

4. $-\dfrac{7}{12} - \left(+\dfrac{5}{6}\right) =$

Answers: Subtracting Positive and Negative Fractions Problems

1.
$$+\frac{3}{4} = +\frac{9}{12}$$
$$-\frac{1}{3} = -\frac{4}{12}$$
$$\overline{\qquad\quad +\frac{5}{12}}$$

2. $+\dfrac{1}{6} - \left(-\dfrac{1}{3}\right) = +\dfrac{1}{6} - \left(-\dfrac{2}{6}\right) = +\dfrac{1}{6} + \dfrac{2}{6} = \dfrac{3}{6} = \dfrac{1}{2}$

3. $-\dfrac{1}{4} - \left(+\dfrac{2}{3}\right) = -\dfrac{3}{12} - \left(+\dfrac{8}{12}\right) = -\dfrac{3}{12} + \left(-\dfrac{8}{12}\right) = -\dfrac{11}{12}$

4. $-\dfrac{7}{12} - \left(+\dfrac{5}{6}\right) = -\dfrac{7}{12} - \left(+\dfrac{10}{12}\right) = -\dfrac{7}{12} + \left(-\dfrac{10}{12}\right) = -\dfrac{17}{12}$ or $-1\frac{5}{12}$

Adding and Subtracting Mixed Numbers

Adding Mixed Numbers

● To *add mixed numbers,* the same rule (find the LCD) shown on p. 36 applies, but make sure that you always add the whole numbers to get your final answer. *For example:*

$$2\tfrac{1}{2} = 2\tfrac{2}{4} \quad \left\{\begin{array}{l}\text{one-half is changed}\\ \text{to two-fourths}\end{array}\right.$$
$$+\ 3\tfrac{1}{4} = 3\tfrac{1}{4}$$
$$\overline{\qquad 5\tfrac{3}{4}} \quad \left\{\begin{array}{l}\text{remember to add the}\\ \text{whole numbers}\end{array}\right.$$

Sometimes you may end up with a mixed number which includes an improper fraction. In that case, you must change the improper fraction to a mixed number and combine it with the sum of the integers. *For example:*

$$2\frac{1}{2} = 2\frac{2}{4}$$
$$+ \ 5\frac{3}{4} = 5\frac{3}{4}$$
$$7\frac{5}{4}$$

And since $\frac{5}{4} = 1\frac{1}{4}$

$$7\frac{5}{4} = 7 + 1\frac{1}{4} = 8\frac{1}{4}$$

Remember, the rules for adding signed numbers apply for mixed numbers as well.

Practice: Adding Mixed Numbers Problems

1. $3\frac{1}{2}$
    $+ \ 1\frac{2}{6}$

2. $4\frac{3}{5}$
    $+ \ 2\frac{1}{10}$

3. $+4\frac{5}{6} + (-2\frac{1}{3}) =$

4. $- \ 14\frac{3}{4}$
    $+ \ 21\frac{7}{8}$

Answers: Adding Mixed Numbers Problems

1. $3\frac{1}{2} = \quad 3\frac{3}{6}$
    $+ \ 1\frac{2}{6} = + \ 1\frac{2}{6}$
          $4\frac{5}{6}$

2. $4\frac{3}{5} = \quad 4\frac{6}{10}$
    $+ \ 2\frac{1}{10} = + \ 2\frac{1}{10}$
          $6\frac{7}{10}$

3. $+ \ 4\frac{5}{6} + (-2\frac{1}{3}) = +4\frac{5}{6} + (-2\frac{2}{6}) = + \ 4\frac{5}{6} - 2\frac{2}{6} = 2\frac{3}{6} = 2\frac{1}{2}$

4. $- \ 14\frac{3}{4} = -14\frac{6}{8}$
    $+ \ 21\frac{7}{8} = +21\frac{7}{8}$
            $7\frac{1}{8}$

Subtracting Mixed Numbers

● When you subtract mixed numbers, sometimes you may have to "borrow" from the whole number, just like you sometimes borrow from the next column when subtracting ordinary numbers. *For example:*

$$\begin{array}{r} {\scriptstyle 4\ \ 11} \\ 6\cancel{3}1 \\ -\ 129 \\ \hline 522 \end{array} \qquad \begin{array}{r} {\scriptstyle 3\frac{7}{6}} \\ \cancel{4}^{1}\!/_{6} \\ -\ 2\frac{5}{6} \\ \hline 1\frac{2}{6} = 1\frac{1}{3} \end{array}$$

you borrowed 1   you borrowed one in
from the 10's   the form $\frac{6}{6}$ from
column   the 1's column

To subtract a mixed number from a whole number, you have to "borrow" from the whole number. *For example:*

$$\begin{array}{r} 6\ \ \ =\ 5\frac{5}{5} \\ -\ 3\frac{1}{5} =\ 3\frac{1}{5} \\ \hline 2\frac{4}{5} \end{array} \leftarrow \begin{cases} \text{borrow one in the form of} \\ \frac{5}{5}\ \text{from the 6} \end{cases}$$

$\begin{cases} \text{remember to subtract the} \\ \text{remaining whole numbers} \end{cases}$

Remember that the rules for signed numbers apply here also and that subtracting can be done across as well as down.

Practice: Subtracting Mixed Numbers Problems

1. $3\frac{7}{8}$
    $-\ 1\frac{2}{8}$

2. $4\frac{3}{4} - 1\frac{1}{2} =$

3. $15\frac{1}{4}$
    $-\ 6\frac{1}{2}$

4. $24\frac{1}{8} - 16\frac{3}{4} =$

5. $102\frac{3}{6}$
    $-\ -53\frac{1}{2}$

Answers: Subtracting Mixed Numbers Problems

1. $3\frac{7}{8}$
    $-\ 1\frac{2}{8}$
     $2\frac{5}{8}$

2. $4\frac{3}{4} - 1\frac{1}{2} = 4\frac{3}{4} - 1\frac{2}{4} = 3\frac{1}{4}$

3. $\begin{array}{r} 15\frac{1}{4} = \\ -\ 6\frac{1}{2} = \end{array} \begin{array}{r} 15\frac{1}{4} = \\ -\ 6\frac{2}{4} = \end{array} \begin{array}{r} 1\overset{4\frac{5}{4}}{\cancel{5\frac{1}{4}}} \\ -\ 6\frac{2}{4} \\ \hline 8\frac{3}{4} \end{array}$

4. $24\frac{1}{8} - 16\frac{3}{4} = 24\frac{1}{8} - 16\frac{6}{8} = 2\overset{3\frac{9}{8}}{\cancel{4\frac{1}{8}}} - 16\frac{6}{8} = 7\frac{3}{8}$

5. $\begin{array}{r} 102\frac{3}{6} = \\ -\ -53\frac{1}{2} = \end{array} \begin{array}{r} 102\frac{3}{6} = \\ -\ -53\frac{3}{6} = \end{array} \begin{array}{r} 102\frac{3}{6} \\ +\ 53\frac{3}{6} \\ \hline 155\frac{6}{6} = 156 \end{array}$

Multiplying Fractions and Mixed Numbers

Multiplying Fractions

- To *multiply fractions,* simply multiply the numerators, then multiply the denominators. Reduce to lowest terms if necessary. *For example:*

$$\frac{2}{3} \times \frac{5}{12} = \frac{10}{36} \qquad \text{reduce } \frac{10}{36} \text{ to } \frac{5}{18}$$

This answer had to be reduced as it wasn't in lowest terms. Since whole numbers can also be written as fractions ($3 = \frac{3}{1}$, $4 = \frac{4}{1}$, etc.), the problem $3 \times \frac{3}{8}$ would be worked by changing 3 to $\frac{3}{1}$.

- *Canceling when multiplying fractions:* You could first have "canceled." That would have eliminated the need to reduce your answer. To cancel, find a number that divides evenly into one numerator and one denominator. In this case, 2 will divide evenly into 2 in the numerator (it goes in one time) and 12 in the denominator (it goes in 6 times). *Thus:*

$$\frac{\overset{1}{\cancel{2}}}{3} \times \frac{5}{\underset{6}{\cancel{12}}} = \frac{5}{18}$$

Remember, you may cancel only when *multiplying* fractions. The rules for multiplying signed numbers hold here too. *For example:*

$$\frac{1}{4} \times \frac{2}{7} = \frac{1}{\underset{2}{\cancel{4}}} \times \frac{\overset{1}{\cancel{2}}}{7} = \frac{1}{14} \quad \text{and} \quad \left(-\frac{\overset{1}{\cancel{3}}}{\underset{2}{\cancel{8}}}\right) \times \left(-\frac{\overset{1}{\cancel{4}}}{\underset{3}{\cancel{9}}}\right) = +\frac{1}{6}$$

Practice: Multiplying Fractions Problems

1. $\dfrac{3}{5} \times \dfrac{1}{2} =$

2. $\dfrac{7}{8} \times \dfrac{2}{3} =$

3. $-\dfrac{4}{7} \times \dfrac{14}{3} =$

4. $\dfrac{7}{10} \times \dfrac{5}{6} \times \dfrac{1}{3} =$

5. $7 \times \dfrac{2}{14} =$

Answers: Multiplying Fractions Problems

1. $\dfrac{3}{5} \times \dfrac{1}{2} = \dfrac{3}{10}$

2. $\dfrac{7}{8} \times \dfrac{2}{3} = \dfrac{7}{\overset{4}{\cancel{8}}} \times \dfrac{\overset{1}{\cancel{2}}}{3} = \dfrac{7}{12}$

3. $-\dfrac{4}{7} \times \dfrac{14}{3} = -\dfrac{4}{\underset{1}{\cancel{7}}} \times \dfrac{\overset{2}{\cancel{14}}}{3} = -\dfrac{8}{3}$

4. $\dfrac{7}{10} \times \dfrac{5}{6} \times \dfrac{1}{3} = \dfrac{7}{\underset{2}{\cancel{10}}} \times \dfrac{\overset{1}{\cancel{5}}}{6} \times \dfrac{1}{3} = \dfrac{7}{36}$

5. $7 \times \dfrac{2}{14} = \dfrac{\overset{1}{\cancel{7}}}{1} \times \dfrac{2}{\underset{2}{\cancel{14}}} = \dfrac{2}{2} = 1$

Multiplying Mixed Numbers

- To *multiply mixed numbers,* first change any mixed number to an improper fraction. Then multiply as previously shown.

$$3\tfrac{1}{3} \times 2\tfrac{1}{4} = {}^{10}\!/_3 \times {}^9\!/_4 = {}^{90}\!/_{12} = 7{}^6\!/_{12} = 7\tfrac{1}{2}$$

or

$$\dfrac{\overset{5}{\cancel{10}}}{\underset{1}{\cancel{3}}} \times \dfrac{\overset{3}{\cancel{9}}}{\underset{2}{\cancel{4}}} = \dfrac{15}{2} = 7\tfrac{1}{2}$$

Change the answer, if in improper fraction form, back to a mixed number and reduce if necessary. Remember, the rules for multiplication of signed numbers apply here as well.

Practice: Multiplying Mixed Numbers Problems

1. $2\tfrac{1}{2} \times 3\tfrac{1}{4} =$

2. $3\tfrac{1}{5} \times 6\tfrac{1}{2} =$

3. $-5\tfrac{1}{4} \times 3\tfrac{3}{7} =$

4. $(-4{}^9\!/_{10}) \times (-3\tfrac{3}{7}) =$

Answers: Multiplying Mixed Numbers Problems

1. $2\frac{1}{2} \times 3\frac{1}{4} = \frac{5}{2} \times \frac{13}{4} = \frac{65}{8} = 8\frac{1}{8}$

2. $3\frac{1}{5} \times 6\frac{1}{2} = \frac{16}{5} \times \frac{13}{2} = \frac{\overset{8}{\cancel{16}}}{5} \times \frac{13}{\underset{1}{\cancel{2}}} = \frac{104}{5} = 20\frac{4}{5}$

3. $-5\frac{1}{4} \times 3\frac{3}{7} = -\frac{21}{4} \times \frac{24}{7} = -\frac{\overset{3}{\cancel{21}}}{\underset{1}{\cancel{4}}} \times \frac{\overset{6}{\cancel{24}}}{\underset{1}{\cancel{7}}} = -18$

4. $(-4\frac{9}{10}) \times (-3\frac{3}{7}) = \left(-\frac{49}{10}\right) \times \left(-\frac{24}{7}\right) = \left(\frac{\overset{7}{\cancel{49}}}{\underset{5}{\cancel{10}}}\right) \times \left(\frac{\overset{12}{\cancel{24}}}{\underset{1}{\cancel{7}}}\right) = \frac{84}{5} = 16\frac{4}{5}$

Dividing Fractions and Mixed Numbers

Dividing Fractions

● To *divide fractions,* invert (turn upside down) the second fraction (the one "divided by") and multiply. Then reduce, if necessary. *For example:*

$$\frac{1}{6} \div \frac{1}{5} = \frac{1}{6} \times \frac{5}{1} = \frac{5}{6} \qquad \frac{1}{6} \div \frac{1}{3} = \frac{1}{\underset{2}{\cancel{6}}} \times \frac{\overset{1}{\cancel{3}}}{1} = \frac{1}{2}$$

Here too the rules for division of signed numbers apply.

Practice: Dividing Fractions Problems

1. $\frac{1}{2} \div \frac{1}{3} =$

2. $\frac{3}{4} \div \frac{1}{2} =$

3. $\frac{3}{7} \div \frac{3}{14} =$

4. $\frac{3}{4} \div \left(-\frac{5}{8}\right) =$

Answers: Dividing Fractions Problems

1. $\frac{1}{2} \div \frac{1}{3} = \frac{1}{2} \times \frac{3}{1} = \frac{3}{2} = 1\frac{1}{2}$

2. $\frac{3}{4} \div \frac{1}{2} = \frac{3}{\underset{2}{\cancel{4}}} \times \frac{\overset{1}{\cancel{2}}}{1} = \frac{3}{2} = 1\frac{1}{2}$

3. $\dfrac{3}{7} \div \dfrac{3}{14} = \dfrac{\cancel{3}^{1}}{\cancel{7}_{1}} \times \dfrac{\cancel{14}^{2}}{\cancel{3}_{1}} = \dfrac{2}{1} = 2$

4. $\dfrac{3}{4} \div \left(-\dfrac{5}{8}\right) = \dfrac{3}{4} \times \left(-\dfrac{8}{5}\right) = \dfrac{3}{\cancel{4}_{1}} \times \left(-\dfrac{\cancel{8}^{2}}{5}\right) = -\dfrac{6}{5} = -1\tfrac{1}{5}$

Dividing Complex Fractions

● Sometimes a division of fractions problem may appear in this form (these are called *complex fractions*).

$$\dfrac{\dfrac{3}{4}}{\dfrac{7}{8}}$$

If so, consider the line separating the two fractions to mean "divided by." Therefore, this problem may be rewritten as

$$\dfrac{3}{4} \div \dfrac{7}{8} =$$

Now, follow the same procedure as shown on p. 46.

$$\dfrac{3}{4} \div \dfrac{7}{8} = \dfrac{3}{\cancel{4}_{1}} \times \dfrac{\cancel{8}^{2}}{7} = \dfrac{6}{7}$$

Practice: Dividing Complex Fractions Problems

1. $\dfrac{\dfrac{3}{4}}{\dfrac{1}{2}}$
2. $\dfrac{\dfrac{5}{6}}{\dfrac{1}{3}}$
3. $\dfrac{\dfrac{1}{2}}{\dfrac{3}{8}}$
4. $\dfrac{\dfrac{7}{8}}{\dfrac{1}{2}}$

Answers: Dividing Complex Fractions Problems

1. $\dfrac{\dfrac{3}{4}}{\dfrac{1}{2}} = \dfrac{3}{4} \div \dfrac{1}{2} = \dfrac{3}{\cancel{4}_{2}} \times \dfrac{\cancel{2}^{1}}{1} = \dfrac{3}{2} = 1\tfrac{1}{2}$

2.
$$\dfrac{\dfrac{5}{6}}{\dfrac{1}{3}} = \dfrac{5}{6} \div \dfrac{1}{3} = \dfrac{5}{\overset{}{\underset{2}{6}}} \times \dfrac{\overset{1}{\cancel{3}}}{1} = \dfrac{5}{2} = 2\frac{1}{2}$$

3.
$$\dfrac{\dfrac{1}{2}}{\dfrac{3}{8}} = \dfrac{1}{2} \div \dfrac{3}{8} = \dfrac{1}{\underset{1}{\cancel{2}}} \times \dfrac{\overset{4}{\cancel{8}}}{3} = \dfrac{4}{3} = 1\frac{1}{3}$$

4.
$$\dfrac{\dfrac{7}{8}}{\dfrac{1}{2}} = \dfrac{7}{8} \div \dfrac{1}{2} = \dfrac{7}{\underset{4}{\cancel{8}}} \times \dfrac{\overset{1}{\cancel{2}}}{1} = \dfrac{7}{4} = 1\frac{3}{4}$$

Dividing Mixed Numbers

- To *divide mixed numbers*, first change them to improper fractions. Then follow the rule for dividing fractions. *For example:*

1. $3\frac{3}{5} \div 2\frac{2}{3} = \dfrac{18}{5} \div \dfrac{8}{3} = \dfrac{\overset{9}{\cancel{18}}}{5} \times \dfrac{3}{\underset{4}{\cancel{8}}} = \dfrac{27}{20} = 1\frac{7}{20}$

2. $2\frac{1}{5} \div 3\frac{1}{10} = \dfrac{11}{5} \div \dfrac{31}{10} = \dfrac{11}{\underset{1}{\cancel{5}}} \times \dfrac{\overset{2}{\cancel{10}}}{31} = \dfrac{22}{31}$

Notice that after you invert and have a multiplication of fractions problem, you may then cancel tops with bottoms when appropriate.

Practice: Dividing Mixed Numbers Problems

1. $3\frac{1}{2} \div \frac{3}{4} =$ 3. $(-5\frac{4}{5}) \div (2\frac{1}{2}) =$

2. $1\frac{1}{6} \div 4\frac{1}{2} =$ 4. $(-3\frac{1}{5}) \div (-3\frac{1}{3}) =$

Answers: Dividing Mixed Numbers Problems

1. $3\frac{1}{2} \div \frac{3}{4} = \dfrac{7}{2} \div \dfrac{3}{4} = \dfrac{7}{\underset{1}{\cancel{2}}} \times \dfrac{\overset{2}{\cancel{4}}}{3} = \dfrac{14}{3} = 4\frac{2}{3}$

2. $1\frac{1}{6} \div 4\frac{1}{2} = \dfrac{7}{6} \div \dfrac{9}{2} = \dfrac{7}{\underset{3}{6}} \times \dfrac{\overset{1}{2}}{9} = \dfrac{7}{27}$

3. $(-5\frac{4}{5}) \div (2\frac{1}{2}) = \left(-\dfrac{29}{5}\right) \div \left(\dfrac{5}{2}\right) = \left(-\dfrac{29}{5}\right) \times \left(\dfrac{2}{5}\right) = -\dfrac{58}{25} = -2\frac{8}{25}$

4. $(-3\frac{1}{5}) \div (-3\frac{1}{3}) = \left(-\dfrac{16}{5}\right) \div \left(-\dfrac{10}{3}\right) = \left(-\dfrac{\overset{8}{16}}{5}\right) \times \left(-\dfrac{3}{\underset{5}{10}}\right) = \dfrac{24}{25}$

Simplifying Fractions and Complex Fractions

● If either numerator or denominator consists of several numbers, these numbers must be combined into one number. Then reduce if necessary. *For example:*

1. $\dfrac{28 + 14}{26 + 17} = \dfrac{42}{43}$

2. $\dfrac{\dfrac{1}{4} + \dfrac{1}{2}}{\dfrac{1}{3} + \dfrac{1}{4}} = \dfrac{\dfrac{1}{4} + \dfrac{2}{4}}{\dfrac{4}{12} + \dfrac{3}{12}} = \dfrac{\dfrac{3}{4}}{\dfrac{7}{12}} = \dfrac{3}{4} \div \dfrac{7}{12} = \dfrac{3}{\underset{1}{4}} \times \dfrac{\overset{3}{12}}{7} = \dfrac{9}{7} = 1\frac{2}{7}$

3. $\dfrac{2 + \frac{1}{2}}{3 + \frac{1}{4}} = \dfrac{2\frac{1}{2}}{3\frac{1}{4}} = \dfrac{\frac{5}{2}}{\frac{13}{4}} = \frac{5}{2} \div 1\frac{3}{4} = \dfrac{5}{\underset{1}{2}} \times \dfrac{\overset{2}{4}}{13} = \frac{10}{13}$

4. $\dfrac{3 - \frac{3}{4}}{-4 + \frac{1}{2}} = \dfrac{2\frac{1}{4}}{-3\frac{1}{2}} = \dfrac{\frac{9}{4}}{-\frac{7}{2}} = \frac{9}{4} \div -\frac{7}{2} = \dfrac{9}{\underset{2}{4}} \times -\dfrac{\overset{1}{2}}{7} = -\frac{9}{14}$

5. $\dfrac{1}{1 + \dfrac{1}{1 + \frac{1}{4}}} = \dfrac{1}{1 + \dfrac{1}{\frac{5}{4}}} = \dfrac{1}{1 + (1 \div \frac{5}{4})} = \dfrac{1}{1 + (1 \times \frac{4}{5})} = \dfrac{1}{1 + \frac{4}{5}} =$

$\dfrac{1}{1\frac{4}{5}} = \dfrac{1}{\frac{9}{5}} = 1 \div \frac{9}{5} = 1 \times \frac{5}{9} = \frac{5}{9}$

Practice: Simplifying Fractions and Complex Fractions Problems

1. $\dfrac{-3 - 2}{-6 + 5} =$

3. $\dfrac{^9/_{20}}{.8} =$

2. $\dfrac{3 + \frac{1}{2}}{5 + \frac{5}{6}} =$

4. $\dfrac{1 + \dfrac{1}{2 + \frac{1}{2}}}{3} =$

Answers: Simplifying Fractions and Complex Fractions Problems

1. $\dfrac{-3 - 2}{-6 + 5} = \dfrac{-5}{-1} = 5$

2. $\dfrac{3 + \frac{1}{2}}{5 + \frac{5}{6}} = \dfrac{3\frac{1}{2}}{5\frac{5}{6}} = \dfrac{7}{2} \div \dfrac{35}{6} = \dfrac{\cancel{7}^1}{\cancel{2}_1} \times \dfrac{\cancel{6}^3}{\cancel{35}_5} = \dfrac{3}{5}$

3. $\dfrac{^9/_{20}}{.8} = \dfrac{^9/_{20}}{^8/_{10}} = \dfrac{9}{20} \div \dfrac{8}{10} = \dfrac{9}{\cancel{20}_2} \times \dfrac{\cancel{10}^1}{8} = \dfrac{9}{16}$

4. $\dfrac{1 + \dfrac{1}{2 + \frac{1}{2}}}{3} = \dfrac{1 + \dfrac{1}{\frac{5}{2}}}{3} = \dfrac{1 + \left(1 \div \frac{5}{2}\right)}{3} = \dfrac{1 + \left(1 \times \frac{2}{5}\right)}{3} =$

$\dfrac{1 + \left(\frac{2}{5}\right)}{3} = \dfrac{1\frac{2}{5}}{3} = \dfrac{\frac{7}{5}}{3} = \dfrac{7}{5} \div \dfrac{3}{1} = \dfrac{7}{5} \times \dfrac{1}{3} = \dfrac{7}{15}$

Decimals

Changing Decimals to Fractions

- *Fractions* may also be written in *decimal* form (decimal fractions) by using a symbol called a *decimal point*. All numbers to the left of the decimal point are whole numbers. All numbers to the right of the decimal point are fractions with denominators of only 10, 100, 1,000, 10,000, etc. *For example:*

$$.6 = \frac{6}{10} = \frac{3}{5} \qquad .0007 = \frac{7}{10,000}$$

$$.7 = \frac{7}{10} \qquad .00007 = \frac{7}{100,000}$$

$$.07 = \frac{7}{100} \qquad .25 = \frac{25}{100} = \frac{1}{4}$$

$$.007 = \frac{7}{1,000}$$

Read it: .8   Write it: $\frac{8}{10}$ Reduce it: $\frac{4}{5}$

All rules for signed numbers also apply to decimals.

Practice: Changing Decimals to Fractions Problems

Change the following decimals to fractions. Reduce if necessary.

1. .4   2. .09   3. .75   4. .062

Answers: Changing Decimals to Fractions Problems

1. $.4 = \frac{4}{10} = \frac{2}{5}$ 3. $.75 = \frac{75}{100} = \frac{3}{4}$

2. $.09 = \frac{9}{100}$ 4. $.062 = \frac{62}{1,000} = \frac{31}{500}$

Adding and Subtracting Decimals

● To *add or subtract decimals*, just line up the decimal points and then add or subtract in the same manner you would add or subtract regular numbers. *For example:*

$$23.6 + 1.75 + 300.002 = \begin{array}{r} 23.6 \\ 1.75 \\ 300.002 \\ \hline 325.352 \end{array}$$

Adding in zeros can make the problem easier to work:

$$\begin{array}{r} 23.600 \\ 1.750 \\ 300.002 \\ \hline 325.352 \end{array}$$

and
$$54.26 - 1.1 = \quad \begin{array}{r} 54.26 \\ -\ 1.10 \\ \hline 53.16 \end{array}$$

and
$$78.9 - 37.43 = \quad \begin{array}{r} 8 \\ 78.\cancel{9}{}^{1}0 \\ -37.4\ 3 \\ \hline 41.4\ 7 \end{array}$$

A whole number has an understood decimal point to its right. *For example:*

$$17 - 8.43 = \quad \begin{array}{r} 6\ \ 9 \\ 1\cancel{7}.\cancel{0}{}^{1}0 \\ -\ \ 8.4\ 3 \\ \hline 8.5\ 7 \end{array}$$

Practice: Adding and Subtracting Decimals Problems

1. $19.6 + 5.02 =$ 3. $.16 - .043 =$

2. $108 + 71.04 =$ 4. $12 - .061 =$

Answers: Adding and Subtracting Decimals Problems

1. 24.62   2. 179.04   3. .117   4. 11.939

Multiplying Decimals

- To *multiply decimals,* just multiply as usual. Then count the total number of digits above the line which are to the right of all decimal points. Place your decimal point in your answer so there is the same number of digits to the right of it as there was above the line. *For example:*

$$\begin{array}{r} 40.012 \leftarrow 3 \text{ digits} \\ \times \quad 3.1 \leftarrow 1 \text{ digit} \\ \hline 40012 \\ 120036 \\ \hline 124.0372 \leftarrow 4 \text{ digits} \end{array}$$

{ total of 4 digits above the line that are to the right of the decimal point

{ decimal point placed so there is same number of digits to the right of the decimal point

Practice: Multiplying Decimals Problems

1. 30.1
    ×2.65

2. 30 × 9.061 =

3. (.906) × (−.1) =

4. (−.012) × (−.003) =

Answers: Multiplying Decimals Problems

1. 79.765   2. 271.83   3. −.0906   4. .000036

Dividing Decimals

● *Dividing decimals* is the same as dividing other numbers, except that if the divisor (the number you're dividing by) has a decimal, move it to the right as many places as necessary until it is a whole number. Then move the decimal point in the dividend (the number being divided into) the same number of places. Sometimes you may have to add zeros to the dividend (the number inside the division sign). *For example:*

$$1.25\overline{)5.} = 125\overline{)500.}^{\;4.}$$

or

$$0.002\overline{)26.} = 2\overline{)26000.}^{\;13000.}$$

Practice: Dividing Decimals Problems

1. Divide 8 by .4

2. .2)6.84

3. .5/.004

4. 90.804)181.608

Answers: Dividing Decimals Problems

1. 20   2. 34.2   3. 125   4. 2

Changing Fractions to Decimals

● To *change a fraction to a decimal,* simply do what the operation says. In other words, $^{13}/_{20}$ means 13 divided by 20. So do just that (insert decimal points and zeros accordingly). *For example:*

$$20\overline{)13.00}^{.65} = .65 \qquad 5/8 = 8\overline{)5.000}^{.625} = .625$$

Practice: Changing Fractions to Decimals

Change each fraction to a decimal.

1. ¼   2. ³⁄₁₀   3. ⅜   4. ⁷⁄₁₁

Answers: Changing Fractions to Decimals

1. .25   2. .3   3. .375   4. .6363 . . .
(sometimes written .$\overline{63}$)

Percentage

● A fraction whose denominator is 100 is called a *percent*. The word *percent* means hundredths (per hundred). *For example:*

$$37\% = {}^{37}/_{100}$$

Changing Decimals to Percents

● To change decimals to percents:
1. Move the decimal point two places to the right.
2. Insert a percent sign.

For example:

.75 = 75%   1.85 = 185%   .003 = .3%
.05 = 5%   20.3 = 2,030%

Practice: Changing Decimals to Percents Problems

Change each decimal to percent.

1. .32   2. .8   3. .006   4. 1.75

Answers: Changing Decimals to Percents Problems

1. 32%   2. 80%   3. .6%   4. 175%

Changing Percents to Decimals

● To *change percents to decimals:*
  1. Eliminate the percent sign.
  2. Move the decimal point two places to the left (sometimes adding zeros will be necessary).

For example:

75% = .75   23% = .23   5% = .05   .2% = .002

Practice: Changing Percents to Decimals Problems

Change each percent to a decimal.

1. 25%   2. 80%   3. 2%   4. .4%   5. 300%

Answers: Changing Percents to Decimals Problems

1. .25   2. .80 or .8   3. .02   4. .004   5. 3.00 or 3

Changing Fractions to Percents

● To *change a fraction to a percent:*
  1. Change to a decimal.
  2. Change the decimal to a percent.

For example:

$\frac{1}{2}$ = .5 = 50% $\frac{5}{2}$ = 2.5 = 250%
$\frac{2}{5}$ = .4 = 40% $\frac{1}{20}$ = .05 = 5%

Practice: Changing Fractions to Percents Problems

Change each fraction to a percent.

1. $\frac{1}{4}$ 2. $\frac{3}{8}$ 3. $\frac{7}{20}$ 4. $\frac{7}{2}$

Answers: Changing Fractions to Percents Problems

1. 25%   2. 37$\frac{1}{2}$% or 37.5%   3. 35%   4. 350%

Changing Percents to Fractions

- To *change percents to fractions:*
  1. Drop the percent sign.
  2. Write over one hundred.
  3. Reduce if necessary.

For example:

$60\% = {}^{60}\!/_{100} = {}^{3}\!/_{5}$ $230\% = {}^{230}\!/_{100} = {}^{23}\!/_{10}$ $13\% = {}^{13}\!/_{100}$

Practice: Changing Percents to Fractions Problems

Change each percent to a fraction.

1. 30%   2. 5%   3. 125%   4. 19%

Answers: Changing Percents to Fractions Problems

1. $30\% = \dfrac{30}{100} = \dfrac{3}{10}$ 3. $125\% = \dfrac{125}{100} = \dfrac{5}{4}$

2. $5\% = \dfrac{5}{100} = \dfrac{1}{20}$ 4. $19\% = \dfrac{19}{100}$

Important Equivalents That Can Save You Time

- Memorizing the following can eliminate unnecessary computations.

$\frac{1}{100} = .01 = 1\%$

$\frac{1}{10} = .1 = 10\%$

$\frac{1}{5} = \frac{2}{10} = .2 = .20 = 20\%$

$\frac{3}{10} = .3 = .30 = 30\%$

$\frac{2}{5} = \frac{4}{10} = .4 = .40 = 40\%$

$\frac{1}{2} = \frac{5}{10} = .5 = .50 = 50\%$

$\frac{3}{5} = \frac{6}{10} = .6 = .60 = 60\%$

$\frac{7}{10} = .7 = .70 = 70\%$

$\frac{4}{5} = \frac{8}{10} = .8 = .80 = 80\%$

$\frac{9}{10} = .9 = .90 = 90\%$

$\frac{1}{4} = {}^{25}\!/_{100} = .25 = 25\%$

$\frac{3}{4} = {}^{75}\!/_{100} = .75 = 75\%$

$\frac{1}{3} = .33\frac{1}{3} = 33\frac{1}{3}\%$

$\frac{2}{3} = .66\frac{2}{3} = 66\frac{2}{3}\%$

$\frac{1}{8} = .125 = .12\frac{1}{2} = 12\frac{1}{2}\%$

$\frac{3}{8} = .375 = .37\frac{1}{2} = 37\frac{1}{2}\%$

$\frac{5}{8} = .625 = .62\frac{1}{2} = 62\frac{1}{2}\%$

$\frac{7}{8} = .875 = .87\frac{1}{2} = 87\frac{1}{2}\%$

$\frac{1}{6} = .16\frac{2}{3} = 16\frac{2}{3}\%$

$\frac{5}{6} = .83\frac{1}{3} = 83\frac{1}{3}\%$

$1 = 1.00 = 100\%$

$2 = 2.00 = 200\%$

$3\frac{1}{2} = 3.5 = 3.50 = 350\%$

Finding Percent of a Number

- To *determine percent of a number,* change the percent to a fraction or decimal (whichever is easier for you) and multiply. Remember, the word *of* means multiply. *For example:*

What is 20% of 80?

$$^{20}\!/_{100} \times 80 = {}^{1600}\!/_{100} = 16 \text{ or } .20 \times 80 = 16.00 = 16$$

What is 12% of 50?

$$^{12}\!/_{100} \times 50 = {}^{600}\!/_{100} = 6 \text{ or } .12 \times 50 = 6.00 = 6$$

What is ½% of 18?

$$\frac{1/2}{100} \times 18 = {}^{1}\!/_{200} \times 18 = {}^{18}\!/_{200} = {}^{9}\!/_{100} \text{ or } .005 \times 18 = .09$$

Practice: Finding Percent of a Number Problems

1. What is 10% of 30?
2. What is 70% of 20?
3. What is ¼% of 1,000?
4. What is 250% of 12?

Answers: Finding Percent of a Number Problems

1. x = (.10)(30) = 3
2. x = (.70)(20) = 14
3. x = (.0025)(1,000) = 2.5
4. x = (2.50)(12) = 30

Other Applications of Percent

- Turn the question word-for-word into an equation. For *what* substitute the letter *x;* for *is* substitute an *equal sign;* for *of* substitute a *multiplication sign.* Change percents to decimals or fractions, whichever you find easier. Then solve the equation. *For example:*

18 is what percent of 90?   18 = x(90)
$$^{18}\!/_{90} = x$$
$$^{1}\!/_{5} = x$$
$$20\% = x$$

10 is 50% of what number?   10 = .50(x)
$$^{10}\!/_{.50} = x$$
$$20 = x$$

What is 15% of 60? $x = {}^{15}\!/_{100} \times 60 = {}^{90}\!/_{10} = 9$
or $.15(60) = 9$

Practice: Other Applications of Percent Problems

1. 20 is what percent of 80?   3. 18 is what percent of 45?
2. 15 is 20% of what number?   4. What is 65% of 20?

Answers: Other Applications of Percent Problems

1. $20 = x(80)$

   $\dfrac{20}{80} = x$

   $\dfrac{1}{4} = x$

   $x = 25\%$

2. $15 = (.20)x$

   $\dfrac{15}{.20} = x$

   $x = 75$

3. $18 = x(45)$

   $\dfrac{18}{45} = x$

   $\dfrac{2}{5} = x$

   $x = 40\%$

4. $x = (.65)20$

   $x = 13$

Percent—Proportion Method

● Another simple method commonly used to solve percent problems
is the *proportion* or *is/of method*. First set up a blank proportion
and then fill in the empty spaces by using the following steps.

$$\frac{?}{?} = \frac{?}{?}$$

30 is what percent of 50?

1. What is next to the percent(%) is put over 100. (The word *what*
is the unknown, or x.)

$$\frac{x}{100} = \frac{?}{?}$$

2. Whatever comes immediately after the word *of* goes on the bottom of one side of the proportion.

$$\frac{x}{100} = \frac{?}{50}$$

3. Whatever is left (comes next to the word *is*) goes on top, on one side of the proportion.

$$\frac{x}{100} = \frac{30}{50}$$

4. Then solve the proportion.

$$\frac{x}{100} = \frac{30}{50}$$

(In this particular instance, it can be observed that $\frac{30}{50} = \frac{60}{100}$, so the answer is 60%. Solving mechanically on this problem would not be time effective.)

This method works for the three basic types of percent questions.

1. 30 is what percent of 50?
2. 30 is 20% of what number?
3. What number is 30% of 50? (In this type it is probably easier to simply multiply the numbers.)

Practice: Percent—Proportion Method Problems

1. 40 is what percent of 200?
2. What percent of 25 is 10?
3. What number is 15% of 30?
4. 60 is 20% of what number?
5. 70% of what number is 35?

Answers: Percent—Proportion Method Problems

1. 20%.
   40 is what percent of 200?

$$\frac{x}{100} = \frac{40}{200}$$

Since $\frac{40}{200}$ can be reduced to $\frac{20}{100}$, x = 20. (This particular problem does not need to be solved mechanically.)

2. 40%
    What percent of 25 is 10?

$$\frac{x}{100} = \frac{10}{25}$$

$$25x = 1,000$$

$$\frac{\cancel{25}x}{\cancel{25}} = \frac{\cancel{1,000}^{40}}{\cancel{25}}$$

$$x = 40$$

(You might have solved this by observing that $4 \times 25 = 100$, therefore $^{40}/_{100} = ^{10}/_{25}$.)

3. 4.5
    What number is 15% of 30?

$$\frac{15}{100} = \frac{x}{30}$$

$$450 = 100x$$

$$\frac{450}{100} = \frac{\cancel{100}x}{\cancel{100}}$$

$$x = 4.5$$

4. 300
    60 is 20% of what number?

$$\frac{20}{100} = \frac{60}{x} \qquad \text{or} \qquad \frac{20}{100} = \frac{60}{x}$$

$$20x = 6,000$$

$$\frac{\cancel{20}x}{\cancel{20}} = \frac{6,000}{20} \qquad\qquad \frac{1}{5} = \frac{60}{x}$$

$$x = 300 \qquad\qquad\qquad x = 300$$

5. 50
    70% of what number is 35?

$$\frac{70}{100} = \frac{35}{x} \quad \text{or} \quad \frac{70}{100} = \frac{35}{x}$$

$$70x = 3,500 \qquad\qquad \frac{7}{10} = \frac{35}{x}$$

$$\frac{\cancel{70}x}{\cancel{70}} = \frac{3,500}{70}$$

$$7x = 350$$

$$x = 50 \qquad\qquad x = 50$$

(Again, this problem could have been solved by observing that $^{70}/_{100}$ can be reduced to $^{35}/_{50}$.)

Finding Percent Increase or Percent Decrease

● To find the *percent change* (increase or decrease), use this formula:

$$\frac{\text{change}}{\text{starting point}} = \text{percent change}$$

For example:

What is the percent decrease of a $500 item on sale for $400?

Change: $500 - 400 = 100$

$$\frac{\text{change}}{\text{starting point}} = \frac{100}{500} = \frac{1}{5} = 20\% \text{ decrease}$$

What is the percent increase of Jon's salary if it went from $150 a month to $200 a month?

Change: $200 - 150 = 50$

$$\frac{\text{change}}{\text{starting point}} = \frac{50}{150} = \frac{1}{3} = 33\frac{1}{3}\% \text{ increase}$$

Note that the terms *percentage rise, percentage difference,* and *percentage change* are the same as *percent change.*

Practice: Finding Percent Increase or Percent Decrease Problems

1. Find the percent decrease from 200 to 180.
2. What is the percent difference between a first month's rent of $250 and a second month's rent of $300?

3. What is the percent increase in rainfall from January (2.5 inches) to February (4.0 inches)?

4. What is the percent change from 2,100 to 1,890?

Answers: Finding Percent Increase or Percent Decrease Problems

1. $\dfrac{\text{change}}{\text{starting point}} = \dfrac{20}{200} = \dfrac{1}{10} = 10\%$

2. $\dfrac{\text{change}}{\text{starting point}} = \dfrac{50}{250} = \dfrac{1}{5} = 20\%$

3. $\dfrac{\text{change}}{\text{starting point}} = \dfrac{1.5}{2.5} = \dfrac{15}{25} = \dfrac{3}{5} = 60\%$

4. $\dfrac{\text{change}}{\text{starting point}} = \dfrac{210}{2,100} = \dfrac{1}{10} = 10\%$

Scientific Notation

- Very large or very small numbers are sometimes written in *scientific notation.* A number written in scientific notation is a number between 1 and 10 and multiplied by a power of 10. *For example:*

1. 2,100,000 written in scientific notation is 2.1×10^6.
   Simply place the decimal point to get a number between 1 and 10 and then count the digits to the right of the decimal to get the power of 10.

   2,100,000   *moved 6 digits to the left*

2. .0000004 written in scientific notation is 4×10^{-7}.
   Simply place the decimal point to get a number between 1 and 10 and then count the digits from the original decimal point to the new one.

   .0000004   *moved 7 digits to the right*

   Notice that whole numbers have positive exponents and fractions have negative exponents.

3. 2/2,500 written in scientific notation is 8×10^{-4}. Simply divide 2,500 into 2 giving .0008. Then change to 8×10^{-4}.

Practice: Scientific Notation Problems

Change the following to scientific notation.

1. 35,000   2. 1,112,000,000   3. .00047   4. 1/200

Change the following from scientific notation.

5. 2.6×10^4 6. 3.11×10^7 7. 6.1×10^{-4} 8. 7.22×10^{-6}

Answers: Scientific Notation Problems

1. 3.5×10^4 5. 26,000
2. 1.112×10^9 6. 31,100,000
3. 4.7×10^{-4} 7. .00061
4. 5×10^{-3} 8. .00000722

Multiplication in Scientific Notation

- To *multiply* numbers in *scientific notation,* simply multiply the numbers together to get the first number and add the powers of ten to get the second number. *For example:*

1. $(2 \times 10^2)(3 \times 10^4) =$

$$(2 \times 10^2)(3 \times 10^4) = 6 \times 10^6$$

2. $(6 \times 10^5)(5 \times 10^7) =$

$$(6 \times 10^5)(5 \times 10^7) = 30 \times 10^{12}$$

This answer must be changed to scientific notation (first number from 1 to 9).

$$30 \times 10^{12} = 3.0 \times 10^{13}$$

3. $(4 \times 10^{-4})(2 \times 10^5) =$

$$(4 \times 10^{-4})(2 \times 10^5) = 8 \times 10^1$$

Practice: Multiplication in Scientific Notation Problems

1. $(3 \times 10^5)(2 \times 10^7) =$ 4. $(6 \times 10^8)(4 \times 10^{-2}) =$
2. $(3.5 \times 10^2)(2.1 \times 10^4) =$ 5. $(2 \times 10^2)(4 \times 10^4)(5 \times 10^6) =$
3. $(5 \times 10^4)(9 \times 10^2) =$ 6. $(1.6 \times 10^{-3})(4.2 \times 10^{-4}) =$

Answers: Multiplication in Scientific Notation Problems

1. 6×10^{12} 4. $24 \times 10^6 = \underline{2.4 \times 10^7}$
2. 7.35×10^6 5. $40 \times 10^{12} = \underline{4.0 \times 10^{13}}$
3. $45 \times 10^6 = \underline{4.5 \times 10^7}$ 6. 6.72×10^{-7}

Division in Scientific Notation

● To *divide* numbers *in scientific notation,* simply divide the numbers to get the first number and subtract the powers of ten to get the second number. *For example:*

1. $(8 \times 10^5) \div (2 \times 10^2) =$

$$(8 \times 10^5) \div (2 \times 10^2) = 4 \times 10^3$$

2. $\dfrac{7 \times 10^9}{4 \times 10^3} = 1.75 \times 10^6$

3. $(6 \times 10^7) \div (3 \times 10^9) =$

$$(6 \times 10^7) \div (3 \times 10^9) = 2 \times 10^{-2}$$

4. $(2 \times 10^4) \div (5 \times 10^2) =$

$$(2 \times 10^4) \div (5 \times 10^2) = .4 \times 10^2$$

This answer must be changed to scientific notation.

$.4 \times 10^2 = 4 \times 10^1$

5. $(8.4 \times 10^5) \div (2.1 \times 10^{-4}) =$

$$(8.4 \times 10^5) \div (2.1 \times 10^{-4}) = 4 \times 10^{5-(-4)} = 4 \times 10^9$$

Practice: Division in Scientific Notation Problems

1. $(8 \times 10^7) \div (4 \times 10^3) =$

2. $\dfrac{9.3 \times 10^8}{3.1 \times 10^5} =$

3. $(7.5 \times 10^{12}) \div (1.5 \times 10^{15}) =$
4. $(1.2 \times 10^5) \div (4 \times 10^3) =$
5. $(9 \times 10^2) \div (2 \times 10^8) =$
6. $(6 \times 10^4) \div (2 \times 10^{-3}) =$

Answers: Division in Scientific Notation Problems

1. 2×10^4 4. $.3 \times 10^2 = 3 \times 10^1$
2. 3×10^3 5. 4.5×10^{-6}
3. 5×10^{-3} 6. 3×10^7 (exponents: $4 - (-3) = 4 + 3 = 7$)

Powers and Exponents

● An *exponent* is a positive or negative number placed above and to the right of a quantity. It expresses the power to which the quantity is to be raised or lowered. In 4^3, 3 is the exponent. It shows that 4 is to be used as a factor three times. $4 \times 4 \times 4$ (multiplied by itself twice). 4^3 is read as *four to the third power* (or *four cubed* as discussed below). *Some examples:*

$$2^4 = 2 \times 2 \times 2 \times 2 = 16$$
$$3^2 = 3 \times 3 = 9$$
$$3^5 = 3 \times 3 \times 3 \times 3 \times 3 = 243$$

Remember that $x^1 = x$ and $x^0 = 1$ when x is any number (other than 0).

For example:

$$2^1 = 2 \qquad 2^0 = 1$$
$$3^1 = 3 \qquad 3^0 = 1$$
$$4^1 = 4 \qquad 4^0 = 1$$

- If the exponent is negative, such as 3^{-2}, then the number and exponent may be dropped under the number 1 in a fraction to remove the negative sign. The number can be simplified as follows:

$$3^{-2} = \frac{1}{3^2} = \frac{1}{9}$$

A few more examples:

$$2^{-3} = \frac{1}{2^3} = \frac{1}{8}$$

$$3^{-4} = \frac{1}{3^4} = \frac{1}{81}$$

$$4^{-2} = \frac{1}{4^2} = \frac{1}{16}$$

Squares and Cubes

- Two specific types of powers should be noted, *squares and cubes*. To *square a number* just multiply it by itself (exponent would be 2). For example, 6 squared (written 6^2) is 6×6, or 36. 36 is called a perfect square (the square of a whole number). Following is a list of perfect squares:

$0^2 = 0$	$5^2 = 25$	$9^2 = 81$
$1^2 = 1$	$6^2 = 36$	$10^2 = 100$
$2^2 = 4$	$7^2 = 49$	$11^2 = 121$
$3^2 = 9$	$8^2 = 64$	$12^2 = 144$ etc.
$4^2 = 16$		

To *cube a number* just multiply it by itself twice (exponent would be 3). For example, 5 cubed (written 5^3) is $5 \times 5 \times 5$, or 125. 125 is called a perfect cube (the cube of a whole number). Following is a list of perfect cubes:

$0^3 = 0$	$4^3 = 64$
$1^3 = 1$	$5^3 = 125$
$2^3 = 8$	$6^3 = 216$
$3^3 = 27$	$7^3 = 343$ etc.

Practice: Powers and Exponents Problems

Give each answer without exponents.

1. $5^4 =$ 4. $7^0 =$
2. $2^5 =$ 5. $5^{-2} =$
3. $6^1 =$

Answers: Powers and Exponents Problems

1. $5^4 = 5 \times 5 \times 5 \times 5 = 625$ 4. $7^0 = 1$
2. $2^5 = 2 \times 2 \times 2 \times 2 \times 2 = 32$
3. $6^1 = 6$ 5. $5^{-2} = \dfrac{1}{5^2} = \dfrac{1}{25}$

Operations with Powers and Exponents

- To *multiply* two numbers with exponents, *if the base numbers are the same,* simply keep the base number and add the exponents. *For example:*

  1. $2^3 \times 2^5 = 2^8$ $(2 \times 2 \times 2) \times (2 \times 2 \times 2 \times 2 \times 2) = 2^8$
  2. $3^2 \times 3^4 = 3^6$
  3. $5^4 \times 5^3 = 5^7$

- To *divide* two numbers with exponents, *if the base numbers are the same,* simply keep the base number and subtract the second exponent from the first. *For example:*

  1. $3^4 \div 3^2 = 3^2$ 2. $4^8 \div 4^5 = 4^3$ 3. $\dfrac{9^6}{9^2} = 9^4$

- To *multiply or divide* numbers with exponents, *if the base numbers are different,* you must simplify each number with an exponent first and then perform the operation. *For example:*

  1. $3^2 \times 2^2 = 9 \times 4 = 36$
  2. $6^2 \div 2^3 = 36 \div 8 = 4\frac{4}{8} = 4\frac{1}{2}$

  (Some shortcuts are possible.)

- To *add or subtract* numbers with exponents, *whether the base numbers are the same or different,* you must simplify each number with an exponent first and then perform the indicated operation.

For example:

1. $3^2 - 2^3 = 9 - 8 = 1$
2. $4^3 + 3^2 = 64 + 9 = 73$

● If a *number with an exponent is taken to another power* $(4^2)^3$, simply keep the original base number and multiply the exponents. *For example:*

1. $(4^2)^3 = 4^6$
2. $(3^3)^2 = 3^6$

Practice: Operations with Powers and Exponents Problems

Simplify, but leave with a number and one exponent when possible.

1. $2^4 \times 2^7 =$	5. $4^6 \div 4^2 =$	9. $(4^2)^4 =$
2. $3^6 \times 3^4 =$	6. $5^2 \div 5^4 =$	10. $(5^3)^5 =$
3. $5^3 \times 5 =$	7. $4^2 \times 3^3 =$	11. $(3^4)^3 =$
4. $2^9 \div 2^4 =$	8. $2^4 \div 3^2 =$	12. $(6^2)^3 =$

Answers: Operations with Powers and Exponents Problems

1. 2^{11}	7. $432 \ (16 \times 27)$
2. 3^{10}	8. $1\frac{7}{9} \ (16 \div 9)$
3. $5^4 \ (5^3 \times 5 = 5^3 \times 5^1 = 5^4)$	9. 4^8
4. 2^5	10. 5^{15}
5. 4^4	11. 3^{12}
6. 5^{-2} or $\dfrac{1}{5^2}$	12. 6^6

Square Roots and Cube Roots

● Note that square and cube roots and operations with them are often included in algebra sections, and the following will be discussed further in that section.

Square Roots

● To find the *square root* of a number, you want to find some number that when multiplied by itself gives you the original number. In other words, to find the square root of 25, you want to find the number that when multiplied by itself gives you 25. The square root of 25, then, is 5. The symbol for square root is $\sqrt{}$. Following is a list of perfect (whole number) square roots:

$$\sqrt{0} = 0 \qquad \sqrt{16} = 4 \qquad \sqrt{64} = 8$$
$$\sqrt{1} = 1 \qquad \sqrt{25} = 5 \qquad \sqrt{81} = 9$$
$$\sqrt{4} = 2 \qquad \sqrt{36} = 6 \qquad \sqrt{100} = 10 \quad \text{etc.}$$
$$\sqrt{9} = 3 \qquad \sqrt{49} = 7$$

Following is a list of some perfect square decimals:

$$\sqrt{.01} = .1 \qquad \sqrt{.16} = .4 \qquad \sqrt{.49} = .7$$
$$\sqrt{.04} = .2 \qquad \sqrt{.25} = .5 \qquad \sqrt{.64} = .8$$
$$\sqrt{.09} = .3 \qquad \sqrt{.36} = .6 \qquad \sqrt{.81} = .9$$

(Note: $\sqrt{.1} \neq .1$, $\sqrt{.4} \neq .2$, etc.)

● Other roots are similarly defined and identified by the index given. *Special Note:* If no sign (or a positive sign) is placed in front of the square root, then the positive answer is required. Only if a negative sign is in front of the square root is the negative answer required. This notation is used on most standardized exams and will be adhered to in this book. *For example:*

1. $\sqrt{9} = 3$ $\qquad\qquad$ 2. $\sqrt{16} = 4$

$\quad -\sqrt{9} = -3$ $\qquad\qquad\quad -\sqrt{16} = -4$

Cube Roots

● To find the *cube root* of a number, you want to find some number that when multiplied by itself twice gives you the original number. In other words, to find the cube root of 8, you want to find the number that when multiplied by itself twice gives you 8. The cube root of 8, then, is 2, since $2 \times 2 \times 2 = 8$. Notice that the symbol for cube root is the square root sign with a small three (called the index) above and to the left $\sqrt[3]{}$. (In square root, an index of two is understood and usually not written.) Following is a list of perfect (whole number) cube roots:

$$\sqrt[3]{0} = 0 \qquad \sqrt[3]{27} = 3$$
$$\sqrt[3]{1} = 1 \qquad \sqrt[3]{64} = 4$$
$$\sqrt[3]{8} = 2 \qquad \sqrt[3]{125} = 5$$

Approximating Square Roots

- To find the square root of a number that is not an exact square, it will be necessary to find an approximate answer by using the procedure explained below.

1. Approximate $\sqrt{42}$.

   The $\sqrt{42}$ is between $\sqrt{36}$ and $\sqrt{49}$. $\sqrt{36} < \sqrt{42} < \sqrt{49}$

   $\sqrt{36} = 6$
   $\sqrt{49} = 7$

   Therefore, $6 < \sqrt{42} < 7$, and since 42 is halfway between 36 and 49, $\sqrt{42}$ is halfway between $\sqrt{36}$ and $\sqrt{49}$. To check, multiply: $6.5 \times 6.5 = 42.25$, or about 42.

   Square roots of nonperfect squares can be approximated or looked up in tables. You may wish to keep these two in mind:

   $$\sqrt{2} \simeq 1.414 \qquad \sqrt{3} \simeq 1.732$$

Practice: Approximating Square Root Problems

1. $\sqrt{22}$ 2. $\sqrt{71}$ 3. $\sqrt{13}$ 4. $\sqrt{\dfrac{400}{24}}$

Answers: Approximating Square Root Problems

1. 4.7

   $\sqrt{16} < \sqrt{22} < \sqrt{25}$
   $4 < \sqrt{22} < 5$
   $4 < 4.7 < 5$

   Check:

   ```
     4.7
   ×  4.7
     329
    188
   22.09 ≃ 22
   ```

2. 8.4

   $\sqrt{64} < \sqrt{71} < \sqrt{81}$
   $8 < \sqrt{71} < 9$
   $8 < 8.4 < 9$

   Check:

   ```
     8.4
   ×  8.4
     336
    672
   70.56 ≃ 71
   ```

3. 3.6

$\sqrt{9} < \sqrt{13} < \sqrt{16}$
$3 < \sqrt{13} < 4$
$3 < 3.6 < 4$

Check:

```
      3.6
  ×   3.6
      216
     108
    12.96 ≃ 13
```

4. 4.1

$\sqrt{\dfrac{400}{24}} = \sqrt{16.7}$
$\sqrt{16} < \sqrt{16.7} < \sqrt{25}$
$4 < \sqrt{16.7} < 5$
$4 < 4.1 < 5$

Check:

```
      4.1
  ×   4.1
      41
     164
    16.81 ≃ 16.7
```

Simplifying Square Roots

● Sometimes you will have to simplify square roots or write them in simplest form. In fractions, $\frac{2}{4}$ can be reduced to $\frac{1}{2}$. In square roots, $\sqrt{32}$ can be simplified to $4\sqrt{2}$. To *simplify a square root,* first factor the number under the $\sqrt{}$ into a counting number times the largest perfect square number that will divide into the number without leaving a remainder. (Perfect square numbers are 1, 4, 9, 16, 25, 36, 49 . . .). *For example:*

$$\sqrt{32} = \sqrt{16 \times 2}$$

Then take the square root of the perfect square number.

$$\sqrt{16 \times 2} = \sqrt{16} \times \sqrt{2} = 4 \times \sqrt{2}$$

and finally write as a single expression: $4\sqrt{2}$

Remember that most square roots cannot be simplified, as they are already in simplest form, such as $\sqrt{7}$, $\sqrt{10}$, $\sqrt{15}$.

Practice: Simplifying Square Roots Problems

Simplify the following.

1. $\sqrt{18}$ 2. $\sqrt{75}$ 3. $\sqrt{96}$ 4. $\sqrt{50}$

Answers: Simplifying Square Roots Problems

1. $3\sqrt{2}$

$$\begin{aligned} \sqrt{18} &= \sqrt{9 \times 2} \\ &= \sqrt{9} \times \sqrt{2} \\ &= 3 \times \sqrt{2} \\ &= 3\sqrt{2} \end{aligned}$$

3. $4\sqrt{6}$

$$\begin{aligned} \sqrt{96} &= \sqrt{16 \times 6} \\ &= \sqrt{16} \times \sqrt{6} \\ &= 4 \times \sqrt{6} \\ &= 4\sqrt{6} \end{aligned}$$

2. $5\sqrt{3}$

$$\begin{aligned} \sqrt{75} &= \sqrt{25 \times 3} \\ &= \sqrt{25} \times \sqrt{3} \\ &= 5 \times \sqrt{3} \\ &= 5\sqrt{3} \end{aligned}$$

4. $5\sqrt{2}$

$$\begin{aligned} \sqrt{50} &= \sqrt{25 \times 2} \\ &= \sqrt{25} \times \sqrt{2} \\ &= 5 \times \sqrt{2} \\ &= 5\sqrt{2} \end{aligned}$$

Statistics

Some Basics: Measures of Central Tendencies

- Any measure indicating a center of a distribution is called a *measure of central tendency*. The three basic measures of central tendency are

    mean (or arithmetic mean)
    median
    mode

Mean

- The *mean* (arithmetic mean) is what is usually called the average. The arithmetic mean is the most frequently used measure of central tendency. It is generally reliable, easy to use, and is more stable than the median. To determine the arithmetic mean, simply total the items and then divide by the number of items. *For example:*

    1. What is the arithmetic mean of 0, 12, 18, 20, 31, and 45?

        $$0 + 12 + 18 + 20 + 31 + 45 = 126$$
        $$126 \div 6 = 21$$
        The arithmetic mean is 21.

2. What is the arithmetic mean of 25, 27, 27, and 27?

$$25 + 27 + 27 + 27 = 106$$
$$106 \div 4 = 26\frac{1}{2}$$

The arithmetic mean is $26\frac{1}{2}$.

3. What is the arithmetic mean of 20 and -10?

$$20 + (-10) = +10$$
$$10 \div 2 = 5$$

The arithmetic mean is 5.

Practice: Arithmetic Mean Problems

1. Find the arithmetic mean of 3, 6, and 12.
2. Find the arithmetic mean of 2, 8, 15, and 23.
3. Find the arithmetic mean of 26, 28, 36, and 40.
4. Find the arithmetic mean of 3, 7, -5, and -13.

Answers: Arithmetic Mean Problems

1. 7 $(21 \div 3)$ 3. $32\frac{1}{2}$ $(130 \div 4)$
2. 12 $(48 \div 4)$ 4. -2 $(-8 \div 4)$

Weighted Mean

● When one or a number of items is used several times, those items have more "weight." This establishment of relative importance or weighting is used to compute the *weighted mean. For example:*

What is the mean of three tests averaging 70% plus seven tests averaging 85%?

In effect you have here ten exams, three of which score 70% and seven of which score 85%. Rather than adding all ten scores, to determine the above "weighted mean," simply multiply 3 times 70% to find the total of those items (210); then multiply 7 times 85% to find their total (595). Now add the two totals (805) and divide by the number of items overall (10). The weighted mean is thus 80.5%.

Practice: Weighted Mean Problems

1. For the first nine months of the year, the average monthly rainfall was two inches. For the last three months of that year, rainfall

averaged four inches per month. What was the mean monthly rainfall for the entire year?

2. Six students averaged 90% on a class test. Four other students averaged 70% on the test. What was the mean score of all ten students?

Answers: Weighted Mean Problems

1. $9 \times 2'' = 18''$
   $\underline{3 \times 4'' = 12''}$
   Total = 30″ divided by 12 months in all = 2.5″ monthly mean

2. $6 \times 90 = 540$
   $\underline{4 \times 70 = 280}$
   Total = 820 divided by 10 students = 82%

Median

- The *median* of a set of numbers arranged in ascending or descending order is the middle number (if there is an odd number of items in the set). If there is an even number of items in the set, their median is the arithmetic mean of the middle two numbers. The median is easy to calculate and is not influenced by extreme measurements. *For example:*

1. Find the median of 3, 4, 6, 9, 21, 24, 56.
   9 is the median.

2. Find the median of 4, 5, 6, 10.
   5½ is the median.

Practice: Median Problems

Find the median of each group of numbers.

1. 9, 3, 5   3. 100, 101, 102, 20
2. 18, 16, 0, 7, 12   4. 71, −5, −3, −100

Answers: Median Problems

1. 5—3,⑤,9

2. 12—0, 7, ⑫, 16, 18

3. 100.5—20, 100, $\overset{100.5}{\widehat{}}$101, 102

4. −4—−100, −5, $\overset{-4}{\widehat{}}$−3, 71

Mode

- The set, class, or classes that appear most, or whose frequency is the greatest is the *mode* or modal class. (Mode is not greatly influenced by extreme cases but is probably the least important or least used of the three types.) *For example:*

Find the mode of 3, 4, 8, 9, 9, 2, 6, 11

The mode is 9 because it appears more often than any other number.

Practice: Mode Problems

Find the mode of each group of numbers.

1. 2, 2, 3
2. 8, 4, 3, 5, 4, 6
3. 7, 8, 4, −3, 2, −3
4. 100, 101, 100, 102, 100, 101

Answers: Mode Problems

1. 2   2. 4   3. −3   4. 100

Range

- For a set of numbers, the *range* is the difference between the largest and the smallest number. The range depends solely on the extreme values. *For example:*

Find the range of the following numbers. 3, 5, 7, 3, 2
7 − 2 = 5 The range is 5.

Practice: Range Problems

1. Find the range of 2, 45, 106, 99
2. Find the range of 6, 101, 152, −5

Answers: Range Problems

1. 106 − 2 = 104   2. 152 − (−5) = 157

Practice: Measures of Central Tendencies Problems

Find the mean, mode, median, and range of each of the following sets.

1. 7, 8, 8, 14, 18   2. 9, 10, 106, 120, 120   3. $-3, -1, 0, 2, 2, 3$

Answers: Measure of Central Tendencies Problems

1. Mean = 11
   $55 \div 5 = 11$
   Mode = 8
   Median = 8
   Range = 11
   $18 - 7 = 11$

2. Mean = 73
   $365 \div 5 = 73$
   Mode = 120
   Median = 106
   Range = 111
   $120 - 9 = 111$

3. Mean = .5
   $3 \div 6 = .5$
   Mode = 2
   Median = 1
   average of 0 and 2
   Range = 6
   $3 - (-3) = 6$

Measures

Measurement Systems

CUSTOMARY SYSTEM, OR
ENGLISH SYSTEM

Length
   12 inches (in) = 1 foot (ft)
   3 feet = 1 yard (yd)
   36 inches = 1 yard
   1,760 yards = 1 mile (mi)
   5,280 feet = 1 mile

Weight
   16 ounces (oz) = 1 pound (lb)
   2000 pounds = 1 ton (T)

Capacity
   2 cups = 1 pint (pt)
   2 pints = 1 quart (qt)
   4 quarts = 1 gallon (gal)

Time
    365 days = 1 year
    52 weeks = 1 year
    10 years = 1 decade
    100 years = 1 century

Converting Units of Measure

Examples:

1. If 36 inches equals 1 yard, then 3 yards equals how many inches?

    Intuitively: $3 \times 36 = 108$ inches

    By proportion: $\dfrac{3}{x} = \dfrac{1}{36}$

    Remember to place the same units across from each other—inches across from inches, etc. Then solve.

$$\frac{3}{x} = \frac{1}{36}$$

$$108 = x$$

$$x = 108 \text{ inches}$$

2. If 2.2 pounds equals 1 kilogram, then 10 pounds equals approximately how many kilograms?

    Intuitively: $10 \div 2.2 = 4.5$ kilograms

    By proportion: $\dfrac{x}{10} = \dfrac{1}{2.2}$

$$2.2x = 10$$

$$\frac{2.2x}{2.2} = \frac{10}{2.2}$$

$$x = 4.5 \text{ kilograms}$$

3. Change 3 decades into weeks.

    Since 1 decade equals 10 years and 1 year equals 52 weeks, then 3 decades equal 30 years.

30 years × 52 weeks = 1,560 weeks in 30 years or 3 decades

Notice that this was converted step-by-step. It could have been done in one step.

$$3 \times 10 \times 52 = 1,560 \text{ weeks}$$

Practice: Simple Conversion Problems

1. If 1,760 yards equal 1 mile, how many yards are in 5 miles?
2. If 1 kilometer equals approximately .6 mile, approximately how many kilometers are there in 3 miles?
3. How many cups are in 3 gallons?
4. How many ounces are in 6 pounds?
5. If 1 kilometer equals 1,000 meters and 1 dekameter equals 10 meters, how many dekameters are in
   a. 1 kilometer
   b. 3 kilometers

Answers: Simple Conversion Problems

1. $1,760 \times 5 = 8,800$ yards in 5 miles.

2. $\dfrac{1}{.6} = \dfrac{x}{3}$

   $.6x = 3$

   $\dfrac{.6x}{.6} = \dfrac{3}{.6}$

   $x = 5$ kilometers

3. $4 \times 3 \times 2 \times 2 = 48$ cups in 3 gallons.

4. $6 \times 16 = 96$ ounces in 6 pounds.

5. a. $\dfrac{1}{10} = \dfrac{x}{1,000}$

      $10x = 1,000$

      $\dfrac{10x}{10} = \dfrac{1,000}{10}$

      $x = 100$ dekameters

   b. $\dfrac{1}{10} = \dfrac{x}{3,000}$

      $10x = 3,000$

      $\dfrac{10x}{10} = \dfrac{3,000}{10}$

      $x = 300$ dekameters

ARITHMETIC REVIEW TEST

Questions

1. The numbers 1, 2, 3, 4, . . . are called _____.

2. The numbers 0, 1, 2, 3, . . . are called _____.

3. The numbers . . . −2, −1, 0, 1, 2, . . . are called _____.

4. Fractions and integers fall into a category called _____.

5. $\sqrt{3}$ and π are examples of _____.

6. A prime number is a number that can be divided evenly by _____.

7. A composite number is divisible by _____.

8. The first four square numbers greater than zero are _____, _____, _____, _____.

9. The first four cube numbers greater than zero are _____, _____, _____, _____.

10. Give the symbol or symbols for each of the following.
    (a) is equal to _____
    (b) is not equal to _____
    (c) is greater than _____
    (d) is less than _____
    (e) is greater than or equal to _____
    (f) is less than or equal to _____
    (g) is parallel to _____

11. "5 times 4" can be written a number of ways. Show three of them. _____, _____, _____

12. List the properties that are represented by each of the following.
    (a) $3 + 0 = 3$
    (b) $4 \times 1 = 4$
    (c) $3 + 6 = 6 + 3$
    (d) $4 + (6 + 2) = (4 + 6) + 2$
    (e) $3 + (-3) = 0$
    (f) $4(3 + 5) = 4(3) + 4(5)$

(g) $7 \times \frac{1}{7} = 1$

(h) $6 \times 8 = 8 \times 6$

(i) $(2 \times 6) \times 3 = 2 \times (6 \times 3)$

13. In the number 543,216, which digit is in the ten thousands place?

14. Express 367 in expanded notation.

15. $(4 \times 10^2) + (3 \times 10^0) + (2 \times 10^{-2}) =$

16. Simplify $3[5 + 2(3 - 1)]$

17. Simplify $2 + 3\{2 + 4[6 + 4(2 + 1)]\}$

18. Simplify $8 + 2 \times 6 + 10^2 + (2 + 3) \times 5$

19. Round off 7.1779 to the nearest thousandth.

20. Complete the number line below

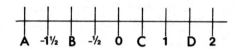

A -1½ B -½ 0 C 1 D 2

21. $-8 + 5 =$

22. $8 - 17 =$

23. $-6 - 5 =$

24. $12 - (-6) =$

25. -19
    $- +24$

26. $12 - (4 - 7 + 6) =$

27. $(-18)(5) =$

28. $-15 \div -3 =$

29. $0 \div 5 =$

30. $\frac{8}{0} =$

31. The number 8,424 is divisible by which numbers between 1 and 10?

32. An improper fraction has _____.

33. Change $^{17}/_3$ to a mixed number.

34. Change $9^1/_4$ to an improper fraction.

35. Reduce $^{14}/_{35}$.

36. Change $^1/_4$ to twelfths.

37. List all the factors of 30.

38. Find the greatest common factor of 18 and 24.

39. List the first four multiples of 7.

40. Find the least common multiple of 6 and 8.

41. $^3/_7 + ^4/_5 =$

42. $-\dfrac{6}{7} + \dfrac{1}{4} =$

43. $^5/_8 - ^1/_3 =$

44. $^1/_4 - ^2/_3 =$

45. $3^1/_5 + 4^3/_8 =$

46. $-5^1/_2 + 4^1/_4 =$

47. $6^1/_4 - 3^3/_5 =$

48. $^3/_5 \times ^{25}/_{36} =$

49. $-\dfrac{1}{6} \times -\dfrac{2}{7} =$

50. $8 \times ^1/_6 =$

51. $-6^1/_2 \times 2^4/_{13} =$

52. $^4/_9 \div ^5/_8 =$

53. $\dfrac{^3/_4}{^4/_5}$

54. $4^1/_3 \div 3^3/_4 =$

55. Simplify $\dfrac{1}{2 + \dfrac{1}{4 + \frac{1}{2}}}$

56. Change .35 to a fraction in lowest terms.

57. $4.6 + 3.924 + 1.88 =$

58. $6.009 - 4.11 =$

59. $8.9 \times .32 =$

60. $23.44 \div .4 =$

61. Change ⅝ to a decimal.

62. Change .66 to a fraction in lowest terms.

63. Change .6 to a percent.

64. Change 57% to a decimal.

65. Change ⁷⁄₂₅ to a percent.

66. Change 78% to a fraction in lowest terms.

67. What is 45% of 30?

68. 15 is what percent of 120?

69. 21 is 30% of what number?

70. What is the percent increase from 120 to 150?

71. Express 360,000 in scientific notation.

72. Express .0002 in scientific notation.

73. $(3 \times 10^5)(2 \times 10^7) =$

74. $(7 \times 10^3)(5 \times 10^8) =$

75. $(1.5 \times 10^{-6})(3 \times 10^8) =$

76. $(9 \times 10^8) \div (3 \times 10^3) =$

77. $\dfrac{9 \times 10^2}{5 \times 10^8} =$

78. $(3 \times 10^7) \div (5 \times 10^{-4}) =$

79. $4^3 =$

80. $8^0 =$

81. $5^{-2} =$

82. $7^3 \times 7^5 =$ (with exponent)

83. $5^8 \div 5^3 =$ (with exponent)

84. $8^2 \times 3^2 =$

85. $2^6 - 5^2 =$

86. $(4^3)^2 =$ (with exponent)

87. $\sqrt{64} =$

88. $\sqrt[3]{27} =$

89. Approximate $\sqrt{50}$ to the nearest tenth.

90. Simplify $\sqrt{60}$.

91. Find the arithmetic mean, mode, median, and range of the following set of numbers. 7, 4, 3, 9, 6, 8, 9

92. How many ounces in 12 pounds?

93. If 1 decimeter is 10 centimeters and 1 centimeter is 10 millimeters, then how many millimeters are there in a decimeter?

Answers

Page numbers following each answer refer to the review section applicable to this problem type.

1. natural or counting numbers (p. 15)

2. whole numbers (p. 15)

3. integers (p. 15)

4. rational numbers (p. 15)

5. irrational numbers (p. 15)

6. one and itself (p. 15)

7. more than just 1 and itself (p. 15)

8. 1, 4, 9, 16 (p. 15)

9. 1, 8, 27, 64 (p. 15)

10. (a) =, (b) $\neq$, (c) >, (d) <, (e) $\geq$, (f) $\leq$, (g) $\parallel$ (p. 16)

11. 5 × 4, 5 · 4, 5(4) (p. 16)

12. (a) additive identity (p. 16)
    (b) multiplicative identity (p. 17)
    (c) commutative property of addition (p. 16)
    (d) associative property of addition (p. 16)
    (e) additive inverse (p. 16)
    (f) distributive property of multiplication and addition (p. 18)
    (g) multiplicative inverse (p. 16)
    (h) commutative property of multiplication (p. 16)
    (i) associative property of multiplication (p. 16)

13. 4 (p. 19)

14. $(3 \times 10^2) + (6 \times 10^1) + (7 \times 10^0)$ (p. 19)

15. 403.02 (p. 19)

16. 27 (p. 20)

17. 224 (p. 20)

18. 145 (p. 21)

19. 7.178 (p. 22)

20. A = -2, B = -1, C = $\frac{1}{2}$, D = $1\frac{1}{2}$ (p. 23)

21. -3 (p. 24)

22. -9 (p. 25)

23. -11 (p. 25)

24. $+18$ (p. 26)

25. -43 (p. 25)

26. 9 (p. 26)

27. -90 (p. 26)

28. 5 (p. 26)

29. 0 (p. 27)

30. undefined (p. 27)

31. 2, 3, 4, 6, 8, 9 (p. 27)

32. a numerator larger than the denominator (p. 30)

33. $5\frac{2}{3}$ (p. 30)

34. $\frac{37}{4}$ (p. 30)

35. $\frac{2}{5}$ (p. 31)

36. $\frac{3}{12}$ (p. 32)

37. 1, 2, 3, 5, 6, 10, 15, 30 (p. 32)

38. 6 (p. 34)

39. 7, 14, 21, 28 (p. 35)

40. 24 (p. 35)

41. $\frac{43}{35} = 1\frac{8}{35}$ (p. 36)

42. $-\dfrac{17}{28}$ (p. 37)

43. $\frac{7}{24}$ (p. 38)

44. $-\dfrac{5}{12}$ (p. 38)

45. $7\frac{23}{40}$ (p. 41)

46. $-1\frac{1}{4}$ (p. 41)

47. $2\frac{13}{20}$ (p. 43)

48. $\frac{5}{12}$ (p. 44)

49. $\frac{1}{21}$ (p. 44)

50. $\frac{4}{3} = 1\frac{1}{3}$ (p. 44)

51. -15 (p. 45)

52. $\frac{32}{45}$ (p. 46)

53. $\frac{15}{16}$ (p. 47)

54. $^{52}\!/_{45} = 1^{7}\!/_{45}$ (p. 48)

55. $^{9}\!/_{20}$ (p. 49)

56. $^{7}\!/_{20}$ (p. 50)

57. 10.404 (p. 51)

58. 1.899 (p. 51)

59. 2.848 (p. 52)

60. 58.6 (p. 53)

61. .625 (p. 53)

62. $^{33}\!/_{50}$ (p. 50)

63. 60% (p. 54)

64. .57 (p. 55)

65. 28% (p. 55)

66. $^{39}\!/_{50}$ (p. 56)

67. 13.5 or 13½ (p. 57)

68. 12.5% (p. 57)

69. 70 (p. 57)

70. 25% (p. 61)

71. 3.6×10^{5} (p. 62)

72. 2×10^{-4} (p. 62)

73. 6×10^{12} (p. 63)

74. $35 \times 10^{11} = \underline{3.5 \times 10^{12}}$ (p. 63)

75. 4.5×10^{2} (p. 63)

76. 3×10^{5} (p. 64)

77. 1.8×10^{-6} (p. 64)

78. $.6 \times 10^{11} = \underline{6 \times 10^{10}}$ (p. 64)

79. 64 (p. 65)

80. 1 (p. 65)

81. $\frac{1}{25}$ or $1/(5^2)$ (p. 65)

82. 7^8 (p. 67)

83. 5^5 (p. 67)

84. 576 (p. 67)

85. 39 (p. 67)

86. 4^6 (p. 67)

87. 8 (p. 68)

88. 3 (p. 69)

89. 7.1 (p. 69)

90. $2\sqrt{15}$ (p. 71)

91. mean = $6\frac{4}{7}$, mode = 9, median = 7, range = 6 (p. 72)

92. 192 ounces (p. 77)

93. 100 millimeters (p. 77)

ARITHMETIC GLOSSARY OF TERMS

ADDITIVE INVERSE: The opposite (negative) of the number. Any number plus its additive inverse equals 0.

ASSOCIATIVE PROPERTY: Grouping of elements does not make any difference in the outcome. Only true for multiplication and addition.

BRACES: Grouping symbols used after the use of brackets. Also used to represent a set. { }

BRACKETS: Grouping symbols used after the use of parentheses. [ ]

CANCELING: In multiplication of fractions, dividing the same number into both a numerator and a denominator.

COMMON DENOMINATOR: A number that can be divided evenly by all denominators in the problem.

COMMON FACTORS: Factors which are the same for two or more numbers.

COMMON MULTIPLES: Multiples which are the same for two or more numbers.

COMMUTATIVE PROPERTY: Order of elements does not make any difference in the outcome. Only true for multiplication and addition.

COMPLEX FRACTION: A fraction having a fraction or fractions in the numerator and/or denominator.

COMPOSITE NUMBER: A number divisible by more than just 1 and itself. (4, 6, 9, . . .) 0 and 1 are *not* composite numbers.

CUBE: The result when a number is multiplied by itself twice.

CUBE ROOT: The number that when multiplied by itself twice gives you the original number. For example, 5 is the cube root of 125. Its symbol is $\sqrt[3]{}$. $\sqrt[3]{125} = 5$

DECIMAL FRACTION: Fraction with a denominator 10, 100, 1,000, etc., written using a decimal point. For example, .3, .275.

DECIMAL POINT: A point used to distinguish decimal fractions from whole numbers.

DENOMINATOR: The bottom symbol or number of a fraction.

DIFFERENCE: The result of subtraction.

DISTRIBUTIVE PROPERTY: The process of distributing the number on the outside of the parentheses to each number on the inside. $a(b + c) = ab + ac$

EVEN NUMBER: An integer (positive whole numbers, zero, and negative whole numbers) divisible by 2 with no remainder.

EXPANDED NOTATION: Pointing out the place value of a digit by writing the number as the digit times its place value. $342 = (3 \times 10^2) + (4 \times 10^1) + (2 \times 10^0)$

EXPONENT: A positive or negative number placed above and to the right of a number. Expresses the power to which the quantity is to be raised or lowered.

FACTOR (noun): A number or symbol which divides evenly into a larger number. For example, 6 is a factor of 24.

FACTOR (verb): To find two or more quantities whose product equals the original quantity.

FRACTION: A symbol expressing part of a whole. Consists of a numerator and a denominator. For example, $\frac{3}{5}$ or $\frac{9}{4}$.

GREATEST COMMON FACTOR: The largest factor common to two or more numbers.

HUNDREDTH: The second decimal place to the right of the decimal point. For example, .08 is eight hundredths.

IDENTITY ELEMENT FOR ADDITION: 0. Any number added to 0 gives the original number.

IDENTITY ELEMENT FOR MULTIPLICATION: 1. Any number multiplied by 1 gives the original number.

IMPROPER FRACTION: A fraction in which the numerator is greater than the denominator. For example, $\frac{3}{2}$.

INTEGER: A whole number, either positive, negative, or zero.

INVERT: Turn upside down, as in "invert $\frac{2}{3}$" = $\frac{3}{2}$.

IRRATIONAL NUMBER: A number that is not rational (cannot be written as a fraction x/y, with x a natural number and y an integer). For example, $\sqrt{3}$ or π.

LEAST COMMON MULTIPLE: The smallest multiple that is common to two or more numbers.

LOWEST COMMON DENOMINATOR: The smallest number that can be divided evenly by all denominators in the problem.

MEAN (arithmetic): The average of a number of items in a group (total the items and divide by the number of items).

MEDIAN: The middle item in an ordered group. If the group has an even number of items, the median is the average of the two middle terms.

MIXED NUMBER: A number containing both a whole number and a fraction. For example, $5\frac{1}{2}$.

MODE: The number appearing most frequently in a group.

MULTIPLES: Numbers found by multiplying a number by 2, by 3, by 4, etc.

MULTIPLICATIVE INVERSE: The reciprocal of the number. Any number multiplied by its multiplicative inverse equals 1.

NATURAL NUMBER: A counting numbers. 1, 2, 3, 4, etc.

NEGATIVE NUMBER: A number less than zero.

NUMBER LINE: A visual representation of the positive and negative numbers and zero. The line may be thought of as an infinitely long ruler with negative numbers to the left of zero and positive numbers to the right of zero.

NUMERATOR: The top symbol or number of a fraction.

ODD NUMBER: An integer (whole number) not divisible evenly by 2.

OPERATION: Multiplication, addition, subtraction, or division.

ORDER OF OPERATIONS: The priority given to an operation relative to other operations. For example, multiplication takes precedence (is performed before) addition.

PARENTHESES: Grouping symbols. ( )

PERCENTAGE: A common fraction with 100 as its denominator. For example, 37% is $^{37}/_{100}$.

PLACE VALUE: The value given a digit by the position of a digit in the number.

POSITIVE NUMBER: A number greater than zero.

POWER: A product of equal factors. $4 \times 4 \times 4 = 4^3$, read "four to the third power" or "the third power of four." *Power* and *exponent* are sometimes used interchangeably.

PRIME NUMBER: A number that can be divided by only itself and one. For example, 2, 3, 5, 7, etc. 0 and 1 are *not* prime.

PRODUCT: The result of multiplication.

PROPER FRACTION: A fraction in which the numerator is less than the denominator. For example, $\frac{2}{3}$.

PROPORTION: Written as two equal ratios. For example, 5 is to 4 as 10 is to 8, or $5/4 = 10/8$.

QUOTIENT: The result of division.

RANGE: The difference between the largest and the smallest number in a set of numbers.

RATIO: A comparison between two numbers or symbols. May be written x:y, x/y, or x is to y.

RATIONAL NUMBER: An integer or fraction such as $\frac{7}{7}$ or $\frac{9}{4}$ or $\frac{5}{1}$. Any number that can be written as a fraction $\frac{x}{y}$ with x a natural number and y an integer.

REAL NUMBER: Any rational or irrational number.

RECIPROCAL: The multiplicative inverse of a number. For example, $\frac{2}{3}$ is the reciprocal of $\frac{3}{2}$.

REDUCING: Changing a fraction into its lowest terms. For example, $\frac{2}{4}$ is reduced to $\frac{1}{2}$.

ROUNDING OFF: Changing a number to a nearest place value as specified. A method of approximating.

SCIENTIFIC NOTATION: A number between 1 and 10 and multiplied by a power of 10. Used for writing very large or very small numbers. For example, 2.5×10^4.

SQUARE: The result when a number is multiplied by itself.

SQUARE ROOT: The number which when multiplied by itself gives you the original number. For example, 5 is the square root of 25. Its symbol is $\sqrt{}$. $\sqrt{25} = 5$

SUM: The result of addition.

TENTH: The first decimal place to the right of the decimal point. For example, .7 is seven tenths.

WEIGHTED MEAN: The mean of a set of numbers which have been weighted (multiplied by their relative importance or times of occurrence).

WHOLE NUMBER: 0, 1, 2, 3, etc.

ALGEBRA

ALGEBRA DIAGNOSTIC TEST

Questions

1. Express algebraically: five increased by three times x

2. Evaluate: $x^2 - 3x - 4$ if $x = 5$

3. Evaluate: $\dfrac{x}{3} - \dfrac{x + 2y}{y}$ if $x = 2$ and $y = 6$

4. Evaluate $|3 - 5|$

5. Solve for x: $2x - 9 = 21$

6. Solve for y: $\dfrac{4}{7}y + 6 = 18$

7. Solve for x: $8x - 8 = 4x + 3$

8. Solve for x: $|x| - 2 = 5$

9. Solve for a: $\dfrac{a - 1}{3} + \dfrac{a + 2}{6} = 2$

10. Solve for y: $\dfrac{3}{y} + \dfrac{2}{y + 2} = 2$

11. Solve for x: $wx + r = t$

12. Solve for m: x is to y as a is to m

13. Solve for y: $\dfrac{8}{y} = \dfrac{3}{7}$

14. Solve this system for x and y:
$8x + 2y = 7$
$3x - 4y = 5$

15. $\dfrac{4xy^2z}{-7xy^2z}$

92

16. Solve this system for x, y, and z:

$$2x - y + z = 5$$
$$x + y + z = 2$$
$$x + 2y + 4z = 7$$

17. $12x + 4x - 23x - (-3x) =$

18. $6x^2y(4xy^2) =$

19. $(2x^3y^4)^3 =$

20. $(-2i)(3i) =$

21. $\dfrac{a^7b^3}{a^2b} =$

22. $\dfrac{x^3}{x^{-6}} =$

23. Change $x^{3/5}$ to radical form.

24. $4^{-1/2} =$

25. $\dfrac{-5(a^3b^2)(2a^2b^5)}{a^4b^3} =$

26. $(4x - 7z) - (3x - 4z) =$

27. $(4x + 2y)(3x - y) =$

28. $\dfrac{16x^2y + 18xy^3}{2xy} =$

29. $(\lambda^2 + 3\lambda - 18) \div (\lambda + 6) =$

30. Factor completely: $8x^3 - 12x^2$

31. Factor: $16a^2 - 81$

32. Factor: $x^2 - 2x - 63$

33. Factor: $3a^2 - 4a + 1$

34. Factor: $m^2 - 2mn - 3n^2$

35. Factor: $m^3 - p^3$

36. Solve for r: $r^2 - 10r = -24$

37. Solve for x: $x^2 - 49 = 0$

38. Solve for x: $x^2 + 2x + 2 = 0$

39. Reduce: $\dfrac{x^2 - 3x + 2}{3x - 6}$

40. Reduce: $\dfrac{x^2 + 2x + cx + 2c}{xc + 2c}$

41. $\dfrac{x^3}{2y} \cdot \dfrac{5y^2}{6x} =$

42. $\dfrac{x - 5}{x} \cdot \dfrac{x + 2}{x^2 - 2x - 15} =$

43. $\dfrac{6x - 3}{2} \div \dfrac{2x - 1}{x} =$

44. $\dfrac{3x - 2}{x + 1} - \dfrac{2x - 1}{x + 1} =$

45. $\dfrac{5}{x} + \dfrac{7}{y} =$

46. $\dfrac{3}{a^3b^5} + \dfrac{2}{a^4b^2} =$

47. $\dfrac{2x}{x - 1} - \dfrac{x}{x + 2} =$

48. Solve for x: $2x + 3 < 11$

49. Solve for x: $3x + 4 \geq 5x - 8$

50. Solve for x: $x^2 - x \leq 2$

51. Graph: $\{x: 2 \leq x < 9\}$

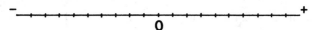

52. Solve for y and graph the answer: $|y - 3| > 1$

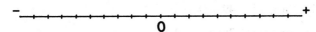

53. Graph: $\{x: -1 < x \le 6, x \text{ is an integer}\}$

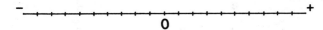

54. Give the coordinates represented by points A and B.

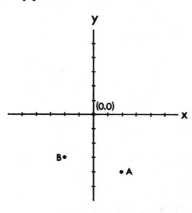

55. Graph: $y = x + 2$

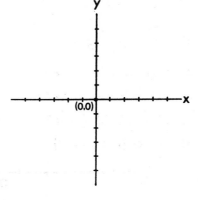

56. Find the slope of this line: $2x - y = 3$

57. Graph: $x + y \leq 1$

58. Graph: $y = x^2 - 1$

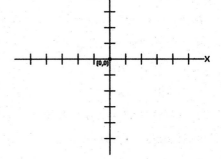

59. Simplify: $\sqrt{18 + 2}$

60. $\sqrt{3} \cdot \sqrt{12} =$

61. $\dfrac{\sqrt{27}}{\sqrt{3}} =$

62. $\dfrac{\sqrt{2}}{\sqrt{2} + 1} =$

63. $\sqrt{18} + \sqrt{2} =$

In problems 64 through 67, each variable is nonnegative.

64. $\sqrt{36a^2b^8} =$

65. $\sqrt{50a^3b^7} =$

66. $\sqrt{5xy} \cdot \sqrt{8x^2yz} =$

67. $3\sqrt{2} \cdot 4\sqrt{5} =$

68. If $\sqrt{x} + 3 = 8$, then x =

In problems 69 through 71, the relation is $A = \{(1, 2)(2, 3)(-1, 4)\}$

69. Is the relation a function?

70. List the domain.

71. List the range.

72. If $f(x) = x^2 + 1$, then $f(3) =$

73. If $\log_2 8 = x$, then x =

74. $-4 - 3 - 2 - 1 + 0 + \ldots 20 =$

75. If $(-3,3)$ and $(5,-3)$ are the end points of a line segment in a plane, state the length of the segment.

76. Find the geometric mean between 6 and 24.

77. $(a - b)^3 =$

Answers

Page numbers following each answer refer to the review section applicable to this problem type.

1. $5 + 3x$ (p. 102)

2. 6 (p. 104)

3. $\dfrac{-10}{6} = \dfrac{-5}{3} = -1\tfrac{2}{3}$ (p. 104)

4. 2 (p. 180)

5. $x = 15$ (p. 107)

6. $y = 21$ (p. 107)

7. $x = \dfrac{11}{4} = 2\tfrac{3}{4}$ (p. 107)

8. $7, -7$ (p. 181)

9. 4 (p. 172)

10. $2, -\tfrac{3}{2}$ (p. 155, p. 172)

11. $x = \dfrac{t - r}{w}$ (p. 114)

12. $m = \dfrac{ay}{x}$ (p. 117)

13. $y = \dfrac{56}{3} = 18\tfrac{2}{3}$ (p. 118)

14. $x = 1, y = -\dfrac{1}{2}$ (p. 121)

15. $-3xy^2z$ (p. 132)

16. $(1, -1, 2)$ (p. 127)

17. $-4x$ (p. 132)

18. $24x^3y^3$ (p. 133)

19. $8x^9y^{12}$ (p. 133)

20. 6 (p. 225)

21. a^5b^2 (p. 134)

22. x^9 (p. 136)

23. $\sqrt[5]{x^3}$ (p.217)

24. $1/2$ (p. 219)

25. $-10ab^4$ (p. 134)

26. $x - 3z$ (p. 138)

27. $12x^2 + 2xy - 2y^2$ (p. 140)

28. $8x + 9y^2$ (p. 142)

29. $(x - 3)$ (p. 143)

30. $4x^2(2x - 3)$ (p. 147)

31. $(4a - 9)(4a + 9)$ (p. 147)

32. $(x - 9)(x + 7)$ (p. 148)

33. $(3a - 1)(a - 1)$ (p. 148)

34. $(m + n)(m - 3n)$ (p. 148)

35. $(m - p)(m^2 + mp + p^2)$ (p. 152)

36. $\{6, 4\}$ (p. 155)

37. $\{7, -7\}$ (p. 155)

38. $(-1 + i)(-1 - i)$ (p. 229)

39. $\dfrac{x - 1}{3}$ (p. 160)

40. $\dfrac{x + c}{c}$ (p. 153, p. 160)

41. $\dfrac{5x^2y}{12}$ (p. 162)

42. $\dfrac{x + 2}{x(x + 3)}$ or $\dfrac{x + 2}{x^2 + 3x}$ (p. 162)

43. $\dfrac{3x}{2}$ (p. 164)

44. $\dfrac{x - 1}{x + 1}$ (p. 166)

45. $\dfrac{5y + 7x}{xy}$ (p. 166)

46. $\dfrac{3a + 2b^3}{a^4b^5}$ (p. 166)

47. $\dfrac{x^2 + 5x}{(x - 1)(x + 2)}$ (p. 166)

48. $\{x: x < 4\}$ (p. 176)

49. $\{x: x \le 6\}$ (p. 176)

50. $\{x: -1 \le x \le 2\}$ (p. 237)

51. 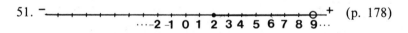 (p. 178)

52. (p. 183)

53. (p. 180)

54. A. $(2, -4)$
    B. $(-2, -3)$ (p. 186)

55.

x	y
0	2
1	3
2	4

(p.189)

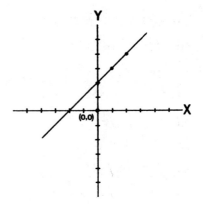

56. 2 (p. 193)

(p. 189)

57.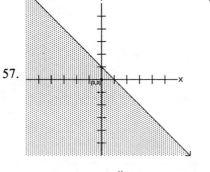

(p. 190)

58.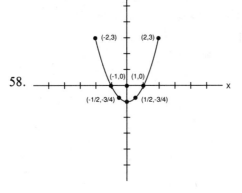

59. $\sqrt{20} = 2\sqrt{5}$ (p. 206)

60. $\sqrt{36} = 6$ (p. 206)

61. $\sqrt{9} = 3$ (p. 213)

62. $2 - \sqrt{2}$ (p. 214)

63. $4\sqrt{2}$ (p. 209)

64. $6ab^4$ (p. 206)

65. $5ab^3\sqrt{2ab}$ (p. 206)

66. $\sqrt{40x^3y^2z} = 2xy\sqrt{10xz}$ (p. 211)

67. $12\sqrt{10}$ (p. 211)

68. $x = 25$ (p. 215)

69. yes (p. 241)

70. $\{1, 2, -1\}$ (p. 241)

71. $\{2, 3, 4\}$ (p. 241)

72. 10 (p. 245)

73. 3 (p. 248)

74. 200 (p. 251)

75. 10 (p. 199)

76. 12 (p. 251)

77. $(a^3 - 3a^2b + 3ab^2 - b^3)$ (p. 255)

ALGEBRA REVIEW

Algebra is essentially arithmetic with some of the numbers replaced by letters or variables. The letters or variables are merely substitutes for numbers. Initially, algebra referred to equation solving, but now it encompasses the language of algebra and the patterns of reasoning. The rules for algebra are basically the same as the rules for arithmetic.

Some Basic Language

Understood Multiplication

- When two or more letters, or a number and letter(s) are written next to each other, they are *understood to be multiplied*. Thus, 8x means 8 timex x. (x8 is never written.) Or ab means a times b. Or 18ab means 18 times a times b.
- To avoid confusion, grouping symbols such as parentheses are sometimes used to separate factors.
- A raised dot also means multiplication. Thus, 6 · 5 means 6 times 5.

Letters to Be Aware of

- Although they may appear in some texts, we recommend that you never use o, e, or i as variables. (Technically, e and i stand for constants or predetermined numbers, and o is too easily confused with 0—zero.) When using z, you may wish to write it as $\not z$ so it is not confused with 2.

Variables and Algebraic Expressions

- A *variable* is a symbol used to denote any element of a given set—often a letter used to stand for a number. Variables are used to change verbal expressions into *algebraic expressions. For example:*

VERBAL EXPRESSION	ALGEBRAIC EXPRESSION
the sum of a number and 7	n + 7 or 7 + n
the number diminished by 10	n − 10
seven times a number	7n
x divided by 4	x/4

Key Words Denoting Addition

sum	larger than	enlarge
plus	gain	rise
more than	increase	grow
greater than		

Key Words Denoting Subtraction

difference	smaller than	lower
minus	fewer than	diminish
lose	decrease	reduced
less than	drop	

Key Words Denoting Multiplication

product	times	of
multiplied by	twice	

Key Words Denoting Division

quotient	ratio
divided by	half

Practice: Expressing Operations Algebraically Problems

Express each of the following algebraically.

1. a number increased by four
2. five less than a number
3. a number reduced by twelve
4. the product of a number and six
5. a number divided by three
6. one half of a number
7. a number multiplied by fourteen
8. the ratio of five to a number
9. twelve decreased by four times y
10. the product of five and the sum of x and y
11. five times c, decreased by one-third of b
12. the average of x, y, and z

Answers: Expressing Operations Algebraically Problems

1. $n + 4$ or $4 + n$
2. $n - 5$
3. $n - 12$
4. $6n$
5. $n/3$
6. $(\frac{1}{2})n$ or $n/2$

7. $14n$
8. $5/n$
9. $12 - 4y$
10. $5(x + y)$ or $(x + y)5$
11. $5c - \frac{1}{3}$ or $5c - (\frac{1}{3})b$
12. $(x + y + z)/3$

Evaluating Expressions

- To *evaluate* an *expression,* just replace the unknowns with grouping symbols, insert the value for the unknowns and do the arithmetic.

Examples:

1. Evaluate: $ab + c$ if $a = 5$, $b = 4$, and $c = 3$.

   $(5)(4) + 3 =$
   $20 + 3 =$
   23

2. Evaluate: $2x^2 + 3y + 6$ if $x = 2$ and $y = 9$.

   $2(2)^2 + 3(9) + 6 =$
   $2(4) + 27 + 6 =$
   $8 + 27 + 6 =$
   $35 + 6 =$
   41

3. Evaluate: $-4p^2 + 5q - 7$ if $p = -3$ and $q = -8$.

   $-4(-3)^2 + 5(-8) - 7 =$
   $-4(9) + 5(-8) - 7 =$
   $-36 - 40 - 7 =$
   $-76 - 7 =$
   -83

4. Evaluate: $\dfrac{a + c}{5} + \dfrac{a}{b + c}$ if $a = 3$, $b = -2$, and $c = 7$.

$$\frac{(3) + (7)}{5} + \frac{3}{(-2) + (7)} =$$

$$\frac{10}{5} + \frac{3}{5} =$$

$$\frac{13}{5} =$$

$2\tfrac{3}{5}$

5. Evaluate: $5x^3y^2$ if $x = -2$ and $y = 3$.

$5(-2)^3(3)^2 =$
$5(-8)(9) =$
$-40(9) =$
-360

Practice: Evaluating Expressions Problems

1. Evaluate: $x^2 + 4x - 7$ if $x = 3$.
2. Evaluate: $y^2 - y + 8$ if $y = 5$.
3. Evaluate: $7s - 2t^2$ if $s = 3$ and $t = 8$.
4. Evaluate: $10m^2 - 5n - 25$ if $m = -6$ and $n = -3$.

5. Evaluate: $\dfrac{x}{2} + \dfrac{x + y}{y}$ if $x = 1$ and $y = 4$

6. Evaluate: $3x^2y^3z$ if $x = 2$, $y = 3$, and $z = -1$.

7. If $x = \dfrac{1}{3}$, then $\dfrac{6x^2}{5} =$

8. If $r = 4$ and $s = 3$, then $\dfrac{3rs}{4r^2s - r} =$

Answers: Evaluating Expressions Problems

1. Evaluate: $x^2 + 4x - 7$ if $x = 3$.

$(3)^2 + 4(3) - 7 =$
$9 + 12 - 7 =$
$21 - 7 =$
14

2. Evaluate: $y^2 - y + 8$ if $y = 5$.

$(5)^2 - (5) + 8 =$
$25 - 5 + 8 =$
$20 + 8 =$
28

3. Evaluate: $7s - 2t^2$ if $s = 3$ and $t = 8$.

$7(3) - 2(8)^2 =$
$7(3) - 2(64) =$
$21 - 128 =$
-107

4. Evaluate: $10m^2 - 5n - 25$ if $m = -6$ and $n = -3$.

$10(-6)^2 - 5(-3) - 25 =$
$10(36) + 15 - 25 =$
$360 + 15 - 25 =$
$375 - 25 =$
350

5. Evaluate: $\dfrac{x}{2} + \dfrac{x + y}{y}$ if $x = 1$ and $y = 4$.

$\dfrac{1}{2} + \dfrac{1 + 4}{4} =$

$\dfrac{1}{2} + \dfrac{5}{4} =$ (finding common denominator)

$\dfrac{2}{4} + \dfrac{5}{4} =$

$\dfrac{7}{4} =$

$1\frac{3}{4}$

6. Evaluate: $3x^2y^3z$ if $x = 2$, $y = 3$, and $z = -1$.

$3(2)^2(3)^3(-1) =$
$3(4)(27)(-1) =$
$12(27)(-1) =$
$324(-1) =$
-324

7. If $x = \dfrac{1}{3}$, then $\dfrac{6x^2}{5} =$

$\dfrac{6(\frac{1}{3})^2}{5} = \dfrac{6(\frac{1}{9})}{5} = \dfrac{\frac{6}{9}}{5} = \dfrac{\frac{2}{3}}{5} =$

$\dfrac{\frac{2}{3}}{\frac{5}{1}} = \dfrac{2}{3} \div \dfrac{5}{1} = \dfrac{2}{3} \times \dfrac{1}{5} = \dfrac{2}{15}$

8. If $r = 4$ and $s = 3$, then $\dfrac{3rs}{4r^2s - r} =$

$\dfrac{3(4)(3)}{4(4)^2(3) - 4} = \dfrac{12(3)}{4(16)(3) - 4} = \dfrac{36}{64(3) - 4} = \dfrac{36}{192 - 4} =$

$\dfrac{36}{188} = \dfrac{18}{94} = \dfrac{9}{47}$

Equations

Solving Equations

● An *equation* is a mathematical sentence, a relationship between numbers and/or symbols. Remember that an equation is like a balance scale, with the equal sign (=) being the fulcrum, or center. Thus, if you do the *same thing to both sides* of the equal sign (say, add 5 to each side), the equation will still be balanced.

Examples:

1. $x - 5 = 23$

To solve the equation $x - 5 = 23$, you must get x by itself on one side; therefore, add 5 to both sides:

$$\begin{array}{r} x - 5 = 23 \\ + 5 \quad +5 \\ \hline x \quad = 28 \end{array}$$

In the same manner, you may subtract, multiply, or divide *both* sides of an equation by the same (nonzero) number, and the equation will not change. Sometimes you may have to use more than one step to solve for an unknown.

2. $3x + 4 = 19$

Subtract 4 from both sides to get the 3x by itself on one side:

$$
\begin{array}{r}
3x + 4 = 19 \\
-\ 4 \quad -4 \\
\hline
3x \quad\ \ = 15
\end{array}
$$

Then divide both sides by 3 to get x:

$$\frac{3x}{3} = \frac{15}{3}$$

$$x = 5$$

Remember: Solving an equation is using opposite operations, until the letter is on a side by itself (for addition, subtract; for multiplication, divide, etc.).

To check, substitute your answer into the original equation.

$$
\begin{array}{r}
3x + 4 = 19 \\
3(5) + 4 = 19 \\
15 + 4 = 19 \\
19 \overset{\checkmark}{=} 19
\end{array}
$$

3. $\dfrac{x}{5} - 4 = 2$

Add 4 to both sides.

$$
\begin{array}{r}
\dfrac{x}{5} - 4 = 2 \\[4pt]
+\ 4\ +4 \\
\hline
\dfrac{x}{5} \quad\ \ = 6
\end{array}
$$

Multiply both sides by 5 to get x.

$$(5)\frac{x}{5} = (5)6$$

$$x = 30$$

4. $\frac{3}{5}x - 6 = 12$

Add 6 to each side.

$$\begin{array}{r} \frac{3}{5}x - 6 = 12 \\ + 6 \quad +6 \\ \hline \frac{3}{5}x \qquad = 18 \end{array}$$

Multiply each side by $\frac{5}{3}$.

$$\left(\frac{5}{3}\right)\frac{3}{5}x = \left(\frac{5}{3}\right)18$$

$$x = \left(\frac{5}{\cancel{3}_1}\right)\frac{\cancel{18}^6}{1}$$

$$x = 30$$

5. $5x = 2x - 6$

Add $-2x$ to each side.

$$\begin{array}{r} 5x = \quad 2x - 6 \\ -2x \quad -2x \\ \hline 3x = \qquad -6 \end{array}$$

Divide both sides by 3.

$$\frac{3x}{3} \quad \frac{-6}{3}$$

$$x = -2$$

6. $6x + 3 = 4x + 5$

Add -3 to each side.

$$\begin{array}{r} 6x + 3 = 4x + 5 \\ - 3 \qquad - 3 \\ \hline 6x \qquad = 4x + 2 \end{array}$$

Add $-4x$ to each side.

$$
\begin{array}{rcl}
6x & = & 4x + 2 \\
-4x & & -4x \\
\hline
2x & = & 2
\end{array}
$$

Divide each side by 2.

$$\frac{2x}{2} = \frac{2}{2}$$

$$x = 1$$

7. $3(2x + 1) - (4 - 2x) = 3$

Simplify.

$$6x + 3 - 4 + 2x = 3$$

Combine like terms.

$$6x + 3 - 4 + 2x = 3$$
$$8x - 1 = 3$$

Add 1 to both sides.

$$
\begin{array}{rcl}
8x - 1 & = & 3 \\
+ 1 & & +1 \\
\hline
8x & = & 4
\end{array}
$$

Divide each side by 8.

$$\frac{8x}{8} = \frac{4}{8}$$

$$x = \frac{4}{8}$$

Reduce

$$x = \frac{1}{2}$$

8. $\dfrac{3x}{2} = 6 - x$

Multiply the complete equation by 2.

$$2\left(\dfrac{3x}{2}\right) = (6 - x)2$$

$$3x = 12 - 2x$$

Add 2x to each side.

$$
\begin{array}{r}
3x = 12 - 2x \\
+2x \qquad + 2x \\
\hline
5x = 12
\end{array}
$$

Divide each side by 5.

$$\dfrac{5x}{5} = \dfrac{12}{5}$$

$$x = \dfrac{12}{5} \text{ or } 2\tfrac{2}{5}$$

9. If $3ac + 2 = 4$, then $c =$

Add $- 2$ to each side.

$$
\begin{array}{r}
3ac + 2 = 4 \\
- 2 -2 \\
\hline
3ac \quad = 2
\end{array}
$$

Divide each side by 3a.

$$\dfrac{3ac}{3a} = \dfrac{2}{3a}$$

$$c = \dfrac{2}{3a}$$

10. If $6 = \dfrac{2 + x}{x}$, then x =

Multiply each side by x.

$$x(6) = \left(\dfrac{2 + x}{x}\right) x$$

$$6x = 2 + x$$

Subtract x from each side.

$$\begin{array}{r} 6x = 2 + x \\ -\ x \quad\quad -\ x \\ \hline 5x = 2 \end{array}$$

Divide each side by 5.

$$\dfrac{5x}{5} = \dfrac{2}{5}$$

$$x = \dfrac{2}{5}$$

Practice: Solving Equations Problems

Solve each equation for y.

1. $y + 8 = 19$
2. $y - 9 = 21$
3. $4y + 8 = 32$

4. $-\dfrac{y}{5} = 8$

5. $\dfrac{2}{3} y + 1 = 13$

6. $4y = 52$
7. $7y = 4y - 12$
8. $5y - 4 = 3y + 4$

9. $3y - \dfrac{3}{5} y = 8$

10. $\dfrac{3y}{4} + 2 = 4 - 2y$

11. If $\dfrac{5 + 2y}{y} = 8$, then y =

12. If $\dfrac{y - 4}{y + 3} = 6$, then y =

Answers: Solving Equations Problems

1. $y + 8 = 19$
$\underline{-8 \quad -8}$
$y = 11$

2. $y - 9 = 21$
$\underline{+9 \quad +9}$
$y = 30$

3. $4y + 8 = 32$
$\underline{-8 \quad -8}$
$4y = 24$

$\dfrac{4y}{4} = \dfrac{24}{4}$

$y = 6$

4. $-\dfrac{y}{5} = 8$

$\left(\dfrac{-\cancel{5}^{1}}{1}\right)-\dfrac{y}{\cancel{5}_{1}} = 8(-5)$

$y = -40$

5. $\dfrac{2}{3}y + 1 = 13$
$\underline{\phantom{\frac{2}{3}y}-1 \quad -1}$
$\dfrac{2}{3}y = 12$

$\left(\dfrac{3}{2}\right)\dfrac{2}{3}y = 12\left(\dfrac{3}{2}\right)$

$y = 18$

6. $\dfrac{4y}{4} = \dfrac{52}{4}$

$y = 13$

7. $7y = 4y - 12$
$\underline{-4y \quad -4y}$
$3y = - 12$

$\dfrac{3y}{3} = \dfrac{-12}{3}$

$y = -4$

8. $5y - 4 = 3y + 4$
$\underline{+4 + 4}$
$5y = 3y + 8$

$5y = 3y + 8$
$\underline{-3y \quad -3y}$
$2y = 8$

$\dfrac{2y}{2} = \dfrac{8}{2}$

$y = 4$

9. $3y - \dfrac{3}{5}y = 8$

$5\left(3y - \dfrac{3}{5}y\right) = (8)5$

$15y - 3y = 40$

$12y = 40$

$\dfrac{12y}{12} = \dfrac{40}{12}$

$y = 3\,{}^{4}/_{12} \text{ or } 3\tfrac{1}{3}$

10. $\dfrac{3y}{4} + 2 = 4 - 2y$

$4\left(\dfrac{3y}{4} + 2\right) = (4 - 2y)4$

$3y + 8 = 16 - 8y$

$\begin{array}{r} 3y + 8 = 16 - 8y \\ -8 \quad\ \ -8 \\ \hline 3y \quad\ = 8 - 8y \end{array}$

$\begin{array}{r} 3y = 8 - 8y \\ +\ 8y \quad\ + 8y \\ \hline 11y = 8 \end{array}$

$\dfrac{11y}{11} = \dfrac{8}{11}$

$y = \dfrac{8}{11}$

11. If $\dfrac{5 + 2y}{y} = 8$, then $y =$

$y\left(\dfrac{5 + 2y}{y}\right) = (8)y$

$5 + 2y = 8y$

$\begin{array}{r} 5 + 2y = 8y \\ -\ 2y\ -2y \\ \hline 5 \quad\ \ = 6y \end{array}$

or

$6y = 5$

$\dfrac{6y}{6} = \dfrac{5}{6}$

$y = \dfrac{5}{6}$

12. If $\dfrac{y - 4}{y + 3} = 6$, then $y =$

$(y + 3)\left(\dfrac{y - 4}{y + 3}\right) = (6)(y + 3)$

$y - 4 = 6y + 18$

$\begin{array}{r} y -\ \ 4 = 6y + 18 \\ -18 \qquad\ -18 \\ \hline y - 22 = 6y \end{array}$

$\begin{array}{r} y - 22 = 6y \\ -y \qquad\ -y \\ \hline -22 = 5y \end{array}$

or

$5y = -22$

$\dfrac{5y}{5} = \dfrac{-22}{5}$

$y = \dfrac{-22}{5}$ or $-4\frac{2}{5}$

Literal Equations

- *Literal equations* have no numbers, only symbols (letters).

Examples:

1. Solve for Q: QP − X = Y

First add X to both sides.

$$QP - X = Y$$
$$\underline{+ X \qquad + X}$$
$$QP \qquad = Y + X$$

Then divide both sides by P.

$$\frac{QP}{P} = \frac{Y + X}{P}$$

$$Q = \frac{Y + X}{P}$$

Operations opposite to those in the original equation were used to isolate Q. (To remove the −X, we *added* a +X to both sides of the equation; since we had Q times P, we *divided* both sides by P.)

2. Solve for y: $\frac{y}{x} = c$

Multiply both sides by x to get y alone.

$$(x)\frac{y}{x} = (x)c$$

$$y = xc$$

3. Solve for x: $\frac{b}{x} = \frac{p}{q}$

To solve this equation quickly, you cross multiply. To cross multiply:
   a. bring the denominators up next to the opposite side numerators and
   b. multiply

$$\frac{b}{x} = \frac{p}{q}$$

$$bq = px$$

Then divide both sides by p to get x alone.

$$\frac{bq}{p} = \frac{px}{p}$$

$$\frac{bq}{p} = x \text{ or } x = \frac{bq}{p}$$

Cross multiplying can be used only when the format is two fractions separated by an equal sign, such as in a proportion.

4. Solve for c: $\dfrac{g}{m} = \dfrac{k}{c}$

Cross multiply. $gc = mk$

Divide both sides by g. $\dfrac{gc}{g} = \dfrac{mk}{g}$

Thus, $c = \dfrac{mk}{g}$

Be aware that cross multiplying is most effective only when the letter you are solving for is on the *bottom* (the denominator) of a fraction. If it is on top (numerator), it is easier simply to clear the denominator under the unknown you're solving for.

4. Solve for x: $\dfrac{x}{k} = \dfrac{p}{q}$

Multiply both sides by k. $(k)\dfrac{x}{k} = (k)\dfrac{p}{q}$

$$x = \frac{kp}{q}$$

In this problem, there was no need to cross multiply.

Practice: Literal Equations Problems

1. Solve for z: $\dfrac{b}{z} = \dfrac{d}{e}$ 3. Solve for c: $\dfrac{a}{b} = \dfrac{c}{d}$

2. Solve for q: $\dfrac{m}{n} = \dfrac{r}{q}$ 4. Solve for c: $\dfrac{d}{x} = \dfrac{y}{c}$

Answers: Literal Equations Problems

1. $\dfrac{b}{z} = \dfrac{d}{e}$

$be = dz$

$\dfrac{be}{d} = \dfrac{dz}{d}$

$\dfrac{be}{d} = z$

2. $\dfrac{m}{n} = \dfrac{r}{q}$

$mq = nr$

$\dfrac{mq}{m} = \dfrac{nr}{m}$

$q = \dfrac{nr}{m}$

3. $\dfrac{a}{b} = \dfrac{c}{d}$

$(d)\dfrac{a}{b} = (d)\dfrac{c}{d}$

$\dfrac{ad}{b} = c$

4. $\dfrac{d}{x} = \dfrac{y}{c}$

$dc = yx$

$\dfrac{dc}{d} = \dfrac{yx}{d}$

$c = \dfrac{yx}{d}$

Ratios and Proportions

Ratios

- A *ratio* is a method of comparing two or more numbers or variables. Ratios are written as a:b or in working form as a fraction:

$$a/b \quad or \quad \frac{a}{b}$$

and are read "a is to b." Notice that whatever comes after the "to" goes second or at the bottom of the fraction.

Proportions

- *Proportions* are written as two ratios (fractions) equal to each other

Examples:

1. Solve this proportion for x: p is to q as x is to y

First the proportion may be rewritten.

$$\frac{p}{q} = \frac{x}{y}$$

Now simply multiply each side by y.

$$(y)\frac{p}{q} = (y)\frac{x}{y} \qquad\qquad \frac{yp}{q} = x$$

2. Solve this proportion for t: s is to t as r is to q

Rewrite.

$$\frac{s}{t} = \frac{r}{q}$$

Cross multiply.

$$sq = rt$$

Divide both sides by r

$$\frac{sq}{r} = \frac{rt}{r}$$

$$\frac{sq}{r} = t$$

Practice: Proportion Problems

1. Solve for p: c is to p as g is to h
2. Solve for s: t is to q as z is to s
3. Solve for h: l is to k as h is to d
4. Solve for b: a is to b as c is to d

Answers: Proportion Problems

1. $\dfrac{c}{p} = \dfrac{g}{h}$

$ch = pg$

$\dfrac{ch}{g} = \dfrac{pg}{g}$

$\dfrac{ch}{g} = p$

2. $\dfrac{t}{q} = \dfrac{z}{s}$

$ts = qz$

$\dfrac{ts}{t} = \dfrac{qz}{t}$

$s = \dfrac{qz}{t}$

3. $\dfrac{l}{k} = \dfrac{h}{d}$

$(d)\dfrac{l}{k} = (d)\dfrac{h}{d}$

$\dfrac{dl}{k} = h$

4. $\dfrac{a}{b} = \dfrac{c}{d}$

$ad = bc$

$\dfrac{ad}{c} = \dfrac{bc}{c}$

$\dfrac{ad}{c} = b$

Solving Proportions for Value

● Use the same rule to solve for the unknown. *For example:*

1. $\dfrac{4}{x} = \dfrac{2}{5}$

Cross multiply.   (4)(5) = 2x

                                   20 = 2x

Divide both sides by 2. $\dfrac{20}{2} = \dfrac{2x}{2}$

                                   10 = x

2. x is directly proportional to y, and x = 2 when y = 3. If y = 10, then x =

$\dfrac{x}{y} = \dfrac{2}{3}$

$\dfrac{x}{10} = \dfrac{2}{3}$

$3x = 20$

$\dfrac{3x}{3} = \dfrac{20}{3}$

$x = \dfrac{20}{3} = 6\tfrac{2}{3}$

Following is a slight twist.

3. m is inversely proportional to n, and m = 6 when n = 3. If m = 3, then n =

This problem involves a different setup. Since m and n are inversely proportional, as m increases n decreases, and as m decreases n increases. Therefore,

mn = k (k = constant value)

6(3) = 18

The constant is 18. Now mn = 18. Therefore, if m = 3,

3(n) = 18

$\dfrac{3n}{3} = \dfrac{18}{3}$

n = 6

Practice: Solving Proportions for Value Problems

Solve for the unknown.

1. $\dfrac{3}{k} = \dfrac{1}{11}$

2. $\dfrac{2}{5} = \dfrac{8}{R}$

3. $\dfrac{14}{5} = \dfrac{7}{t}$

4. $\dfrac{15}{2} = \dfrac{25}{t}$

5. a is directly proportional to b, and a = 4 when b = 3. If b = 14, then a =

6. x is inversely proportional to y, and x = 5 when y = 2. If x = 1, then y =

Answers: Solving Proportions for Value Problems

1. $\dfrac{3}{k} = \dfrac{1}{11}$

   $33 = 1k$ or $33 = k$

2. $\dfrac{2}{5} = \dfrac{8}{R}$

   $2R = 40$

   $\dfrac{2R}{2} = \dfrac{40}{2}$

   $R = 20$

   Note that this problem could have been done intuitively if you noticed that the second ratio (fraction) is four times the first.

   $\dfrac{2 \times 4}{5 \times 4} = \dfrac{8}{\boxed{20}}$

3. $\dfrac{14}{5} = \dfrac{7}{t}$

   $14t = 35$

   $\dfrac{14t}{14} = \dfrac{35}{14}$

   $t = \dfrac{35}{14} = 2\,7/14 = 2\frac{1}{2}$

   Intuitively: $\dfrac{14 \div 2}{5 \div 2} = \dfrac{7}{\boxed{2\frac{1}{2}}}$

4. $\dfrac{15}{2} = \dfrac{25}{t}$

   $15t = 50$

   $\dfrac{15t}{15} = \dfrac{50}{15}$

   $t = \dfrac{50}{15} = 3\,5/15 = 3\frac{1}{3}$

5. $\dfrac{a}{b} = \dfrac{4}{3}$

$\dfrac{a}{14} = \dfrac{4}{3}$

$3a = 56$

$\dfrac{3a}{3} = \dfrac{56}{3}$

$a = 18\tfrac{2}{3}$

6. $xy = k$
$5(2) = 10$
$xy = 10$

If $x = 1$,

$1(y) = 10$
$y = 10$

Solving for Two Unknowns—Systems of Equations

● If you solve *two equations with the same two unknowns in each,* you can solve for both unknowns. One method is:
   a. Multiply one or both equations by some number to make the number in front of one of the letters (unknowns) the same in each equation.
   b. Add or subtract the two equations to eliminate one letter.
   c. Solve for the other unknown.
   d. Insert the value of the first unknown in one of the original equations to solve for the second unknown.

Examples:

1. Solve for x and y: $3x + 3y = 24$
$2x + y = 13$

First multiply the bottom equation by 3. Now the y is preceded by a 3 in each equation

$3x + 3y = 24$ $3x + 3y = 24$
$3(2x) + 3(y) = 3(13)$ $6x + 3y = 39$

Now we can subtract equations, eliminating the y terms.

$$
\begin{array}{r}
3x + 3y = 24 \\
-6x + -3y = -39 \\
\hline
-3x \qquad = -15
\end{array}
$$

$$\dfrac{-3x}{-3} = \dfrac{-15}{-3}$$

$$x = 5$$

Now insert x = 5 in one of the original equations to solve for y

$$2x + y = 13$$
$$2(5) + y = 13$$
$$10 + y = \quad 13$$
$$\underline{-10 \qquad \quad -10}$$
$$y = \quad 3$$

Answer: x = 5, y = 3

Of course, if the number in front of a letter is already the same in each equation, you do not have to change either equation. Simply add or subtract.

2. Solve for x and y: x + y = 7
   x − y = 3

$$x + y = 7$$
$$\underline{x - y = 3}$$
$$2x \qquad = 10$$

$$\frac{2x}{2} = \frac{10}{2}$$

$$x = 5$$

Now, inserting 5 for x in the first equation gives:

$$5 + y = \quad 7$$
$$\underline{-5 \qquad \quad -5}$$
$$y = \quad 2$$

Answer: x = 5, y = 2

You should note that this method will not work when the two equations are, in fact, the same.

3. Solve for a and b: 3a + 4b = 2
   6a + 8b = 4

The second equation is actually the first equation multiplied by 2. In this instance, the system is unsolvable.

4. Solve for p and q: $3p + 4q = 9$
$2p + 2q = 6$

Multiply the second equation by 2.

$$(2)2p + (2)2q = (2)6$$
$$4p + 4q = 12$$

Now subtract the equations.

$$3p + 4q = 9$$
$$(-)4p + 4q = 12$$
$$\overline{-p = -3}$$
$$p = 3$$

Now that you know $p = 3$, you may plug in 3 for p in either of the two original equations to find q.

$$3p + 4q = 9$$
$$3(3) + 4q = 9$$
$$9 + 4q = 9$$
$$4q = 0$$
$$q = 0$$

Answer: $p = 3, q = 0$

Sometimes a system is more easily solved by the substitution method.

5. Solve for x and y: $x = y + 8$
$x + 3y = 48$

From the first equation, substitute $(y + 8)$ for x in the second equation.

$$(y + 8) + 3y = 48$$

Now solve for y. Simplify by combining y's.

$$4y + 8 = 48$$
$$\underline{ - 8 - 8}$$
$$4y = 40$$

$$\frac{4y}{4} = \frac{40}{4}$$

$$y = 10$$

Now insert y = 10 in one of the original equations.

$$x = y + 8$$
$$x = 10 + 8$$
$$x = 18$$

Answer: y = 10, x = 18

Practice: Systems of Equations Problems

Solve for both unknowns.

1. $6a - 2b = 32$
    $3a + 2b = 22$

2. $3a + 3b = 24$
    $2a + b = 13$

3. $3x + 2y = 10$
    $2x + 3y = 5$

4. $6x + 2y = 24$
    $x = -y + 5$

Answers: Systems of Equations Problems

1. $6a - 2b = 32$
    $3a + 2b = 22$

Add the two equations:

$$
\begin{array}{r}
6a - 2b = 32 \\
(+)\ 3a + 2b = 22 \\
\hline
9a \qquad = 54
\end{array}
$$

$$\frac{9a}{9} = \frac{54}{9}$$

$$a = 6$$

Now plug in 6 for a in one of the original equations.

$$3a + 2b = 22$$
$$3(6) + 2b = 22$$

$$
\begin{array}{r}
18 + 2b = 22 \\
-18 \qquad -18 \\
\hline
2b = 4
\end{array}
$$

$$\frac{2b}{2} = \frac{4}{2}$$

$$b = 2$$

Answer: a = 6, b = 2

2. $3a + 3b = 24$
$\ 2a + b = 13$

Multiply the second equation by 3.

$$(3)2a + (3)b = (3)13$$
$$6a + 3b = 39$$

Subtract the first equation from the second.

$$\begin{array}{r} 6a + 3b = 39 \\ (-)\ 3a + 3b = 24 \\ \hline 3a\ = 15 \end{array}$$

$$\frac{3a}{3} = \frac{15}{3}$$

$$a = 5$$

Now plug in 5 for a in one of the original equations:

$$2a + b = 13$$
$$2(5) + b = 13$$

$$\begin{array}{r} 10 + b = 13 \\ -10 -10 \\ \hline b = 3 \end{array}$$

Answer: a = 5, b = 3

3. $3x + 2y = 10$
$\ 2x + 3y = 5$

Multiply the first equation by 2.

$$(2)3x + (2)2y = (2)10$$
$$6x + 4y = 20$$

Multiply the second equation by 3.

$$(3)2x + (3)3y = (3)5$$
$$6x + 9y = 15$$

Subtract the second equation from the first.

$$6x + 4y = 20$$
$$\underline{(-)\ 6x + 9y = 15}$$
$$-5y = 5$$

$$\frac{-5y}{-5} = \frac{5}{-5}$$

$$y = -1$$

Now plug in -1 for y in one of the original equations.

$$3x + 2y = 10$$
$$3x + 2(-1) = 10$$

$$3x - 2 = 10$$
$$\underline{+ 2\ + 2}$$
$$3x = 12$$

$$\frac{3x}{3} = \frac{12}{3}$$

$$x = 4$$

Answer: $y = -1$, $x = 4$

4. $6x + 2y = 24$
    $x = -y + 5$

Substitute the value of x from the second equation into the first equation.

$$6x + 2y = 24$$
$$6(-y + 5) + 2y = 24$$
$$-6y + 30 + 2y = 24$$

$$-4y + 30 = 24$$
$$\underline{- 30\ -30}$$
$$-4y = -6$$

$$\frac{-4y}{-4} = \frac{-6}{-4}$$

$$y = \frac{3}{2} \text{ or } 1\frac{1}{2}$$

Now plug in $1\frac{1}{2}$ for y in one of the original equations.

$$x = -y + 5$$
$$x = -(1\frac{1}{2}) + 5$$
$$x = 3\frac{1}{2}$$

Answer: $y = 1\frac{1}{2}$, $x = 3\frac{1}{2}$

Solving for Three Unknowns—Systems of Equations

● To solve equations with three unknowns, there must be three equations containing the unknowns. One method is:

a. Choose two of the equations and apply the method used in working with equations in two unknowns; combine them to eliminate one of the unknowns.

b. Repeat the process with any other pair, eliminating the same unknown as in step a above.

c. There are now two equations with the same two unknowns, and they may be solved as before.

Examples:

1. Solve for a, b, and c: $2a + b - c = -1$
$$a - b + 2c = 6$$
$$a + 2b + c = 1$$

First pick the first two equations and add them together to eliminate b.

$$\begin{array}{rcl} 2a + b - c &=& -1 \\ a - b + 2c &=& 6 \\ \hline 3a + c &=& 5 \end{array}$$

Next select the second and third equations and arrange them to eliminate the same unknown, b.

$$2(a) - 2(b) + 2(2c) = 2(6)$$
$$a + 2b + c = 1$$

$$\begin{array}{rcl} 2a - 2b + 4c &=& 12 \\ a + 2b + c &=& 1 \\ \hline 3a + 5c &=& 13 \end{array}$$

Now there are two equations with the same two unknowns. Solve these as before.

$$
\begin{array}{ll}
3a + c = 5 & 3a + c = 5 \\
3a + 5c = 13 & -3a - 5c = -13 \\
\hline
 & -4c = -8 \\
\end{array}
$$

$$\frac{-4c}{-4} = \frac{-8}{-4}$$

$$c = 2$$

Now insert c = 2 in one of the two equations and solve for a.

$$3a + c = 5$$
$$3a + (2) = 5$$

$$
\begin{array}{r}
3a + 2 = 5 \\
- 2 = -2 \\
\hline
3a = 3 \\
\end{array}
$$

$$\frac{3a}{3} = \frac{3}{3}$$

$$a = 1$$

With two of the three variables known, the third variable can easily be found by substitution.

$$
\begin{array}{r}
2a + b - c = -1 \\
2(1) + b - (2) = -1 \\
2 + b - 2 = -1 \\
b = -1 \\
\end{array}
$$

Answer: a = 1, b = -1, c = 2

Sometimes a system of equations is more easily solved by using substitution or by using a combination of substitution and addition or subtraction of equations.

2. Solve for x, y, and z:
$$x + 2y = 0$$
$$2x - z = 6$$
$$y + z = -3$$

First solve one of the equations for one of the variables.

$$\begin{array}{r} x + 2y = 0 \\ -2y -2y \\ \hline x = -2y \end{array}$$

Next substitute $-2y$ in the other equation containing x.

$$\begin{array}{r} 2x - z = 6 \\ 2(-2y) - z = 6 \\ -4y - z = 6 \end{array}$$

Now there are two equations with the same two unknowns. By adding the equations, the value of y can be found.

$$\begin{array}{r} y + z = -3 \\ -4y - z = 6 \\ \hline -3y = 3 \end{array}$$

$$\frac{-3y}{-3} = \frac{3}{-3}$$

$$y = -1$$

Substituting $y = -1$ in both of the other equations containing y, the values of x and z can be found.

$$\begin{array}{ll} x + 2y = 0 & y + z = -3 \\ x + 2(-1) = 0 & (-1) + z = -3 \\ x - 2 = 0 & -1 + z = -3 \end{array}$$

$$\begin{array}{rr} x - 2 = 0 & -1 + z = -3 \\ +2 = +2 & +1 = +1 \\ \hline x = 2 & z = -2 \end{array}$$

Answer: $x = 2, y = -1, z = -2$

Practice: Systems of Equations Problems (Three Unknowns)

Solve for all variables.

1. $m - n - p = 2$
   $2m + n + 2p = 9$
   $3m + 2n + 3p = 13$

2. $2r - s = 0$
   $r + t = 1$
   $s - 2t = -6$

Answers: Systems of Equations Problems (Three Unknowns)

1. $m - n - p = 2$
    $2m + n + 2p = 9$
    $3m + 2n + 3p = 13$

Add the first two equations to eliminate n.

$$
\begin{array}{rcr}
m - n - p &=& 2 \\
2m + n + 2p &=& 9 \\
\hline
3m + p &=& 11
\end{array}
$$

Select another pair of equations and eliminate the same variable.

$$
\begin{array}{l}
(2)m - (2)n - (2)p = (2)2 \\
3m + 2n + 3p = 13
\end{array}
\qquad
\begin{array}{rcr}
2m - 2n - 2p &=& 4 \\
3m + 2n + 3p &=& 13 \\
\hline
5m + p &=& 17
\end{array}
$$

Next subtract one equation from the other.

$$
\begin{array}{l}
5m + p = 17 \\
3m + p = 11
\end{array}
\qquad
\begin{array}{rcr}
5m + p &=& 17 \\
-3m - p &=& -11 \\
\hline
= 112m &=& 6
\end{array}
$$

$$
\frac{2m}{2} = \frac{6}{2}
$$

$$
m = 3
$$

Now plug in 3 for m in one of the equations with only m and p.

$$
3m + p = 11
$$
$$
3(3) + p = 11
$$
$$
9 + p = 11
$$

$$
\begin{array}{rcr}
9 + p &=& 11 \\
-9 & & -9 \\
\hline
p &=& 2
\end{array}
$$

Finally, plug in values for m and p in one of the original equations and solve for n.

$$
2m + n + 2p = 9
$$
$$
2(3) + n + 2(2) = 9
$$

$$6 + n + 4 = 9$$
$$n + 10 = 9$$

$$n + 10 = 9$$
$$\underline{-10 = -10}$$
$$n = -1$$

Answer: m = 3, n = −1, p = 2

2. $2r - s = 0$
   $r + t = 1$
   $s - 2t = -6$

Solve one of the equations for either of the unknowns.

$$2r - s = 0$$
$$\underline{-2r = -2r}$$
$$-s = -2r$$

$$\frac{-s}{-1} = \frac{-2r}{-1}$$

$$s = 2r$$

Substitute 2r for s in the equation s − 2t = −6.

$$s - 2t = -6$$
$$(2r) - 2t = -6$$

$$\frac{2r}{2} - \frac{2t}{2} = \frac{-6}{2}$$

$$r - t = -3$$

Add the two equations with the same variables, r and t.

$$r + t = 1$$
$$\underline{r - t = -3}$$
$$2r = -2$$

$$\frac{2r}{2} = \frac{-2}{2}$$

$$r = -1$$

Now plug in -1 for r in the two original equations in which it is found.

$$
\begin{array}{ll}
2r - s = 0 & r + t = 1 \\
2(-1) - s = 0 & (-1) + t = 1 \\
-2 - s = 0 &
\end{array}
$$

$$
\begin{array}{ll}
-2 - s = 0 & -1 + t = 1 \\
+ s = +s & +1 = +1 \\
\hline
-2 = s & t = 2
\end{array}
$$

Answer: $r = -1, s = -2, t = 2$

Monomials and Polynomials

- A *monomial* is an algebraic expression that consists of only one term. (A term is a numerical or literal expression with its own sign.) For instance, 9x, $4a^2$, and $3mpxz^2$ are all monomials
- A *polynomial* consists of two or more terms. For instance, $x + y$, $y^2 - x^2$, and $x^2 + 3x + 5y^2$ are all polynomials.
- A *binomial* is a polynomial that consists of exactly two terms. For instance, $x + y$ is a binomial.
- A *trinomial* is a polynomial that consists of exactly three terms. For instance, $y^2 + 9y + 8$ is a trinomial.
- The number in front of the variable is called the *coefficient*. In 9y, 9 is the coefficient.

     Polynomials are usually arranged in one of two ways.
- *Ascending order* is basically when the power of a term increases for each succeeding term. For example, $x + x^2 + x^3$ or $5x + 2x^2 - 3x^3 + x^5$ are arranged in ascending order.
- *Descending order* is basically when the power of a term decreases for each succeeding term. For example, $x^3 + x^2 + x$ or $2x^4 + 3x^2 + 7x$ are arranged in descending order. Descending order is more commonly used.

Adding and Subtracting Monomials

- To *add* or *subtract monomials,* follow the same rules as with signed numbers (p. 22), *provided that the terms are alike.* Notice that you add or subtract the coefficients only and leave the variables the same.

Examples:

1. $15x^2yz$
    $-18x^2yz$
    $\overline{-3x^2yz}$

3. $9y$
    $-\ 3y$
    $\overline{6y}$

2. $3x + 2x = 5x$

4. $17q + 8q - 3q - (-4q) =$
    $22q - (-4q) =$
    $22q + 4q = 26q$

Remember that the rules for signed numbers apply to monomials as well.

Practice: Adding and Subtracting Monomials Problems

Perform the indicated operation.

1. $-9m^2s + 5m^2s =$

2. $+7qt^2 - 3qt^2 + 20qt^2 =$

3. $18pc$
    $\underline{(-)\ 7pc}$

4. $-7x^2y$
    $\underline{(-)\ -3x^2y}$

Answers: Adding and Subtracting Monomials Problems

1. $-4m^2s$ 2. $24qt^2$ 3. $11pc$ 4. $-4x^2y$

Multiplying Monomials

- Reminder: The rules and definitions for powers and exponents introduced in arithmetic (pp. 63 65) also apply in algebra. For example, $5 \cdot 5 = 5^2$ and $x \cdot x = x^2$. Similarly, $a \cdot a \cdot a \cdot b \cdot b = a^3b^2$.

- To *multiply monomials,* add the exponents of the same bases.

Examples:

1. $(x^3)(x^4) = x^7$

2. $(x^2y)(x^3y^2) = x^5y^3$

3. $(6k^5)(5k^2) = 30k^7$ (multiply numbers)

4. $-4(m^2n)(-3m^4n^3) = 12m^6n^4$

5. $(c^2)(c^3)(c^4) = c^9$

6. $(3a^2b^3c)(b^2c^2d) = 3a^2b^5c^3d$

Note that in example 4 the product of -4 and -3 is $+12$, the product of m^2 and m^4 is m^6, and the product of n and n^3 is n^4, since any monomial having no exponent indicated is assumed to have an exponent of 1.

- When monomials are being *raised to a power,* the answer is obtained by multiplying the exponents of each part of the monomial by the power to which it is being raised.

Examples:

1. $(a^7)^3 = a^{21}$
2. $(x^3y^2)^4 = x^{12}y^8$
3. $(2x^2y^3)^3 = (2)^3x^6y^9 = 8x^6y^9$

Practice: Multiplying Monomials Problems

1. $(m^3)(m^{10}) =$
2. $(a^5b^6)(a^4b^2) =$
3. $(5k^2)(8k^4) =$
4. $-2(x^2y^3)(6xy^4) =$
5. $(2x^2)(-4x)(x^3y) =$
6. $(d^4)^5 =$
7. $(c^3d^2)^5 =$
8. $(3a^2bc^3)^2 =$

Answers: Multiplying Monomials Problems

1. m^{13}
2. a^9b^8
3. $40k^6$
4. $-12x^3y^7$
5. $-8x^6y$
6. d^{20}
7. $c^{15}d^{10}$
8. $9a^4b^2c^6$

Dividing Monomials

- To *divide monomials,* subtract the exponent of the divisor from the exponent of the dividend of the same base.

Examples:

1. $\dfrac{y^{15}}{y^4} = y^{11}$ or $y^{15} \div y^4 = y^{11}$

2. $\dfrac{x^5 y^2}{x^3 y} = x^2 y$

3. $\dfrac{36 a^4 b^6}{-9ab} = -4a^3 b^5$ (divide the numbers)

4. $\dfrac{fg^{15}}{g^3} = fg^{12}$

5. $\dfrac{x^5}{x^8} = \dfrac{1}{x^3}$ (may also be expressed x^{-3})

6. $\dfrac{-3\,(xy)(xy^2)}{xy}$

You can simplify the numerator first.

$$\frac{-3(xy)(xy^2)}{xy} = \frac{-3x^2 y^3}{xy} = -3xy^2$$

Or, since the numerator is all multiplication, we can cancel.

$$\frac{-3(\cancel{xy})(xy^2)}{\cancel{xy}} = -3xy^2$$

Practice: Dividing Monomials Problems

1. $\dfrac{x^8}{x^3} =$

2. $a^9 \div a^6 =$

3. $\dfrac{m^5 n^4}{m^2 n^3} =$

4. $\dfrac{-10 x^4 z^9}{5 x^3 z^4} =$

5. $\dfrac{x^8 y^3}{x^5} =$

6. $3p^5 q^3 \div 12 p^4 q^9 =$

7. $\dfrac{s^4 t^6}{s^7 t^3} =$

8. $\dfrac{2(x^2 y)(3x^2 y^3)}{x^2 y^2} =$

Answers: Dividing Monomials Problems

1. x^5

2. a^3

3. m^3n

4. $-2xz^5$

5. x^3y^3

6. $\dfrac{\cancel{3}p^{\cancel{5}^1}\cancel{q^{\cancel{2}}}}{_4\cancel{12}p^4q^{\cancel{6}}} = \dfrac{1p}{4q^6} = \dfrac{p}{4q^6}$ or $.25pq^{-6}$

7. $\dfrac{t^3}{s^3}$ or $s^{-3}t^3$

8. $\dfrac{2(x^2y)(3x^2y^3)}{x^2y^2} = \dfrac{6x^4y^4}{x^2y^2} = 6x^2y^2$ or $\dfrac{2(x^{\cancel{2}}y)(3x^2y^{\cancel{3}^1})}{x^{\cancel{2}}y^{\cancel{2}}} = 6x^2y^2$

Working with Negative Exponents

- Remember, if the exponent is negative, such as x^{-3}, then the variable and exponent may be dropped under the number 1 in a fraction to remove the negative sign as follows:

$$x^{-3} = \frac{1}{x^3}$$

A few examples including some with multiplication and division follow:

1. $a^{-2}b = \dfrac{b}{a^2}$

2. $\dfrac{a^{-3}}{b^4} = \dfrac{1}{a^3b^4}$

3. $(a^2b^{-3})(a^{-1}b^4) = ab$

$$\begin{bmatrix} a^2 \cdot a^{-1} = a \\ b^{-3} \cdot b^4 = b \end{bmatrix}$$

If the negative exponent belongs to a number or variable below the fraction bar, then simply bring the number or variable up and drop the negative sign.

4. $\dfrac{1}{x^{-2}} = x^2$

5. $\dfrac{x^6}{x^{-3}} = x^6 \cdot x^3 = x^9$

6. $(3x^{-2})^{-2} = 3^{-2} \cdot x^{-2 \cdot -2} = 3^{-2} \cdot x^4 = \dfrac{1}{9} \cdot x^4 = \dfrac{x^4}{9}$

7. $\left(\dfrac{1}{3}\right)^{-2} = \dfrac{1}{\left(\dfrac{1}{3}\right)^2} = \dfrac{1}{\dfrac{1}{9}} = \dfrac{9}{1} = 9$

Or simply invert the fraction and drop the negative sign.

$\left(\dfrac{1}{3}\right)^{-2} = \left(\dfrac{3}{1}\right)^2 = 9$

● Any nonzero variable to the zero power equals 1.

8. $x^0 = 1$

9. $2y^0 = 2(1) = 2$

10. $(4xy^2)^0 = 1$

Practice: Working with Negative Exponents Problems

1. $x^2y^{-3}z =$

2. $\dfrac{m^{-7}}{n^4} =$

3. $(x^{-3}y^5)(xy^{-3}) =$

4. $\dfrac{y}{z^{-4}} =$

5. $\dfrac{x^8}{x^{-3}}$

6. $(2x^{-3})^{-3} =$

7. $\left(\dfrac{1}{4}\right)^{-2} =$

8. $\left(\dfrac{2}{3}\right)^{-2}\left(\dfrac{3}{4}\right)^2 =$

9. $\dfrac{x^2y^{-3}}{x^{-3}y^2} =$

10. $(3x)^0 + 3x^0 =$

11. $\dfrac{x^3y^{-2}}{x^0y^2} =$

Answers: Working with Negative Exponents Problems

1. $xy^{-3}z = \dfrac{x^2z}{y^3}$

2. $\dfrac{m^{-2}}{n^4} = -\dfrac{1}{m^2n^4}$

3. $(x^{-3}y)(xy^{-3}) = x^{-2}y^{-2} = \dfrac{1}{x^2y^2}$

4. $\dfrac{y}{z^{-4}} = yz^4$

5. $\dfrac{x^8}{x^{-3}} = x^8 \cdot x^3 = x^{11}$

6. $(2x^{-3})^{-3} = (2)^{-3} \cdot x^9 = \dfrac{1}{2^3} \cdot x^9 = \dfrac{1}{8} \cdot x^9 = \dfrac{x^9}{8}$

7. $\left(\dfrac{1}{4}\right)^{-2} = \left(\dfrac{4}{1}\right)^2 = 16$

8. $\left(\dfrac{2}{3}\right)^{-2}\left(\dfrac{3}{4}\right)^2 = \left(\dfrac{3}{2}\right)^2\left(\dfrac{3}{4}\right)^2 = \left(\dfrac{9}{4}\right)\left(\dfrac{9}{16}\right) = \dfrac{81}{64} = 1\,^{17}\!/_{64}$

9. $\dfrac{x^2y^{-3}}{x^{-3}y^2} = \dfrac{x^2 \cdot x^3}{y^2 \cdot y^3} = \dfrac{x^5}{y^5}$

10. $(3x)^0 + 3x^0 = 1 + 3(1) = 1 + 3 = 4$

11. $\dfrac{x^3y^{-2}}{x^0y^2} = \dfrac{x^3}{(1)y^2 \cdot y^2} = \dfrac{x^3}{y^4}$

Adding and Subtracting Polynomials

- To *add* or *subtract polynomials*, just arrange *like terms* in columns and then add or subtract. (Or simply add or subtract like terms when rearrangement is not necessary.)

Examples:

1. Add:
$$
\begin{array}{r}
a^2 + ab + b^2 \\
3a^2 + 4ab - 2b^2 \\
\hline
4a^2 + 5ab - b^2
\end{array}
$$

2. $(5y - 3x) + (9y + 4x) =$

$(5y - 3x) + (9y + 4x) = 14y + x$ or $x + 14y$

3. Subtract:

$$\begin{array}{r} a^2 + b^2 \\ (-)\ 2a^2 - b^2 \end{array} \qquad \begin{array}{r} a^2 + b^2 \\ (+)\ -2a^2 + b^2 \\ \hline -a^2 + 2b^2 \end{array}$$

4. $(3cd - 6mt) - (2cd - 4mt) =$
   $(3cd - 6mt) + (-2cd + 4mt) =$

   $(3cd - 6mt) + (-2cd + 4mt) = cd - 2mt$

5. $3a^2bc + 2ab^2c + 4a^2bc + 5ab^2c =$

$$\begin{array}{r} 3a^2bc + 2ab^2c \\ +\ 4a^2bc + 5ab^2c \\ \hline 7a^2bc + 7ab^2c \end{array}$$

   or

   $3a^2bc + 2ab^2c + 4a^2bc + 5ab^2c = 7a^2bc + 7ab^2c$

Practice: Adding and Subtracting Polynomials Problems

Perform the indicated operations and simplify.

1. $$\begin{array}{r} 5x^2y^2 - 4ab \\ -6x^2y^2 + 3ab \\ \hline -2x^2y^2 - \underline{ab} \end{array}$$

2. $(7gr - 3nt) + (5gr - 2nt) =$
3. $(9kb^2 + 6ht - 3ab) - (4kb^2 - 6ht + 2ab) =$
4. $7xyz^2 + 8x^2yz + 9xy^2z + 8xyz^2 + 3xy^2z - 3x^2yz =$

Answers: Adding and Subtracting Polynomials Problems

1. $-3x^2y^2 - 2ab$ 3. $5kb^2 + 12ht - 5ab$
2. $12gr - 5nt$ 4. $15xyz^2 + 5x^2yz + 12xy^2z$

Multiplying Polynomials

● To *multiply polynomials,* multiply each term in one polynomial by each term in the other polynomial. Then simplify if necessary.

Examples:

1.

$$
\begin{array}{r}
2x - 2a \\
\times \quad 3x + \ a \\
\hline
+2ax - 2a^2 \\
6x^2 - 6ax \\
\hline
6x^2 - 4ax - 2a^2
\end{array}
$$

similar to

$$
\begin{array}{r}
21 \\
\times 23 \\
\hline
63 \\
42 \\
\hline
483
\end{array}
$$

Or you may wish to use the "F.O.I.L." method with *binomials.* F.O.I.L. means First terms, Outside terms, Inside terms, Last terms. Then simplify if necessary.

2. $(3x + a)(2x - 2a) =$

Multiply *first* terms from each quantity.

$$(3x + a)(2x - 2a) = 6x^2 \underline{\hspace{4cm}}$$

Now *outside* terms.

$$(3x + a)(2x - 2a) = 6x^2 - 6ax \underline{\hspace{3cm}}$$

Now *inside* terms.

$$(3x + a)(2x - 2a) = 6x^2 - 6ax + 2ax \underline{\hspace{1.5cm}}$$

Finally *last* terms.

$$(3x + a)(2x - 2a) = 6x^2 - 6ax + 2ax - 2a^2$$

Now simplify.

$$6x^2 - 6ax + 2ax - 2a^2 = 6x^2 - 4ax - 2a^2$$

3. $(x + y)(x + y + z) =$

$$
\begin{array}{r}
x + y + z \\
\times \qquad x + y \\
\hline
xy + y^2 + yz \\
x^2 + xz + xy \\
\hline
x^2 + xz + 2xy + y^2 + yz
\end{array}
$$

Practice: Multiplying Polynomials Problems

1. $(2x + y)(3x + 5y) =$ 3. $(9x + 5)(3x - 2) =$
2. $(7a + b)(2a - 3b) =$ 4. $(-6y + z^2)(2y - 3z) =$

Answers: Multiplying Polynomials Problems

1.
$$
\begin{array}{r}
2x + y \\
\times \quad 3x + 5y \\
\hline
+10xy + 5y^2 \\
+6x^2 + 3xy \\
\hline
6x^2 + 13xy + 5y^2
\end{array}
$$

2.
$$
\begin{array}{r}
7a + b \\
\times \quad 2a - 3b \\
\hline
-21ab - 3b^2 \\
+14a^2 + 2ab \\
\hline
14a^2 - 19ab - 3b^2
\end{array}
$$

3.
$$
\begin{array}{r}
9x + 5 \\
\times \quad 3x - 2 \\
\hline
-18x - 10 \\
+27x^2 + 15x \\
\hline
27x^2 - 3x - 10
\end{array}
$$

4.
$$
\begin{array}{r}
-6y + z^2 \\
\times \quad 2y - 3z \\
\hline
+ 18yz - 3z^2 \\
-12y^2 + 2yz^2 \\
\hline
-12y^2 + 2yx^2 + 18yz - 3z^3
\end{array}
$$

or $-12y^2 + 18yz + 2yz^2 - 3z^3$

Dividing Polynomials by Monomials

● To *divide a polynomial by a monomial,* just divide each term in the polynomial by the monomial.

Examples:

1. $(6x^2 + 2x) \div 2x =$

$$\frac{6x^2 + 2x}{2x} = \frac{6x^2}{2x} + \frac{2x}{2x} = 3x + 1$$

2. $(16a^7 - 12a^5) \div 4a^2 =$

$$\frac{16a^7 - 12a^5}{4a^2} = \frac{16a^7}{4a^2} - \frac{12a^5}{4a^2} = 4a^5 - 3a^3$$

Practice: Dividing Polynomials by Monomials Problems

1. $(3x - 9) \div 3 =$
2. $(16x^3 + 4x^2 + 8x) \div 2x =$
3. $(14a^2b - 8ab + 4a) \div 2a =$
4. $(84c^2d - 38cd + 18cd^3) \div 2cd =$

Answers: Dividing Polynomials by Monomials Problems

1. $(3x - 9) \div 3 =$

$$\frac{3x - 9}{3} = \frac{3x}{3} - \frac{9}{3} = x - 3$$

2. $(16x^3 + 4x^2 + 8x) \div 2x =$

$$\frac{16x^3 + 4x^2 + 8x}{2x} = \frac{16x^3}{2x} + \frac{4x^2}{2x} + \frac{8x}{2x} = 8x^2 + 2x + 4$$

3. $(14a^2b - 8ab + 4a) \div 2a =$

$$\frac{14a^2b - 8ab + 4a}{2a} = \frac{14a^2b}{2a} - \frac{8ab}{2a} + \frac{4a}{2a} = 7ab - 4b + 2$$

4. $(84c^2d - 38cd + 18cd^3) \div 2cd =$

$$\frac{84c^2d - 38cd + 18cd^3}{2cd} = \frac{84c^2d}{2cd} - \frac{38cd}{2cd} + \frac{18cd^3}{2cd}$$

$$= 42c - 19 + 9d^2$$

Dividing Polynomials by Polynomials

● To *divide a polynomial by a polynomial,* make sure both are in descending order; then use long division (Remember: Divide by the first term, multiply, subtract, bring down.)

Examples:

1. Divide $4a^2 + 18a + 8$ by $a + 4$

First divide a into $4a^2$.

$$\begin{array}{r} 4a \\ a + 4 \overline{)\, 4a^2 + 18a + 8} \end{array}$$

Now multiply 4a times (a + 4).

$$\begin{array}{r} 4a \\ a + 4 \overline{)\, 4a^2 + 18a + 8} \\ 4a^2 + 16a \end{array}$$

Now subtract.

$$\begin{array}{r} 4a \\ a + 4 \overline{)\, 4a^2 + 18a + 8} \\ (-)\ 4a^2 + 16a \\ \hline 2a \end{array}$$

Now bring down the +8.

$$\begin{array}{r} 4a \\ a + 4 \overline{)\, 4a^2 + 18a + 8} \\ (-)\ 4a^2 + 16a \\ \hline 2a + 8 \end{array}$$

Now divide a into 2a.

$$\begin{array}{r} 4a + 2 \\ a + 4 \overline{)\, 4a^2 + 18a + 8} \\ (-)\ 4a^2 + 16a + 8 \\ \hline 2a + 8 \end{array}$$

Now multiply 2 times (a + 4).

$$\begin{array}{r} 4a + 2 \\ a + 4 \overline{)\, 4a^2 + 18a + 8} \\ (-)\ 4a^2 + 16a \\ \hline 2a + 8 \\ 2a + 8 \end{array}$$

Now subtract.

$$
\begin{array}{r}
4a + 2 \\
a + 4\overline{)\,4a^2 + 18a + 8} \\
(-)\ \ 4a^2 + 16a \\
\hline
2a + 8 \\
(-)\ 2a + 8 \\
\hline
0
\end{array}
$$

$$
\begin{array}{r}
4a + 2 \\
a + 4\overline{)\,4a^2 + 18a + 8} \\
(-)\ 4a^2 + 16a \\
\hline
2a + 8 \\
(-)\ 2a + 8 \\
\hline
0
\end{array}
$$

similar to

$$
\begin{array}{r}
23 \\
53\overline{)\,1219} \\
(-)\ 106 \\
\hline
159 \\
(-)\ 159 \\
\hline
0
\end{array}
$$

2. $(3x^2 + 4x + 1) \div (x + 1) =$

$$
\begin{array}{r}
3x + 1 \\
x + 1\overline{)\,3x^2 + 4x + 1} \\
(-)\ 3x^2 + 3x \\
\hline
x + 1 \\
(-)\ x + 1 \\
\hline
0
\end{array}
$$

3. $(2x + 1 + x^2) \div (x + 1) =$

First change to descending order: $x^2 + 2x + 1$
Then divide.

$$
\begin{array}{r}
x + 1 \\
x + 1\overline{)\,x^2 + 2x + 1} \\
(-)\ x^2 + 1x \\
\hline
x + 1 \\
(-)\ x + 1 \\
\hline
0
\end{array}
$$

4. $(m^3 - m) \div (m + 1)$

Note: when terms are missing, be sure to leave proper room between terms.

$$
\begin{array}{r}
m^2 - m \\
m + 1\overline{)\,m^3 + 0m^2 - m} \\
(-)\ m^3 +\ \ m^2 \\
\hline
- m^2 - m \\
(-)\ - m^2 - m \\
\hline
0
\end{array}
$$

5. $(10a^2 - 29a - 21) \div (2a - 7) =$

$$\begin{array}{r} 5a + 3 \\ 2a - 7 \overline{\smash{)}10a^2 - 29a - 21} \\ (-)\ \underline{10a^2 - 35a} \\ 6a - 21 \\ (-)\ \underline{6a - 21} \\ 0 \end{array}$$

Note that remainders are possible.

6. $(x^2 + 2x + 4) \div (x + 1) =$

$$\begin{array}{r} x + 1 \text{ (with remainder 3)} \\ x + 1 \overline{\smash{)}x^2 + 2x + 4} \\ (-)\ \underline{x^2 + x} \\ x + 4 \\ (-)\ \underline{x + 1} \\ 3 \end{array}$$

This answer can be rewritten as $(x + 1) + \dfrac{3}{x + 1}$

Practice: Dividing Polynomials by Polynomials Problems

1. $(x^2 + 18x + 45) \div (x + 3) =$
2. $(21t + 5 + 4t^2) \div (t + 5) =$
3. $(z^3 - 1) \div (z - 1) =$
4. $(t^2 + 4t - 6) \div (t + 2) =$
5. $(14x^2 + 11x + 2) \div (2x + 1) =$

Answers: Dividing Polynomials by Polynomials Problems

1. $(x^2 + 18x + 45) \div (x + 3) =$

$$\begin{array}{r} x + 15 \\ x + 3 \overline{\smash{)}x^2 + 18x + 45} \\ (-)\ \underline{x^2 + 3x} \\ 15x + 45 \\ (-)\ \underline{15x + 45} \\ 0 \end{array}$$

2. $(21t + 5 + 4t^2) \div (t + 5) =$
Reorder: $4t^2 + 21t + 5$

$$
\begin{array}{r}
4t + 1 \\
t + 5 \overline{)\, 4t^2 + 21t + 5} \\
(-)\ \underline{4t^2 + 20t} \\
t + 5 \\
(-)\ \underline{t + 5} \\
0
\end{array}
$$

3. $(z^3 - 1) \div (z - 1) =$

$$
\begin{array}{r}
z^2 + z + 1 \\
z - 1 \overline{)\, z^3 \qquad\quad - 1} \\
(-)\ \underline{z^3 - z^2} \\
z^2 \\
(-)\ \underline{z^2 - z} \\
z - 1 \\
(-)\ \underline{z - 1} \\
0
\end{array}
$$

4. $(t^2 + 4t - 6) \div (t + 2) =$

$$
\begin{array}{r}
t + 2\ \text{(with remainder } -10 \text{ or } (t + 2) - \dfrac{10}{t + 2}) \\
t + 2 \overline{)\, t^2 + 4t - 6} \\
(-)\ \underline{t^2 + 2t} \\
2t - 6 \\
(-)\ \underline{2t + 4} \\
-10
\end{array}
$$

5. $(14x^2 + 11x + 2) \div (2x + 1) =$

$$
\begin{array}{r}
7x + 2 \\
2x + 1 \overline{)\, 14x^2 + 11x + 2} \\
(-)\ \underline{14x^2 + 7x} \\
4x + 2 \\
(-)\ \underline{4x + 2} \\
0
\end{array}
$$

Factoring

- To *factor* means to find two or more quantities whose product equals the original quantity.

Factoring out a Common Factor

- To *factor out a common factor*
  (a) Find the largest common monomial factor of each term.
  (b) Divide the original polynomial by this factor to obtain the second factor. The second factor will be a polynomial.

Examples:

1. $5x^2 + 4x = x(5x + 4)$
2. $2y^3 - 6y = 2y(y^2 - 3)$
3. $x^5 - 4x^3 + x^2 = x^2(x^3 - 4x + 1)$

Practice: Factoring out a Common Factor Problems

Factor the following completely.

1. $a^2 + 26a =$ 3. $3m^3 + 6m^2 + 9m =$
2. $t^2 - 35t =$ 4. $12p^3 + 24p^2 =$

Answers: Factoring out a Common Factor Problems

1. $a(a + 26)$ 3. $3m(m^2 + 2m + 3)$
2. $t(t - 35)$ 4. $12p^2(p + 2)$

Factoring the Difference Between Two Squares

- To *factor the difference between two squares*
  (a) Find the square root of the first term and the square root of the second term.
  (b) Express your answer as the product of: the sum of the quantities from step a, times the difference of those quantities.

Examples:

1. $x^2 - 144 = (x + 12)(x - 12)$
2. $a^2 - b^2 = (a + b)(a - b)$
3. $9y^2 - 1 = (3y + 1)(3y - 1)$

Note: $x^2 + 144$ is *not* factorable.

Practice: Factoring the Difference Between Two Squares Problems

Factor the following.

1. $x^2 - 25 =$ 4. $x^2y^2 - z^2 =$
2. $p^2 - q^2 =$ 5. $4a^2 - 9 =$
3. $144 - h^2 =$ 6. $2t^2 - 50 =$

Answers: Factoring the Difference Between Two Squares Problems

1. $(x + 5)(x - 5)$ 4. $(xy + z)(xy - z)$
2. $(p + q)(p - q)$ 5. $(2a + 3)(2a - 3)$
3. $(12 + h)(12 - h)$ 6. $2(t^2 - 25) = 2(t + 5)(t - 5)$

Factoring Trinomials of the Form $ax^2 + bx + c$

● To *factor trinomials of the form* $ax^2 + bx + c$
   (a) Check to see if you can monomial factor (factor out common terms). Then if $a = 1$ (that is, the first term is simply x^2) use double parentheses and factor the first term. Place these factors in the left sides of the parentheses. For example, $(x \quad)(x \quad)$.
   (b) Factor the last term and place the factors in the right sides of the parentheses.

To decide on the signs of the numbers do the following.
If the sign of the last term is *negative*
   (1) Find two numbers whose product is the last term and whose *difference* is the *coefficient* (number in front) of the middle term.
   (2) Give the larger of these two numbers the sign of the middle term and the *opposite* sign to the other factor.

If the sign of the last term is *positive*
   (1) Find two numbers whose product is the last term and whose *sum* is the coefficient of the middle term.
   (2) Give both factors the sign of the middle term.

Examples:

1. Factor $x^2 - 3x - 10$

First check to see if you can monomial factor (factor out common terms). Since this is not possible, use double parentheses and factor the first term as follows: (x   )(x   ). Next, factor the last term, 10, into 2 times 5 (using step b above, 5 must take the negative sign and 2 must take the positive sign because they will then total the coefficient of the middle term, which is -3) and add the proper signs leaving

$$(x - 5)(x + 2)$$

Multiply *means* (inner terms) and *extremes* (outer terms) to check.

$$(x - 5)(x + 2)$$
$$-5x$$
$$+2x$$
$$\overline{-3x} \text{ (which is the middle term)}$$

To completely check, multiply the factors together.

$$
\begin{array}{r}
x - 5 \\
\times\ \ x + 2 \\
\hline
+ 2x - 10 \\
x^2 - 5x \\
\hline
x^2 - 3x + 10
\end{array}
$$

2. Factor $x^2 + 8x + 15$

$$(x + 3)(x + 5)$$

Notice that $3 \times 5 = 15$ and $3 + 5 = 8$, the coefficient of the middle term. Also note that the signs of both factors are $+$, the sign of the middle term. To check

$$(x + 3)(x + 5)$$
$$+3x$$
$$+5x$$
$$\overline{+8x} \text{ (the middle term)}$$

3. Factor $x^2 - 5x - 14$

$(x - 7)(x + 2)$

Notice that $7 \times 2 = 14$ and $7 - 2 = 5$, the coefficient of the middle term. Also note that the sign of the larger factor, 7, is $-$, while the other factor, 2, has a $+$ sign. To check

$$\underset{\underset{-7x}{\smile}}{(x - 7)(x + 2)}$$

$$\frac{+2x}{-5x} \text{ (the middle term)}$$

If, however, $a \neq 1$ (that is, the first term has a coefficient—for example, $4x^2 + 5x + 1$—then additional trial and error will be necessary.

4. Factor $4x^2 + 5x + 1$

$(2x + \quad)(2x + \quad)$ might work for the first term. But when 1's are used as factors to get the last term—$(2x + 1)(2x + 1)$—the middle term comes out as *4x* instead of *5x*.

$$\underset{\underset{+2x}{\smile}}{(2x + 1)(2x + 1)}$$

$$\frac{+2x}{+4x}$$

Therefore, try $(4x + \quad)(x + \quad)$. Now using 1's as factors to get the last terms gives $(4x + 1)(x + 1)$. Checking for the middle term

$$\underset{\underset{+1x}{\smile}}{(4x + 1)(x + 1)}$$

$$\frac{+4x}{+5x}$$

Therefore, $4x^2 + 5x + 1 = (4x + 1)(x + 1)$.

5. Factor $4a^2 + 6a + 2$

Factoring out a 2 leaves $2(2a^2 + 3a + 1)$

Now factor as usual giving $2(2a + 1)(a + 1)$

To check $(2a + 1)(a + 1)$

$+1a$

$\underline{+2a}$ (the middle
                          term after
$+3a$ 2 was
                          factored out)

6. Factor $5x^3 + 6x^2 + x$

Factoring out an x leaves $x(5x^2 + 6x + 1)$

Now factor as usual giving $x(5x + 1)(x + 1)$

To check $(5x + 1)(x + 1)$

$+1x$

$\underline{+5x}$ (the middle
                          term after
$+6x$ x was
                          factored out

7. Factor $5 + 7b + 2b^2$ (a slight twist)

$(5 + 2b)(1 + b)$

To check $(5 + 2b)(1 + b)$

$+2b$

$\underline{+5b}$

$+7b$ (the middle term)

Note that $(5 + b)(1 + 2b)$ is incorrect because it gives the wrong middle term.

8. Factor $x^2 + 2xy + y^2$

$(x + y)(x + y)$

To check

$$(x + y)(x + y)$$
$$+ \, xy$$
$$\underline{+ \, xy}$$
$$+ \, 2xy \qquad \text{(the middle term)}$$

Note: There are polynomials that are not factorable.

Practice: Factoring Polynomials Problems

Factor each of the following.

1. $x^2 + 8x + 15 =$
2. $x^2 + 2x - 24 =$
3. $r^3 + 14r^2 + 45r =$
4. $x^2 - 16x + 48 =$

5. $1 + 2x + x^2 =$
6. $c^2 - 2cd + d^2 =$
7. $3y^2 + 4yz + z^2 =$
8. $7a^2 - 20a - 3 =$

Answers: Factoring Polynomials Problems

1. $(x + 3)(x + 5)$
2. $(x + 6)(x - 4)$
3. $r(r + 9)(r + 5)$
4. $(x - 4)(x - 12)$

5. $(1 + x)(1 + x)$
6. $(c - d)(c - d)$
7. $(3y + z)(y + z)$
8. $(7a + 1)(a - 3)$

Factoring the Sum or Difference Between Two Cubes

● To factor the sum or difference between two cubes, first find the cube root of each term. The factors will be one binomial and one trinomial. The binomial will be the sum or difference, depending upon the problem, of the two cube roots. The trinomial will be the cube root of the first term squared, the product of the two cube roots disregarding the sign, and the cube root of the last term squared. There will always be just one negative sign in the factors. The second term of either the binomial or the trinomial is negative. The second term of the binomial has the same sign as the original problem.

Examples:

1. Factor $x^3 - y^3$
   $(x - y)(x^2 + xy + y^2)$

2. Factor $a^3 + 8$
   $(a + 2)(a^2 - 2a + 4)$

3. Factor $m^3 + 27p^3$
   $(m + 3p)(m^2 - 3mp + 9p^2)$

4. Factor $8r^3 - s^3$
   $(2r - s)(4r^2 + 2rs + s^2)$

Practice: Factoring the Sum or Difference Between Two Cubes Problems

Factor each of the following.

1. $a^3 + b^3 =$
2. $p^3 - q^3 =$
3. $x^3 - 8y^3 =$

4. $27 + m^3 =$
5. $64 - 27x^3 =$
6. $16 + 2a^3 =$

Answers: Factoring the Sum or Difference Between Two Cubes Problems

1. $(a + b)(a^2 - ab + b^2)$
2. $(p - q)(p^2 + pq + q^2)$
3. $(x - 2y)(x^2 + 2xy + 4y^2)$
4. $(3 + m)(9 - 3m + m^2)$

5. $(4 - 3x)(16 + 12x + 9x^2)$
6. $2(8 + a^3)$
   $2(2 + a)(4 - 2a + a^2)$

Factoring Polynomials by Grouping

● Some polynomials can be factored by grouping the terms. Look for grouping(s) that will allow you to factor part of the expression.

Examples:

1. Factor $ax - a + bx - b$
   $(ax - a) + (bx - b)$
   $a(x - 1) + b(x - 1)$
   $(x - 1)(a + b)$

2. Factor $y^3 - 5y^2 - 2y + 10$
   $(y^3 - 5y^2) + (-2y + 10)$
   $y^2(y - 5) - 2(y - 5)$
   $(y - 5)(y^2 - 2)$

3. Factor $y^2 + 2xy + x^2 - 4$
$(y^2 - 2xy + x^2) - 4$
$(y + x)^2 - 4$

This is the difference between two squares, so

$[(y + x) + 2][(y + x) - 2]$
or $(y + x + 2)(y + x - 2)$

4. Factor $x^2 - y^2 - 10y - 25$
$x^2 - (y^2 + 10y + 25)$
$x^2 - (y + 5)^2$

This is the difference between two squares, so

$[x + (y + 5)][x - (y + 5)]$
or $(x + y + 5)(x - y - 5)$

5. Factor $c^2 - 2cd + d^2 + 10c - 10d + 25$
$(c^2 - 2cd + d^2) + (10c - 10d) + 25$
$(c - d)^2 + 10(c - d) + 25$
$[(c - d) + 5][(c - d) + 5]$
or $(c - d + 5)^2$

Practice: Factoring Polynomials by Grouping Problems

Factor each of the following.

1. $y^2 + 2y + yw + 2w =$
2. $p^4 + p^3 + 3p + 3 =$
3. $x^2 + xy - 3x - 3y =$
4. $a^2 + 4ab + 4b^2 - c^2 =$
5. $z^2 - x^2 - y^2 + 2xy =$
6. $x^2 + 2xy + y^2 + 4x + 4y + 4 =$

Answers: Factoring Polynomials by Grouping Problems

1. $y^2 + 2y + yw + 2w$
$(y^2 + 2y) + (yw + 2w)$
$y(y + 2) + w(y + 2)$
$(y + 2)(y + w)$

2. $p^4 + p^3 + 3p + 3$
$(p^4 + p^3) + (3p + 3)$
$p^3(p + 1) + 3(p + 1)$
$(p + 1)(p^3 + 3)$

3. $x^2 + xy - 3x - 3y$
   $(x^2 + xy) + (-3x - 3y)$
   $x(x + y) - 3(x + y)$
   $(x + y)(x - 3)$

4. $a^2 + 4ab + 4b^2 - c^2$
   $(a^2 + 4ab + 4b^2) - c^2$
   $(a + 2b)^2 - c^2$
   $[(a + 2b) + c][(a + 2b) - c]$
   $(a + 2b + c)(a + 2b - c)$

5. $z^2 - x^2 - y^2 + 2xy$
   $z^2 - x^2 + 2xy - y^2$
   $z^2 + (-x^2 + 2xy - y^2)$
   $z^2 - (x^2 - 2xy + y^2)$
   $z^2 - (x - y)^2$
   $[z - (x - y)][z + (x - y)]$
   $(z - x + y)(z + x - y)$

6. $x^2 + 2xy + y^2 + 4x + 4y + 4$
   $(x^2 + 2xy + y^2) + (4x + 4y) + 4$
   $(x + y)^2 + 4(x + y) + 4$
   $[(x + y) + 2][(x + y) + 2]$
   $(x + y + 2)(x + y + 2)$
   or $(x + y + 2)^2$

Solving Quadratic Equations

- *A quadratic equation* is an equation that could be written as
  $ax^2 + bx + c = 0$. To solve a quadratic equation
  (a) Put all terms on one side of the equal sign, leaving zero on the
      other side.
  (b) Factor.
  (c) Set each factor equal to zero.
  (d) Solve each of these equations.
  (e) Check by inserting your answer in the original equation.

Examples:

1. Solve: $x^2 - 6x = 16$

Now, following the steps, $x^2 - 6x = 16$ becomes $x^2 - 6x - 16 = 0$.

Factor. $(x - 8)(x + 2) = 0$

$$x - 8 = 0 \quad or \quad x + 2 = 0$$
$$x = 8 \qquad\qquad x = -2$$

Then to check $8^2 - 6(8) = 16 \quad or \quad (-2)^2 - 6(-2) = 16$

$$64 - 48 = 16 \qquad\qquad 4 + 12 = 16$$
$$16 = 16 \qquad\qquad\quad 16 = 16$$

Both values 8 and -2 are solutions to the original equation.

2. Solve: $y^2 = -6y - 5$

Setting all terms equal to zero

$$y^2 + 6y + 5 = 0$$

Factoring $(y + 5)(y + 1) = 0$

Setting each factor to 0

$$y + 5 = 0 \quad or \quad y + 1 = 0$$
$$y = -5 \qquad\qquad y = -1$$

To check $(-5)^2 = -6(-5) - 5 \quad or \quad (-1)^2 = -6(-1) - 5$

$$25 = 30 - 5 \qquad\qquad 1 = 6 - 5$$
$$25 = 25 \qquad\qquad\quad 1 = 1$$

A quadratic with a term missing is called an *incomplete quadratic.*

3. Solve: $x^2 - 16 = 0$

Factor. $(x + 4)(x - 4) = 0$

$$x + 4 = 0 \quad or \quad x - 4 = 0$$
$$x = -4 \qquad\qquad x = 4$$

To check $(-4)^2 - 16 = 0 \quad or \quad (4)^2 - 16 = 0$

$$16 - 16 = 0 \qquad\qquad 16 - 16 = 0$$
$$0 = 0 \qquad\qquad\quad 0 = 0$$

4. Solve: $x^2 + 6x = 0$

Factor.

$$x(x + 6) = 0$$

$x = 0$ *or* $x + 6 = 0$

$x = 0$ $x = -6$

To check $(0)^2 + 6(0) = 0$ or $(-6)^2 + 6(-6) = 0$

                 $0 + 0 = 0$ $36 + (-36) = 0$

                 $0 = 0$ $0 = 0$

5. Solve: $2x^2 + 2x - 1 = x^2 + 6x - 5$

First, simplify by putting all terms on one side and combining like terms.

$$\begin{array}{r} 2x^2 + 2x - 1 = x^2 + 6x - 5 \\ -x^2 - 6x + 5 \quad -x^2 - 6x + 5 \\ \hline x^2 - 4x + 4 = 0 \end{array}$$

Now factor.

$$(x - 2)(x - 2) = 0$$

$$x - 2 = 0$$

$$x = 2$$

To check $2(2)^2 + 2(2) - 1 = (2)^2 + 6(2) - 5$

                 $8 + 4 - 1 = 4 + 12 - 5$

                 $11 = 11$

Practice: Solving Quadratic Equations Problems

Solve each of the following

1. $x^2 + 7x = -10$
2. $y^2 - 18y = -45$
3. $x^2 - 25 = 0$
4. $3t^2 + 4t + 1 = 0$
5. $2b^2 - b = 0$
6. $3n^2 - 2n = -1 + 2n^2$
7. $(3x + 2)(x - 1) = 0$
8. $2x^2 - 32 = 0$

Answers: Solving Quadratic Equations Problems

1. $x^2 + 7x = -10$
    $x^2 + 7x + 10 = 0$
    $(x + 2)(x + 5) = 0$

    $x + 2 = 0$ or $x + 5 = 0$
    $x = -2$ $x = -5$

2. $y^2 - 18y = -45$
    $y^2 - 18y + 45 = 0$
    $(y - 15)(y - 3) = 0$

    $y - 15 = 0$ or $y - 3 = 0$
    $y = 15$ $y = 3$

3. $x^2 - 25 = 0$
    $(x + 5)(x - 5) = 0$

    $x + 5 = 0$ or $x - 5 = 0$
    $x = -5$ $x = 5$

4. $3t^2 + 4t + 1 = 0$
    $(3t + 1)(t + 1) = 0$

    $3t + 1 = 0$ or $t + 1 = 0$
    $3t = -1$ $t = -1$

    $t = -\dfrac{1}{3}$ $t = -1$

5. $2b^2 - b = 0$
    $b(2b - 1) = 0$

    $b = 0$ or $2b - 1 = 0$
    $b = 0$ $2b = 1$
    $b = 0$ $b = \frac{1}{2}$

6. $3n^2 - 2n = -1 + 2n^2$
        $\underline{-2n^2 \qquad\qquad\quad -2n^2}$
        $n^2 - 2n = -1$

$$n^2 - 2n + 1 = 0$$
$$(n - 1)(n - 1) = 0$$
$$n - 1 = 0$$
$$n = 1$$

7. $(3x + 2)(x - 1) = 0$

$3x + 2 = 0$ *or* $x - 1 = 0$
$3x = -2$ $x = 1$

$$x = -\frac{2}{3}$$

8. $2x^2 - 32 = 0$
$2(x^2 - 16) = 0$
$2(x - 4)(x + 4) = 0$

$x - 4 = 0$ *or* $x + 4 = 0$
$x = 4$ $x = -4$

Algebraic Fractions

• *Algebraic fractions* are fractions using a variable in the numerator or denominator, such as $3/x$. Since division by 0 is impossible, variables in the denominator have certain restrictions. The denominator can *never* equal 0. Therefore in the fractions

$\dfrac{5}{x}$ x cannot equal 0 ($x \neq 0$)

$\dfrac{2}{x - 3}$ x cannot equal 3 ($x \neq 3$)

$\dfrac{3}{a - b}$ $a - b$ cannot equal 0 ($a - b \neq 0$) so a cannot equal b ($a \neq b$)

$\dfrac{4}{a^2 b}$ a cannot equal 0 and b cannot equal 0 ($a \neq 0$ and $b \neq 0$)

Be aware of these types of restrictions.

Operations with Algebraic Fractions

Reducing Algebraic Fractions

- To *reduce an algebraic fraction* to lowest terms, first factor the numerator and the denominator; then cancel (or divide out) common factors.

Examples:

1. Reduce $\dfrac{4x^3}{8x^2}$

$$\dfrac{\overset{1}{\cancel{4x^3}}^{\,1}}{\underset{2}{\cancel{8x^2}}} = \dfrac{1}{2}\,x$$

2. Reduce $\dfrac{3x - 3}{4x - 4}$

$$\dfrac{3x - 3}{4x - 4} = \dfrac{3(x - 1)}{4(x - 1)} = \dfrac{3(\cancel{x - 1})}{4(\cancel{x - 1})} = \dfrac{3}{4}$$

3. Reduce $\dfrac{x^2 + 2x + 1}{3x + 3}$

$$\dfrac{x^2 + 2x + 1}{3x + 3} = \dfrac{(x + 1)(x + 1)}{3(x + 1)} = \dfrac{(\cancel{x + 1})(x + 1)}{3(\cancel{x + 1})}$$

$$= \dfrac{x + 1}{3}$$

4. Reduce $\dfrac{x^2 - y^2}{x^3 - y^3}$

$$\dfrac{x^2 - y^2}{x^3 - y^3} = \dfrac{(x - y)(x + y)}{(x - y)(x^2 + xy + y^2)} =$$

$$\dfrac{(\cancel{x - y})(x + y)}{(\cancel{x - y})(x^2 + xy + y^2)} = \dfrac{x + y}{x^2 + xy + y^2}$$

WARNING: Do *not* cancel through an addition or subtraction sign. For example:

$$\frac{x + 1}{x + 2} \neq \frac{\cancel{x} + 1}{\cancel{x} + 2} \neq \frac{1}{2}$$

or

$$\frac{x + 6}{6} \neq \frac{x + \cancel{6}}{\cancel{6}} \neq x$$

Practice: Reducing Algebraic Fractions Problems

Reduce each of the following.

1. $\dfrac{8a^2b}{12a^3b}$

2. $\dfrac{5xy^3}{10x^3y}$

3. $\dfrac{10x + 5}{8x + 4}$

4. $\dfrac{x^2 - y^2}{x + y}$

5. $\dfrac{a^2 + a}{2a^2 + 4a + 2}$

6. $\dfrac{x^3 - 9x}{x^3 + 27}$

Answers: Reducing Algebraic Fractions Problems

1. $\dfrac{8a^2b}{12a^3b} = \dfrac{2\cancel{8}\cancel{a^2}\cancel{b}}{3\cancel{12}a^{1}\cancel{b}} = \dfrac{2}{3a}$

2. $\dfrac{5xy^3}{10x^3y} = \dfrac{1\cancel{5}\cancel{x}y^{2}}{2\cancel{10}x^{2}\cancel{y}} = \dfrac{1y^2}{2x^2}$ or $\dfrac{y^2}{2x^2}$

3. $\dfrac{10x + 5}{8x + 4} = \dfrac{5(2x + 1)}{4(2x + 1)} = \dfrac{5\cancel{(2x + 1)}}{4\cancel{(2x + 1)}} = \dfrac{5}{4}$ or $1\frac{1}{4}$

4. $\dfrac{x^2 - y^2}{x + y} = \dfrac{(x - y)(x + y)}{x + y} = \dfrac{(x - y)\cancel{(x + y)}}{\cancel{x + y}} = \dfrac{x - y}{1} = x - y$

5. $\dfrac{a^2 + a}{2a^2 + 4a + 2} = \dfrac{a(a + 1)}{2(a^2 + 2a + 1)} = \dfrac{a(a + 1)}{2(a + 1)(a + 1)} =$

$\dfrac{a\cancel{(a + 1)}}{2(a + 1)\cancel{(a + 1)}} = \dfrac{a}{2(a + 1)}$

6. $\dfrac{x^3 - 9x}{x^3 + 27} = \dfrac{x(x^2 - 9)}{(x + 3)(x^2 - 3x + 9)} = \dfrac{x(x + 3)(x - 3)}{(x + 3)(x^2 - 3x + 9)} =$

$\dfrac{x(x+3)(x - 3)}{(x+3)(x^2 - 3x + 9)} = \dfrac{x(x - 3)}{x^2 - 3x + 9}$ or $\dfrac{x^2 - 3x}{x^2 - 3x + 9}$

Multiplying Algebraic Fractions

- To *multiply algebraic fractions,* first factor the numerator and denominators that are polynomials; then cancel where possible. Multiply the remaining numerators together and denominators together. (If you've canceled properly, your answer will be in reduced form.)

Examples:

1. $\dfrac{2x}{3} \cdot \dfrac{y}{5} = \dfrac{2x}{3} \cdot \dfrac{y}{5} = \dfrac{2xy}{15}$

2. $\dfrac{x^2}{3y} \cdot \dfrac{2y}{3x} = \dfrac{x^2}{3y} \cdot \dfrac{2y}{3x} = \dfrac{2x}{9}$

3. $\dfrac{x + 1}{5y + 10} \cdot \dfrac{y + 2}{x^2 + 2x + 1} = \dfrac{x + 1}{5(y + 2)} \cdot \dfrac{y + 2}{(x + 1)(x + 1)} =$

$\dfrac{\overset{1}{x+1}}{5(y+2)} \cdot \dfrac{\overset{1}{y+2}}{(x+1)(x + 1)} = \dfrac{1}{5(x + 1)}$

Note: In the following problem, remember to factor $x^2 + 2x - xy - 2y$ by grouping.

4. $\dfrac{x^2 + 2x - xy - 2y}{x^2 - 4} \cdot \dfrac{(x - 2)^2}{x^2 - xy} = \dfrac{(x - y)(x + 2)}{(x + 2)(x - 2)} \cdot$

$\dfrac{(x - 2)(x - 2)}{x(x - y)} = \dfrac{\overset{1}{(x-y)}\overset{1}{(x+2)}}{(x+2)(x-2)} \cdot \dfrac{\overset{1}{(x-2)}(x - 2)}{x(x-y)} = \dfrac{x - 2}{x}$

Practice: Multiplying Algebraic Fractions Problems

1. $\dfrac{6x}{11} \cdot \dfrac{2}{5y} =$

4. $\dfrac{x^2 - 4}{6} \cdot \dfrac{3y}{2x + 4} =$

2. $\dfrac{3a^2}{5b} \cdot \dfrac{2b}{9a} =$

5. $\dfrac{x^2 + 4x + 4}{x - 3} \cdot \dfrac{5}{3x + 6} =$

3. $\dfrac{5}{x + 1} \cdot \dfrac{3x + 3}{6} =$

6. $\dfrac{x^3 - 8}{x^2} \cdot \dfrac{x^2 - xy}{x^2 - 2x - xy + 2y}$

Answers: Multiplying Algebraic Fractions Problems

1. $\dfrac{6x}{11} \cdot \dfrac{2}{5y} = \dfrac{12x}{55y}$

2. $\dfrac{3a^2}{5b} \cdot \dfrac{2b}{9a} = \dfrac{\cancel{3}a^{\cancel{2}}}{5\cancel{b}} \cdot \dfrac{2\cancel{b}}{\cancel{9}\cancel{a}} = \dfrac{2a}{15}$

3. $\dfrac{5}{x + 1} \cdot \dfrac{3x + 3}{6} = \dfrac{5}{x + 1} \cdot \dfrac{3(x + 1)}{6} = \dfrac{5}{\cancel{x+1}} \cdot \dfrac{\cancel{3}(\cancel{x+1})}{\cancel{6}_2}$

$= \dfrac{5}{2} = 2\frac{1}{2}$

4. $\dfrac{x^2 - 4}{6} \cdot \dfrac{3y}{2x + 4} = \dfrac{(x + 2)(x - 2)}{6} \cdot \dfrac{3y}{2(x + 2)} =$

$\dfrac{(\cancel{x + 2})(x - 2)}{\cancel{6}_2} \cdot \dfrac{\cancel{3}y}{2(\cancel{x + 2})} = \dfrac{(x - 2)y}{4}$

5. $\dfrac{x^2 + 4x + 4}{x - 3} \cdot \dfrac{5}{3x + 6} = \dfrac{(x + 2)(x + 2)}{x - 3} \cdot \dfrac{5}{3(x + 2)} =$

$\dfrac{(x + 2)(\cancel{x + 2})}{x - 3} \cdot \dfrac{5}{3(\cancel{x + 2})} = \dfrac{5(x + 2)}{3(x - 3)}$

6. $\dfrac{x^3 - 8}{x^2} \cdot \dfrac{x^2 - xy}{x^2 - 2x - xy + 2y} = \dfrac{(x - 2)(x^2 + 2x + 4)}{x^2} \cdot$

$\dfrac{x(x - y)}{(x - y)(x - 2)} = \dfrac{(x - 2)(x^2 + 2x + 4)}{x^{\cancel{2}1}} \cdot \dfrac{\cancel{x}(x - y)}{(x - y)(x - 2)} =$

$$\dfrac{x^2 + 2x + 4}{x}$$

Dividing Algebraic Fractions

● To *divide algebraic fractions,* invert the fraction following the division sign and multiply. Remember, you can cancel only after you invert.

Examples:

1. $\dfrac{3x^2}{5} \div \dfrac{2x}{y} = \dfrac{3x^2}{5} \cdot \dfrac{y}{2x} = \dfrac{3x^{\cancel{2}1}}{5} \cdot \dfrac{y}{2\cancel{x}} = \dfrac{3xy}{10}$

2. $\dfrac{4x - 8}{6} \div \dfrac{x - 2}{3} = \dfrac{4x - 8}{6} \cdot \dfrac{3}{x - 2} = \dfrac{4(x - 2)}{6} \cdot \dfrac{3}{x - 2} =$

$\dfrac{4(x - 2)^1}{\cancel{6}_2} \cdot \dfrac{\cancel{3}^1}{\underset{1}{x - 2}} = \dfrac{4}{2} = 2$

● If the fraction is a compound fraction, first simplify the numerator and/or denominator.

3. $\dfrac{y}{y + \dfrac{1}{2}} = \dfrac{y}{\dfrac{2y}{2} + \dfrac{1}{2}} = \dfrac{y}{\dfrac{2y + 1}{2}} = y \div \dfrac{2y + 1}{2} = \dfrac{y}{1} \cdot \dfrac{2}{2y + 1} = \dfrac{2y}{2y + 1}$

Practice: Dividing Algebraic Fractions Problems

1. $\dfrac{8x^3}{15} \div \dfrac{6x^2}{3} =$

4. $\dfrac{x^2}{x^2 + 5x + 6} \div \dfrac{x}{x + 3} =$

2. $\dfrac{y^2}{5} \div y^2 =$

5. $\dfrac{\dfrac{ab^2}{c}}{\dfrac{b}{ac^2}} =$

3. $\dfrac{2x + 6}{5} \div \dfrac{x + 3}{10} =$

6. $\dfrac{2 + \dfrac{1}{x}}{x + \dfrac{1}{x}} =$

Answers: Dividing Algebraic Fractions Problems

1. $\dfrac{8x^3}{15} \div \dfrac{6x^2}{3} = \dfrac{8x^3}{15} \cdot \dfrac{3}{6x^2} = \dfrac{\overset{4}{\cancel{8}}x^{\cancel{3}^{1}}}{\underset{5}{\cancel{15}}} \cdot \dfrac{\overset{1}{\cancel{3}}}{\underset{3}{\cancel{6}x^{\cancel{2}}}} = \dfrac{4x}{15}$

2. $\dfrac{y^2}{5} \div y^2 = \dfrac{y^2}{5} \div \dfrac{y^2}{1} = \dfrac{y^2}{5} \cdot \dfrac{1}{y^2} = \dfrac{\cancel{y^2}}{5} \cdot \dfrac{1}{\cancel{y^2}} = \dfrac{1}{5}$

3. $\dfrac{2x + 6}{5} \div \dfrac{x + 3}{10} = \dfrac{2x + 6}{5} \cdot \dfrac{10}{x + 3} = \dfrac{2(x + 3)}{5} \cdot \dfrac{10}{x + 3} =$

$\dfrac{2(\cancel{x + 3})}{\underset{1}{\cancel{5}}} \cdot \dfrac{\overset{2}{\cancel{10}}}{\cancel{x + 3}} = \dfrac{4}{1} = 4$

4. $\dfrac{x^2}{x^2 + 5x + 6} \div \dfrac{x}{x + 3} = \dfrac{x^2}{x^2 + 5x + 6} \cdot \dfrac{x + 3}{x} =$

$\dfrac{x^2}{(x + 3)(x + 2)} \cdot \dfrac{x + 3}{x} = \dfrac{x^{\cancel{2}^{1}}}{(\cancel{x + 3})(x + 2)} \cdot \dfrac{\cancel{x + 3}}{\cancel{x}} = \dfrac{x}{x + 2}$

5. $\dfrac{\dfrac{ab^2}{c}}{\dfrac{b}{ac^2}} = \dfrac{ab^2}{c} \div \dfrac{b}{ac^2} = \dfrac{ab^2}{c} \cdot \dfrac{ac^2}{b} = \dfrac{ab^{\cancel{2}}}{\cancel{c}} \cdot \dfrac{ac^{\cancel{2}}}{\cancel{b}} = a^2bc$

6.
$$\frac{2 + \dfrac{1}{x}}{x + \dfrac{1}{x}} = \frac{\dfrac{2x}{x} + \dfrac{1}{x}}{\dfrac{x^2}{x} + \dfrac{1}{x}} = \frac{\dfrac{2x+1}{x}}{\dfrac{x^2+1}{x}} = \frac{2x+1}{x} \div \frac{x^2+1}{x} = \frac{2x+1}{x} \cdot \frac{x}{x^2+1}$$

$$= \frac{2x+1}{\not{x}} \cdot \frac{\not{x}}{x^2+1} = \frac{2x+1}{x^2+1}$$

Adding or Subtracting Algebraic Fractions

- To *add or subtract albegraic fractions having a common denominator,* simply keep the denominator and combine (add or subtract) the numerators. Reduce if necessary.

Examples:

1. $\dfrac{4}{x} + \dfrac{5}{x} = \dfrac{4+5}{x} = \dfrac{9}{x}$

2. $\dfrac{x-4}{x+1} + \dfrac{3}{x+1} = \dfrac{x-4+3}{x+1} = \dfrac{x-1}{x+1}$

3. $\dfrac{3x}{y} - \dfrac{2x-1}{y} = \dfrac{3x-(2x-1)}{y} = \dfrac{3x-2x+1}{y} = \dfrac{x+1}{y}$

Practice: Adding or Subtracting Algebraic Fractions Problems

1. $\dfrac{3}{x} + \dfrac{2}{x} =$

2. $\dfrac{x-1}{y} + \dfrac{3x+2}{y} =$

3. $\dfrac{4x-3}{x} - \dfrac{3x-3}{x} =$

4. $\dfrac{6x-3}{x-4} - \dfrac{x+2}{x-4} =$

Answers: Adding or Subtracting Algebraic Fractions Problems

1. $\dfrac{3}{x} + \dfrac{2}{x} = \dfrac{3+2}{x} = \dfrac{5}{x}$

2. $\dfrac{x-1}{y} + \dfrac{3x+2}{y} = \dfrac{x-1+3x+2}{y} = \dfrac{4x+1}{y}$

3. $\dfrac{4x - 3}{x} - \dfrac{3x - 3}{x} = \dfrac{4x - 3 - (3x - 3)}{x} = \dfrac{4x - 3 - 3x + 3}{x} =$

$\dfrac{x}{x} = 1$

4. $\dfrac{6x - 3}{x - 4} - \dfrac{x + 2}{x - 4} = \dfrac{6x - 3 - (x + 2)}{x - 4} = \dfrac{6x - 3 - x - 2}{x - 4} =$

$\dfrac{5x - 5}{x - 4}$ or $\dfrac{5(x - 1)}{x - 4}$

- To *add or subtract algebraic fractions having different denominators,* first find a lowest common denominator (LCD), change each fraction to an equivalent fraction with the common denominator, then combine each numerator. Reduce if necessary.

Examples:

1. $\dfrac{2}{x} + \dfrac{3}{y} =$

LCD $= xy$

$\dfrac{2}{x} \cdot \dfrac{y}{y} + \dfrac{3}{y} \cdot \dfrac{x}{x} = \dfrac{2y}{xy} \cdot \dfrac{3x}{xy} = \dfrac{2y + 3x}{xy}$

2. $\dfrac{x + 2}{3x} + \dfrac{x - 3}{6x} =$

LCD $= 6x$

$\dfrac{x + 2}{3x} \cdot \dfrac{2}{2} + \dfrac{x - 3}{6x} = \dfrac{2x + 4}{6x} + \dfrac{x - 3}{6x} = \dfrac{2x + 4 + x - 3}{6x} = \dfrac{3x + 1}{6x}$

If there is a common variable factor with more than one exponent, use its greatest exponent.

3. $\dfrac{2}{y^2} - \dfrac{3}{y} =$

LCD $= y^2$

$$\frac{2}{y^2} - \frac{3}{y} \cdot \frac{y}{y} = \frac{2}{y^2} - \frac{3y}{y^2} = \frac{2 - 3y}{y^2}$$

4. $\dfrac{4}{x^3y} + \dfrac{3}{xy^2} =$

LCD $= x^3y^2$

$$\frac{4}{x^3y} \cdot \frac{y}{y} + \frac{3}{xy^2} \cdot \frac{x^2}{x^2} = \frac{4y}{x^3y^2} + \frac{3x^2}{x^3y^2} = \frac{4y + 3x^2}{x^3y^2}$$

5. $\dfrac{x}{x + 1} - \dfrac{2x}{x + 2} =$

LCD $= (x + 1)(x + 2)$

$$\frac{x}{x + 1} \cdot \frac{(x + 2)}{(x + 2)} - \frac{2x}{x + 2} \cdot \frac{(x + 1)}{(x + 1)} =$$

$$\frac{x^2 + 2x}{(x + 1)(x + 2)} - \frac{2x^2 + 2x}{(x + 1)(x + 2)} =$$

$$\frac{x^2 + 2x - 2x^2 - 2x}{(x + 1)(x + 2)} = \frac{-x^2}{(x + 1)(x + 2)}$$

Following is a slight twist.

6. $\dfrac{x^2}{x - 3} + \dfrac{9}{3 - x} =$

$$\frac{x^2}{x - 3} + \frac{9}{-1(x - 3)} = \frac{x^2}{x - 3} - \frac{9}{x - 3} =$$

$$\frac{x^2 - 9}{x - 3} = \frac{(x-3)(x + 3)}{(x-3)} = x + 3$$

Notice that LCD was $x - 3$.

To find the lowest common denominator, it is often necessary to factor the denominators and proceed as follows.

7. $\dfrac{2x}{x^2 - 9} - \dfrac{5}{x^2 + 4x + 3} = \dfrac{2x}{(x + 3)(x - 3)} - \dfrac{5}{(x + 3)(x + 1)} =$

LCD $= (x + 3)(x - 3)(x + 1)$

$\dfrac{2x}{(x + 3)(x - 3)} \cdot \dfrac{(x + 1)}{(x + 1)} - \dfrac{5}{(x + 3)(x + 1)} \cdot \dfrac{(x - 3)}{(x - 3)} =$

$\dfrac{2x^2 + 2x}{(x + 3)(x - 3)(x + 1)} - \dfrac{5x - 15}{(x + 3)(x - 3)(x + 1)} =$

$\dfrac{2x^2 + 2x - (5x - 15)}{(x + 3)(x - 3)(x + 1)} = \dfrac{2x^2 + 2x - 5x + 15}{(x + 3)(x - 3)(x + 1)} =$

$\dfrac{2x^2 - 3x + 15}{(x + 3)(x - 3)(x + 1)}$

Practice: Adding or Subtracting Algebraic Fractions Problems

1. $\dfrac{5}{x} + \dfrac{2}{y} =$

2. $\dfrac{x}{4} - \dfrac{y}{3} =$

3. $\dfrac{y + 5}{2y} + \dfrac{y - 2}{8y} =$

4. $\dfrac{7}{x} + \dfrac{3}{x^3} =$

5. $\dfrac{3x}{x^2y} + \dfrac{2x}{xy^2} =$

6. $\dfrac{x}{3x + 3} + \dfrac{2x}{x + 1} =$

7. $\dfrac{3}{x^2 - 4} - \dfrac{2x}{x^2 + 4x + 4} =$

8. $\dfrac{1}{x} + \dfrac{1}{y} + \dfrac{1}{z} =$

9. $\dfrac{1}{2x} - y =$

10. $\dfrac{x^2}{x - 5} + \dfrac{25}{5 - x} =$

Answers: Adding or Subtracting Algebraic Fractions Problems

1. $\dfrac{5}{x} + \dfrac{2}{y} =$

LCD $= xy$

$$\frac{5}{x} \cdot \frac{y}{y} + \frac{2}{y} \cdot \frac{x}{x} = \frac{5y}{xy} + \frac{2x}{xy} = \frac{5y + 2x}{xy}$$

2. $\dfrac{x}{4} - \dfrac{y}{3} =$

LCD = 12

$$\frac{x}{4} \cdot \frac{3}{3} - \frac{y}{3} \cdot \frac{4}{4} = \frac{3x}{12} - \frac{4y}{12} = \frac{3x - 4y}{12}$$

3. $\dfrac{y + 5}{2y} + \dfrac{y - 2}{8y} =$

LCD = 8y

$$\frac{y + 5}{2y} \cdot \frac{4}{4} + \frac{y - 2}{8y} = \frac{4y + 20}{8y} + \frac{y - 2}{8y} =$$

$$\frac{4y + 20 + y - 2}{8y} = \frac{5y + 18}{8y}$$

4. $\dfrac{7}{x} + \dfrac{3}{x^3} =$

LCD = x^3

$$\frac{7}{x} \cdot \frac{x^2}{x^2} + \frac{3}{x^3} = \frac{7x^2}{x^3} + \frac{3}{x^3} = \frac{7x^2 + 3}{x^3}$$

5. $\dfrac{3x}{x^2y} + \dfrac{2x}{xy^2} =$

LCD = x^2y^2

$$\frac{3x}{x^2y} \cdot \frac{y}{y} + \frac{2x}{xy^2} \cdot \frac{x}{x} = \frac{3xy}{x^2y^2} + \frac{2x^2}{x^2y^2} = \frac{3xy + 2x^2}{x^2y^2}$$

6. $\dfrac{x}{3x + 3} + \dfrac{2x}{x + 1} = \dfrac{x}{3(x + 1)} + \dfrac{2x}{x + 1}$

LCD = $3(x + 1)$

$$\frac{x}{3(x + 1)} + \frac{2x}{x + 1} \cdot \frac{3}{3} = \frac{x}{3(x + 1)} + \frac{6x}{3(x + 1)} =$$

$$\frac{x + 6x}{3(x + 1)} = \frac{7x}{3(x + 1)}$$

7. $\dfrac{3}{x^2 - 4} - \dfrac{2x}{x^2 + 4x + 4} = \dfrac{3}{(x + 2)(x - 2)} - \dfrac{2x}{(x + 2)(x + 2)}$

LCD $= (x + 2)(x - 2)(x + 2)$

$$\frac{3}{(x + 2)(x - 2)} \cdot \frac{(x + 2)}{(x + 2)} - \frac{2x}{(x + 2)(x + 2)} \cdot \frac{(x - 2)}{(x - 2)} =$$

$$\frac{3x + 6}{(x + 2)(x - 2)(x + 2)} - \frac{2x^2 - 4x}{(x + 2)(x + 2)(x - 2)} =$$

$$\frac{3x + 6 - (2x^2 - 4x)}{(x + 2)(x - 2)(x + 2)} = \frac{3x + 6 - 2x^2 + 4x}{(x + 2)(x - 2)(x + 2)} =$$

$$\frac{-2x^2 + 7x + 6}{(x + 2)(x - 2)(x + 2)}$$

8. $\dfrac{1}{x} + \dfrac{1}{y} + \dfrac{1}{z} =$

LCD $= xyz$

$$\frac{1}{x} \cdot \frac{yz}{yz} + \frac{1}{y} \cdot \frac{xz}{xz} + \frac{1}{z} \cdot \frac{xy}{xy} = \frac{yz}{xyz} + \frac{xz}{xyz} + \frac{xy}{xyz} = \frac{yz + xz + xy}{xyz}$$

9. $\dfrac{1}{2x} - y =$

LCD $= 2x$

$$\frac{1}{2x} - \frac{y}{1} = \frac{1}{2x} - \frac{2xy}{2x} = \frac{1 - 2xy}{2x}$$

10. $\dfrac{x^2}{x-5} + \dfrac{25}{5-x} =$

$\dfrac{x^2}{x-5} + \dfrac{25}{-1(x-5)} = \dfrac{x^2}{x-5} - \dfrac{25}{x-5} = \dfrac{x^2-25}{x-5} =$

$\dfrac{(x-5)(x+5)}{(x-5)} = x + 5$

LCD was $= x + 5$

Solving Equations with Fractions

- To solve equations containing fractions, it is best to eliminate the fractions by multiplying through the equation by the LCM (least common multiple). Then proceed as before.

Examples:

1. Solve for x: $\dfrac{x}{2} + \dfrac{x}{3} = 5$ LCM = 6

$6\left(\dfrac{x}{2}\right) + 6\left(\dfrac{x}{3}\right) = 6(5)$

$\overset{3}{6}\left(\dfrac{x}{2}\right) + \overset{2}{6}\left(\dfrac{x}{3}\right) = 6(5)$

$3x + 2x = 30$
$5x = 30$
$x = 6$

2. Solve for y: $\dfrac{2}{5} + \dfrac{2}{y} = 1$ LCM = 5y

$5y\left(\dfrac{2}{5}\right) + 5y\left(\dfrac{2}{y}\right) = 5y(1)$

$\overset{}{5}y\left(\dfrac{2}{5}\right) + 5y\left(\dfrac{2}{y}\right) = 5y(1)$

$\begin{aligned} 2y + 10 &= 5y \\ -2y &= -2y \\ \hline 10 &= 3y \end{aligned}$

$$\frac{10}{3} = y$$

3. Solve for x: $\dfrac{x - 3}{2} = \dfrac{1}{x - 4}$ LCM $= 2(x - 4)$

$$2(x - 4)\left(\frac{x - 3}{2}\right) = 2(x - 4)\left(\frac{1}{x - 4}\right)$$

$$\cancel{2}(x - 4)\left(\frac{x - 3}{\cancel{2}}\right) = 2(x - \cancel{4})\left(\frac{1}{x - \cancel{4}}\right)$$

$$(x - 4)(x - 3) = 2(1)$$

$$x^2 - 7x + 12 = 2$$
$$- 2 = -2$$
$$\overline{x^2 - 7x + 10 = 0}$$

$$(x - 5)(x - 2) = 0$$

$$x - 5 = 0 \qquad x - 2 = 0$$
$$x = 5 \qquad x = 2$$

4. Solve for m: $\dfrac{3}{m} + \dfrac{2}{m + 2} = 2$ LCM $= m(m + 2)$

$$m(m + 2)\left(\frac{3}{m}\right) + m(m + 2)\left(\frac{2}{m + 2}\right) = m(m + 2)(2)$$

$$\cancel{m}(m + 2)\left(\frac{3}{\cancel{m}}\right) + m(\cancel{m + 2})\left(\frac{2}{\cancel{m + 2}}\right) = m(m + 2)(2)$$

$$3(m + 2) + 2m = 2m(m + 2)$$
$$3m + 6 + 2m = 2m^2 + 4m$$
$$6 + 5m = 2m^2 + 4m$$
$$0 = 2m^2 - m - 6$$
$$0 = (2m + 3)(m - 2)$$

$$2m + 3 = 0 \qquad m - 2 = 0$$
$$2m = -3 \qquad m = 2$$
$$m = \frac{-3}{2}$$

Practice: Solving Equations with Fractions Problems

1. $\dfrac{x}{2} + \dfrac{x}{5} = 7$

4. $\dfrac{2}{3n^2} = \dfrac{1}{4n^2} + \dfrac{5}{6n}$

2. $\dfrac{x}{10} + \dfrac{x}{6} + \dfrac{x}{15} = 1$

5. $\dfrac{2a - 3}{a - 3} - 2 = \dfrac{12}{a + 3}$

3. $\dfrac{a}{3} + 1 = \dfrac{a}{4} + 2$

6. $\dfrac{3}{x} + \dfrac{2}{x + 2} = 2$

Answers: Solving Equations with Fractions Problems

1. $\dfrac{x}{2} + \dfrac{x}{5} = 7$ LCM = 10

$$10\left(\dfrac{x}{2}\right) + 10\left(\dfrac{x}{5}\right) = 10(7)$$

$$^5\cancel{10}\left(\dfrac{x}{2}\right) + {}^2\cancel{10}\left(\dfrac{x}{5}\right) = 10(7)$$

$$5x + 2x = 70$$
$$7x = 70$$
$$x = 10$$

2. $\dfrac{x}{10} + \dfrac{x}{6} + \dfrac{x}{15} = 1$ LCM = 30

$$30\left(\dfrac{x}{10}\right) + 30\left(\dfrac{x}{6}\right) + 30\left(\dfrac{x}{15}\right) = 30(1)$$

$$^3\cancel{30}\left(\dfrac{x}{10}\right) + {}^5\cancel{30}\left(\dfrac{x}{6}\right) + {}^2\cancel{30}\left(\dfrac{x}{15}\right) = 30(1)$$

$$3x + 5x + 2x = 30$$
$$10x = 30$$
$$x = 3$$

3. $\dfrac{a}{3} + 1 = \dfrac{a}{4} + 2$ LCM = 12

$$12\left(\dfrac{a}{3}\right) + 12(1) = 12\left(\dfrac{a}{4}\right) + 12(2)$$

$${}^{4}\cancel{12}\left(\dfrac{a}{\cancel{3}}\right) + 12(1) = {}^{3}\cancel{12}\left(\dfrac{a}{\cancel{4}}\right) + 12(2)$$

$$4a + 12 = 3a + 24$$
$$a = 12$$

4. $\dfrac{2}{3n^2} = \dfrac{1}{4n^2} + \dfrac{5}{6n}$ LCM = $12n^2$

$$12n^2\left(\dfrac{2}{3n^2}\right) = 12n^2\left(\dfrac{1}{4n^2}\right) + 12n^2\left(\dfrac{5}{6n}\right)$$

$${}^{4}\cancel{12n^2}\left(\dfrac{2}{\cancel{3n^2}}\right) = {}^{3}\cancel{12n^2}\left(\dfrac{1}{\cancel{4n^2}}\right) + {}^{2}\cancel{12n^2}^{\,1}\left(\dfrac{5}{\cancel{6n}}\right)$$

$$4(2) = 3(1) + 2n(5)$$
$$8 = 3 + 10n$$
$$5 = 10n$$

$$\dfrac{1}{2} = n$$

5. $\dfrac{2a - 3}{a - 3} - 2 = \dfrac{12}{a + 3}$ LCM = $(a - 3)(a + 3)$

$$(a - 3)(a + 3)\left(\dfrac{2a - 3}{a - 3}\right) - 2(a - 3)(a + 3) =$$

$$(a - 3)(a + 3)\left(\dfrac{12}{a + 3}\right)$$

$$(\cancel{a - 3})(a + 3)\left(\dfrac{2a - 3}{\cancel{a - 3}}\right) - 2(a - 3)(a + 3) =$$

$$(a - 3)(\cancel{a + 3})\left(\dfrac{12}{\cancel{a + 3}}\right)$$

$$(a + 3)(2a - 3) - 2(a - 3)(a + 3) = 12(a - 3)$$
$$2a^2 + 3a - 9 - 2(a^2 - 9) = 12a - 36$$
$$2a^2 + 3a - 9 - 2a^2 + 18 = 12a - 36$$
$$3a + 9 = 12a - 36$$
$$45 = 9a$$
$$5 = a$$

6. $\dfrac{3}{x} + \dfrac{2}{x + 2} + 2$ LCM $= x(x + 2)$

$$x(x + 2)\left(\frac{3}{x}\right) + x(x + 2)\left(\frac{2}{x + 2}\right) = x(x + 2)(2)$$

$$\cancel{x}(x + 2)\left(\frac{3}{\cancel{x}}\right) + x\cancel{(x + 2)}\left(\frac{2}{\cancel{x + 2}}\right) = x(x + 2)(2)$$

$$3(x + 2) + 2x = 2x(x + 2)$$
$$3x + 6 + 2x = 2x^2 + 4x$$
$$5x + 6 = 2x^2 + 4x$$
$$0 = 2x^2 - x - 6$$
$$0 = (2x + 3)(x - 2)$$

$$2x + 3 = 0 \qquad\qquad x - 2 = 0$$
$$2x = -3 \qquad\qquad\quad x = 2$$
$$x = \frac{-3}{2}$$

Inequalities

- An *inequality* is a statement in which the relationships are not equal. Instead of using an equal sign ($=$) as in an equation, we use $>$ (greater than) and $<$ (less than), or $\geq$ (greater than or equal to) and $\leq$ (less than or equal to).

Solving Inequalities

- When working with inequalities, treat them exactly like equations (*except,* if you multiply or divide both sides by a negative number, you must *reverse* the direction of the sign).

Examples:

1. Solve for x: $2x + 4 > 6$

$$\begin{array}{r} 2x + 4 > 6 \\ \underline{ -4 \;\; -4} \\ 2x > 2 \end{array}$$

$$\frac{2x}{2} > \frac{2}{2} \qquad x > 1$$

Answers are sometimes written in set builder notation $\{x: x > 1\}$ which is read "all x such that x is greater than 1."

2. Solve for x: $-7x > 14$ (divide by -7 and reverse the sign)

$$\frac{-7x}{-7} < \frac{14}{-7}$$

$$x < -2$$

3. Solve for x: $3x + 2 \geq 5x - 10$

$$\begin{array}{r} 3x + 2 \geq 5x - 10 \\ \underline{ -2 -2} \\ 3x \geq 5x - 12 \end{array}$$

$$\begin{array}{r} 3x \geq 5x - 12 \\ \underline{-5x -5x} \\ -2x \geq -12 \end{array}$$

Notice opposite operations are used. Divide both sides by -2 and reverse the sign.

$$\frac{-2x}{-2} \leq \frac{-12}{-2}$$

$$x \leq 6$$

In set builder notation: $\{x: x \leq 6\}$

Practice: Solving Inequalities Problems

Solve each of the following for x.

1. $7x + 4 > 32$

2. $\frac{2}{3}x + 5 \leq 17$

3. $3 - 2x > 7$

4. $5x + 6 > 2x + 21$

Answers: Solving Inequalities Problems

1.
$$7x + 4 > 32$$
$$\underline{\quad -4 \quad -4 \quad}$$
$$7x \quad\quad > 28$$

$$\frac{7x}{7} > \frac{28}{7}$$

$$x > 4 \text{ or } \{x: x > 4\}$$

3.
$$3 - 2x > 7$$
$$\underline{-3 \quad\quad -3 \quad}$$
$$-2x > 4$$

$$\frac{-2x}{-2} < \frac{4}{-2}$$

$$x < -2 \text{ or } \{x: x < -2\}$$

2.
$$\tfrac{2}{3}x + 5 \leq 17$$
$$\underline{\quad -5 - 5 \quad}$$
$$\tfrac{2}{3}x \quad \leq 12$$

$$\frac{3}{2} \cdot \frac{2}{3}x \leq \frac{\cancel{12}^{6}}{1} \cdot \frac{3}{\cancel{2}}$$

$$x \leq 18 \text{ or } \{x: x \leq 18\}$$

4.
$$5x + 6 > 2x + 21$$
$$\underline{-2x - 6 \quad -2x - 6}$$
$$3x \quad\quad > \quad\quad 15$$

$$\frac{3x}{3} > \frac{15}{3}$$

$$x > 5 \text{ or } \{x: x > 5\}$$

Graphing on a Number Line

• Integers and real numbers can be represented on a *number line*. The point on this line associated with each number is called the graph of the number. Notice that number lines are spaced equally or proportionately.

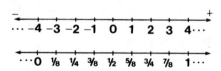

Graphing Inequalities

Examples:

When graphing inequalities involving only integers, dots are used.
1. Graph the set of x such that $1 \le x \le 4$ and x is an integer.
   {x: $1 \le x \le 4$, x is an integer}

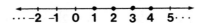

When graphing inequalities involving real numbers, lines, rays, and dots are used. A *dot* is used if the number is included. A *hollow dot* is used if the number is not included.

2. Graph the set of x such that $x \ge 1$.   {x: $x \ge 1$}

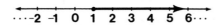

3. Graph the set of x such that $x > 1$.   {x: $x > 1$}

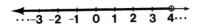

4. Graph the set of x such that $x < 4$.   {x: $x < 4$}

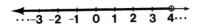

This ray is often called an *open ray* or a *half line*. The hollow dot distinguishes an open ray from a ray.

Intervals

● An *interval* consists of all the numbers that lie within two certain boundaries. If the two boundaries, or fixed numbers, are included, then the interval is called a *closed interval*. If the fixed numbers are not included, then the interval is called an *open interval*.

Closed interval   {x: $-1 \le x \le 2$}

Open interval $\{x: -1 < x < 2\}$

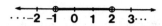

If the interval includes only one of the boundaries, then it is called a *half-open interval*.

Half-open interval $\{x: -1 < x \le 2\}$

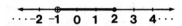

Practice: Graphing Inequalities Problems

Graph each of the following.

1. $\{x: 2 \le x \le 6, x \text{ is an integer}\}$
2. $\{x: -3 < x < 5, x \text{ is an integer}\}$
3. $\{x: x \ge -2\}$
4. $\{x: x < 3\}$
5. $\{x: x \le -1\}$

Answers: Graphing Inequalities Problems

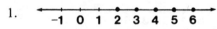

Absolute Value

- The numerical value when direction or sign is not considered is called the *absolute value*. The absolute value of x is written $|x|$. The absolute value of a number is always positive except when the number is 0.

$$|0| = 0 \qquad |x| > 0 \qquad |-x| > 0$$

Examples:

1. $|4| = 4$
2. $|-6| = 6$
3. $|7 - 9| = |-2| = 2$
4. $3 - |-6| = 3 - 6 = -3$ (note that absolute value is taken first)

Practice: Absolute Value Problems

1. $|-9| =$
2. $|6| =$
3. $|-3 + 2| =$
4. $|-6 - 6| =$
5. $|4 - 8| =$
6. $|-5| + 3 =$
7. $9 + |-5| =$
8. $6 - |-8| =$

Answers: Absolute Value Problems

1. 9
2. 6
3. $|-3 + 2| = |-1| = 1$
4. $|-6 - 6| = |-12| = 12$
5. $|4 - 8| = |-4| = 4$
6. $|-5| + 3 = 5 + 3 = 8$
7. $9 + |-5| = 9 + 5 = 14$
8. $6 - |-8| = 6 - 8 = -2$

Solving Equations Containing Absolute Value

● To solve an equation containing absolute value, isolate the absolute value on one side of the equation. Then set its contents equal to both + and − the other side of the equation and solve both equations.

Examples:

1. Solve $|x| + 2 = 5$

Isolate the absolute value.

$$
\begin{aligned}
|x| + 2 &= 5 \\
-2 &= -2 \\
\hline
|x| &= 3
\end{aligned}
$$

Set the contents of the absolute value portion equal to $+3$ and to -3.

$$x = 3 \qquad x = -3$$

Answer: 3, −3

2. Solve $3|x - 1| - 1 = 11$

Isolate the absolute value.

$$3|x - 1| - 1 = 11$$
$$\underline{\quad\quad\quad +1 \quad +1}$$
$$3|x - 1| \quad\quad = 12$$

$$\frac{3|x - 1|}{3} = \frac{12}{3}$$

$$|x - 1| = 4$$

Set the contents of the absolute value portion equal to $+4$ and to -4.

Solving for x

$x - 1 = 4$	$x - 1 = -4$
$\underline{+1 \;\; +1}$	$\underline{+1 = +1}$
$x \quad\;\; = 5$	$x \quad\quad = -3$

Answer: 5, -3

Practice: Solving Equations Containing Absolute Value Problems

Solve each equation for x.

1. $|x| - 3 = 7$ 3. $|x - 1| = 4$
2. $4|x| = 1\text{-}2$ 4. $3|x + 2| - 5 = 22$

Answers: Solving Equations Containing Absolute Value Problems

1. $|x| - 3 = 7$
   $\underline{\quad +3 \;\; +3}$
   $|x| \quad\quad = 10$

   $x = 10 \quad\quad x = -10$

2. $\dfrac{4|x|}{4} = \dfrac{12}{4}$

   $|x| = 3$

   $x = 3 \quad\quad x = -3$

3. $|x - 1| = 4$

$$x - 1 = 4 \qquad x - 1 = -4$$
$$\underline{+ 1 = +1} \qquad \underline{+ 1 = +1}$$
$$x \quad = 5 \qquad x \quad = -3$$

4. $3|x + 2| - 5 = 22$

$$\underline{\qquad\quad + 5 \quad +5}$$
$$3|x + 2| \quad = 27$$

$$\frac{3|x + 2|}{3} = \frac{27}{3}$$

$$|x + 2| = 9$$

$$x + 2 = 9 \qquad x + 2 = -9$$
$$\underline{- 2 \quad -2} \qquad \underline{- 2 = -2}$$
$$x \quad = 7 \qquad x \quad = -11$$

Solving Inequalities Containing Absolute Value

● To solve an inequality containing absolute value, follow the same steps as in solving equations with absolute value except you must remember to reverse the direction of the sign when setting the absolute value opposite the negative.

Examples:

Solve and graph answers.

1. $|x - 1| > 2$

The absolute value is isolated: $x - 1 > 2$

Set the contents of the absolute value portion to both 2 and -2. Be sure to change the direction of the sign when using -2.

Solve for x.
$$x - 1 > 2 \qquad x - 1 < -2$$
$$\underline{+ 1 \quad +1} \qquad \underline{+ 1 \quad +1}$$
$$x \quad > 3 \qquad x \quad < -1$$

Graph answer:

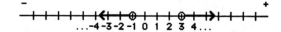

2. $3|x| - 2 \leq 1$

Isolate the absolute value.

$$3|x| - 2 \leq 1$$
$$\underline{ + 2 \quad +2}$$
$$3|x| \quad \leq 3$$

$$\frac{3|x|}{3} \leq \frac{3}{3}$$

$$|x| \leq 1$$

Set the contents of the absolute value portion to both 1 and -1. Be sure to change the direction of the sign when using -1.

$$x \leq 1 \qquad x \geq -1$$

Graph answer:

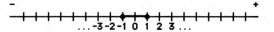

3. $2|1 - x| + 1 \geq 3$

Isolate the absolute value.

$$2|1 - x| + 1 \geq 3$$
$$\underline{ - 1 \quad -1}$$
$$2|1 - x| \quad \geq 2$$

$$\frac{2|1 - x|}{2} \geq \frac{2}{2}$$

$$|1 - x| \geq 1$$

Set the contents of the absolute value portion to both 1 and -1. Be sure to change the direction of the sign when using -1.

Solve for x.

$$1 - x \geq 1 \qquad\qquad 1 - x \leq -1$$
$$\underline{-1 \qquad -1} \qquad\qquad \underline{-1 \qquad -1}$$
$$-x \geq 0 \qquad\qquad -x \leq -2$$

$$\frac{-x}{-1} \geq \frac{0}{-1} \qquad\qquad \frac{-x}{-1} \leq \frac{-2}{-1}$$

$$x \leq 0 \qquad\qquad x \geq 2$$

Graph answer:

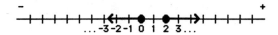

Practice: Solving Inequalities Containing Absolute Value Problems

Solve for x and graph answers.

1. $|x + 1| < 3$
2. $2|x| + 1 \geq 5$

3. $|x - 1| + 2 \leq 3$
4. $3|2 - x| + 1 > 7$

Answers: Solving Inequalities Containing Absolute Value Problems

1. $|x + 1| < 3$

$$
\begin{array}{rr}
x + 1 < 3 & \quad x + 1 > -3 \\
\underline{-1 \quad -1} & \quad \underline{-1 \quad -1} \\
x \quad < 2 & \quad x \quad > -4
\end{array}
$$

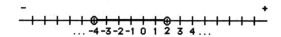

2. $2|x| + 1 \geq 5$

$$
\begin{array}{r}
2|x| + 1 \geq 5 \\
\underline{-1 \quad -1} \\
2|x| \quad \geq 4
\end{array}
$$

$$\frac{2|x|}{2} \geq \frac{4}{2}$$

$$|x| \geq 2$$

$$x \geq 2 \qquad x \leq -2$$

3. $|x - 1| + 2 \leq 3$

$$
\begin{array}{r}
|x - 1| + 2 \leq 3 \\
\underline{-2 \quad -2} \\
|x - 1| \quad \leq 1
\end{array}
$$

$$x - 1 \leq 1 \qquad x - 1 \geq -1$$
$$\underline{\;+1\quad +1\;} \qquad \underline{\;+1\quad +1\;}$$
$$x \quad\leq\quad 2 \qquad x \quad\geq\quad 0$$

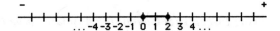

4. $3\,|2 - x| + 1 > 7$

$$3\,|2 - x| + 1 > \quad 7$$
$$\underline{\qquad\qquad -1 \quad -1\;}$$
$$3\,|2 - x| \qquad > \quad 6$$

$$\frac{3\,|2 - x|}{3} > \frac{6}{3}$$

$$|2 - x| > 2$$

$$2 - x > \quad 2 \qquad\qquad 2 - x < -2$$
$$\underline{-2 \qquad\quad -2} \qquad\quad \underline{-2 \qquad\qquad -2}$$
$$-x > \quad 0 \qquad\qquad\quad -x < -4$$

$$\frac{-x}{-1} > \frac{0}{-1} \qquad\qquad \frac{-x}{-1} < \frac{-4}{-1}$$

$$x < 0 \qquad\qquad\qquad x > 4$$

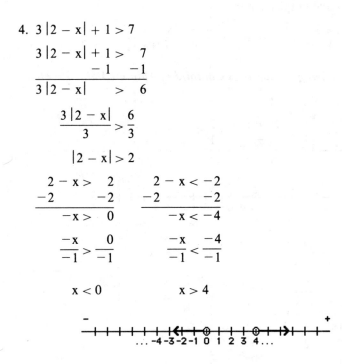

Analytic Geometry

Coordinate Graphs

● Each point on a number line is assigned a number. In the same way, each point in a plane is assigned a pair of numbers. These numbers represent the placement of the point relative to two intersecting lines. In *coordinate graphs,* two perpendicular number lines are used and are called *coordinate axes.* One axis is horizontal and is called the *x axis*. The other is vertical and is called the *y axis*. The point of intersection of the two number lines is called the *origin* and is represented by the coordinates (0, 0).

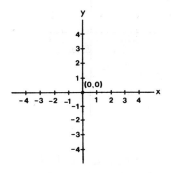

Each point on a plane is located by a unique ordered pair of numbers called the coordinates. Some coordinates are noted below.

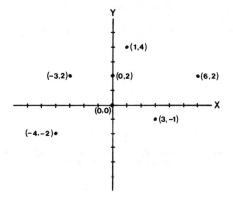

Notice that on the x-axis, numbers to the right of 0 are positive and to the left of 0 are negative. On the y-axis, numbers above 0 are positive and below 0 are negative. Also, note that the first number in the ordered pair is called the *x-coordinate,* or *abscissa,* while the second number is the *y-coordinate,* or *ordinate.* The x-coordinate shows the right or left direction, and the y coordinate shows the up or down direction.

The coordinate graph is divided into four quarters called *quadrants*. These quadrants are labeled below.

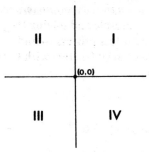

Notice that

In quadrant I, x is always positive and y is always positive.
In quadrant II, x is always negative and y is always positive.
In quadrant III, x and y are both always negative.
In quadrant IV, x is always positive and y is always negative.

Practice: Coordinate Graph Problems

Identify the points (A, B, C, D, E, and F) on the coordinate graph below.

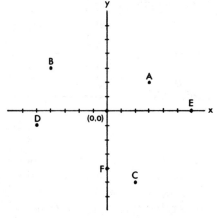

Answers: Coordinate Graph Problems

A. (3, 2)   D. (−5, −1)
B. (−4, 3)   E. (6, 0)
C. (2, −5)   F. (0, −4)

Graphing Equations on the Coordinate Plane

- To *graph an equation on the coordinate plane,* find the solutions by giving a value to one variable and solving the resulting equation for the other value. Repeat this process to find other solutions. (When giving a value for one variable, start with 0, then try 1, etc.) Then graph the solutions.

Examples:

1. Graph the equation x + y = 6.

If x is 0, then y is 6.

$$(0) + y = 6$$
$$y = 6$$

If x is 1, then y is 5.

$$\begin{array}{r} (1) + y = 6 \\ -1 \qquad -1 \\ \hline y = 5 \end{array}$$

If x is 2, then y is 4.

$$\begin{array}{r} (2) + y = 6 \\ -2 \qquad -2 \\ \hline y = 4 \end{array}$$

Using a simple chart is helpful.

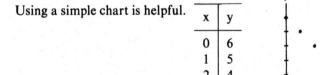

x	y
0	6
1	5
2	4

Now plot these coordinates.

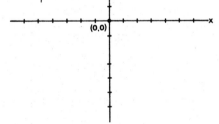

Note: To graph an inequality on the coordinate plane, such as x + y > 6, simply follow the same steps as graphing an equation. After drawing the line between the plotted points, you must find which side of the line is to be shaded. To do this, select a point on the graph and plug the values into the inequality. If the values make the inequality true, then shade that side of the line. If not, shade the other side of the line. For example, in x + y > 6 use the points (0,0). Since 0 + 0 is not greater than 6, you would shade the other side of the line.

Notice that these solutions, when plotted, form a straight line. Equations whose solution sets form a straight line are called *linear equations*. Equations that have a variable raised to a power, show division by a variable, involve variables with square roots, or have variables multiplied together will not form a straight line when their solutions are graphed. These are called *nonlinear equations*.

2. Graph the equation $y = x^2 + 4$.

If x is 0, then y is 4.

$$y = (0)^2 + 4$$
$$y = 0 + 4$$
$$y = 4$$

If x is 1, then y is 5.

$$y = (1)^2 + 4$$
$$y = 1 + 4$$
$$y = 5$$

If x is 2, then y is 8.

$$y = (2)^2 + 4$$
$$y = 4 + 4$$
$$y = 8$$

Use a simple chart.

x	y
0	4
1	5
2	8

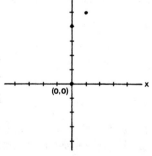

Now plot these coordinates.

Notice that these solutions, when plotted, give a curved line (non-linear). The more points plotted, the easier it is to see and describe the solution set.

Practice: Graphing Equations on the Coordinate Plane Problems

State whether the equations are linear or nonlinear in problems 1–6.

1. $x - 5 = 5$ 4. $xy = 0$
2. $x + 5 = y$ 5. $x + \frac{5}{y} = 0$
3. $x^2 + y = 3$ 6. $y = x + 7$

Graph each of the equations in problems 7–14.

7. $x - y = 3$ 10. $x - 2y = 4$
8. $y = -2x + 1$ 11. $x + 4 = y + 2x - 3$
9. $y = x^2 + 1$ 12. $y = 4$

Answers: Graphing Equations on the Coordinate Plane Problems

1. linear   4. nonlinear
2. linear   5. nonlinear
3. nonlinear   6. linear

7. $x - y = 3$

x	y
3	0
4	1
5	2

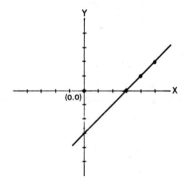

8. $y = -2x + 1$

$x = 0$	$x = 1$
$y = -2(0) + 1$	$y = -2(1) + 1$
$y = 0 + 1$	$y = -2 + 1$
$y = 1$	$y = -1$

$x = 2$
$y = -2(2) + 1$
$y = -4 + 1$
$y = -3$

x	y
0	1
1	-1
2	-3

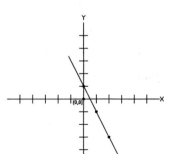

9. $y = x^2 + 1$

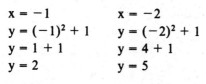

$$x = 0 \qquad\qquad x = 1 \qquad\qquad x = 2$$
$$y = (0)^2 + 1 \qquad y = (1)^2 + 1 \qquad y = (2)^2 + 1$$
$$y = 0 + 1 \qquad\; y = 1 + 1 \qquad\; y = 4 + 1$$
$$y = 1 \qquad\qquad y = 2 \qquad\qquad y = 5$$

$$x = -1 \qquad\qquad x = -2$$
$$y = (-1)^2 + 1 \qquad y = (-2)^2 + 1$$
$$y = 1 + 1 \qquad\quad y = 4 + 1$$
$$y = 2 \qquad\qquad\; y = 5$$

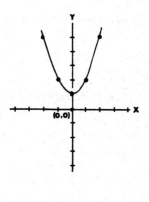

x	y
0	1
1	2
2	5
-1	2
-2	5

10. $x - 2y = 4$

$$y = 0 \qquad\qquad\qquad y = 1$$
$$x - 2(0) = 4 \qquad\quad x - 2(1) = 4$$
$$x - 0 = 4 \qquad\qquad x - 2 = 4$$
$$x = 4$$

$$x - 2 = 4$$
$$\underline{+ 2 + 2}$$
$$x \quad\;\; = 6$$

$$y = -2$$
$$x - 2(-2) = 4$$
$$x + 4 = 4$$
$$x = 0$$

x	y
4	0
6	1
0	-2

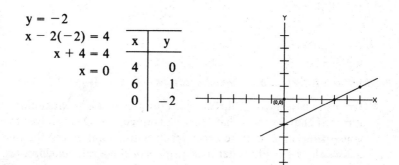

11. $x + 4 = y + 2x - 3$

First simplify by combining like terms.

$$
\begin{array}{rcl}
x + 4 &=& y + 2x - 3 \\
-2x & & \quad\;\; -2x \\
\hline
-x + 4 &=& y \qquad -3 \\
+3 & & \qquad +3 \\
\hline
-x + 7 &=& y
\end{array}
$$

or $7 = x + y$

x	y
0	7
1	6
2	5

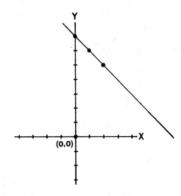

12. $y = 4$

x	y
0	4
1	4
2	4

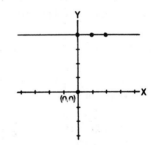

Slope and Intercept of Linear Equations

● There are two relationships between the graph of a linear equation and the equation itself that must be pointed out. One involves the slope of the line, and the other involves the point where the line crosses the y-axis. In order to see either of these relationships, the terms of the equation must be in a certain order.

$$(+)(1)y = (\ )x + (\ )$$

When the terms are written in this order, the equation is said to be in y-form. Y-form is written $y = mx + b$, and the two relationships involve m and b.

Look back at problems 7, 8, and 10 in the last section. Write the equations in y-form.

7. $x - y = 3$
    $-y = -x + 3$
    $y = x - 3$

8. $y = -2x + 1$

10. $x - 2y = 4$
    $-2y = -x + 4$
    $2y = x - 4$
    $y = \frac{1}{2}x - 2$

● Looking at the graphs of these three problems, the lines cross the y-axis at -3, $+1$, and -2, the last term in each equation. If a linear equation is written in the form of $y = mx + b$, b is the y-intercept.

● The slope of a line is defined as

$$\frac{\text{the change in y}}{\text{the change in x}}$$

and the word "change" refers to the difference in the value of y (or x) between two points on the line.

$$\text{The slope of line AB} = \frac{y_A - y_B}{x_A - x_B} \quad \left[\frac{\text{y at point A} - \text{y at point B}}{\text{x at point A} - \text{x at point B}}\right]$$

Note: Points A and B can be any two points on a line; there will be no difference in the slope.

Examples:

To find the slope of the line in problem 7, pick any two points on the line such as A $(3,0)$ and B $(5,2)$ and calculate the slope.

$$\text{slope (problem 7)} = \frac{y_A - y_B}{x_A - x_B} = \frac{(0) - (2)}{(3) - (5)} = \frac{-2}{-2} = 1$$

In problem 8, pick two points such as A $(1,-1)$ and B $(-1,3)$ and calculate the slope.

$$\text{slope (problem 8)} = \frac{y_A - y_B}{x_A - x_B} = \frac{(-1) - (3)}{(1) - (-1)} = \frac{-1 - 3}{1 + 1}$$

$$= \frac{-4}{2} = -2$$

In problem 10, pick two points such as A $(0,-2)$ and B $(4,0)$ and calculate the slope.

$$\text{slope (problem 10)} = \frac{y_A - y_B}{x_A - x_B} = \frac{(-2) - (0)}{(0) - (4)} = \frac{-2}{-4} = \frac{1}{2}$$

Looking back at the equations for problems 7, 8, and 10 written in y-form, it should be evident that the slope of the line is the same as the numerical coefficient of the x term.

7. $y = x - 3$

slope = 1   y-intercept = -3

8. $y = -2x + 1$

slope = -2 y-intercept = 1

10. $y = \frac{1}{2}x - 2$

slope = $\frac{1}{2}$ y-intercept = -2

Graphing Linear Equations Using Slope and Intercept

● Graphing an equation by using its slope and y-intercept is usually quite easy.
  a. State the equation in y-form.
  b. Locate the y-intercept on the graph (that is one of the points on the line).
  c. Write the slope as a ratio (fraction) and use it to locate other points on the line.
  d. Draw the line through the points.

Examples:

Graph the following equations using slope and y-intercept.

1. $x - y = 2$
    $-y = -x + 2$
    $y = x - 2$

    Locate -2 on the y-axis.

    From this point, count:

    slope $= 1$

    or $\dfrac{1 \text{ (for every 1 up)}}{1 \text{ (go 1 to the right)}}$

    or $\dfrac{-1 \text{ (for every 1 down)}}{-1 \text{ (go 1 to the left)}}$

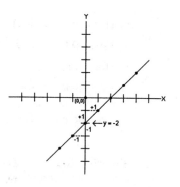

2. $2x - y = -4$
    $-y = -2x - 4$
    $y = 2x + 4$

    Locate $+4$ on the y-axis.

    From this point, count:

    slope $= 2$

    or $\dfrac{2 \text{ (for every 2 up)}}{1 \text{ (go 1 to the right)}}$

    or $\dfrac{-2 \text{ (for every 2 down)}}{-1 \text{ (go 1 to the left)}}$

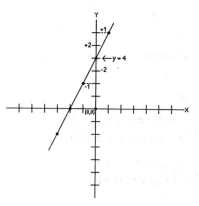

3. $x + 3y = 0$
    $3y = -x + (0)$
    $y = -\frac{1}{3}x + (0)$

Locate 0 on the y-axis.

From this point, count:

slope $= -\dfrac{1}{3}$

or $\dfrac{-1}{3}$ (for every 1 down)
(go 3 to the right)

or $\dfrac{1}{-3}$ (for every 1 up)
(go 3 to the left)

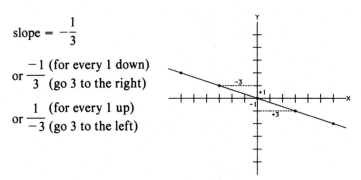

Practice: Graphing Linear Equations Using Slope and Intercept Problems

Graph each of the following using slope and intercept.

1. $x + y = 1$ 2. $3x - y = 1$ 3. $x - 2y = 4$ 4. $2x - 3y = 0$

Answers: Graphing Linear Equations Using Slope and Intercept Problems

1. $x + y = 1$
    $y = -x + 1$

    y-intercept $= 1$

    slope $= -1$

    or $\dfrac{-1}{1}$ (for every 1 down)
    (go 1 to the right)

    or $\dfrac{1}{-1}$ (for every 1 up)
    (go 1 to the left)

2. $3x - y = 1$
$ -y = -3x + 1$
$ y = 3x - 1$

y-intercept $= -1$

slope $= 3$

or $\dfrac{3 \text{ (for every 3 up)}}{1 \text{ (go 1 to the right)}}$

or $\dfrac{-3 \text{ (for every 3 down)}}{-1 \text{ (go 1 to the left)}}$

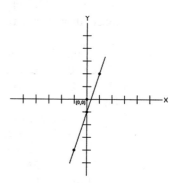

3. $x - 2y = 4$
$ -2y = -x + 4$
$ 2y = x - 4$
$ y = \tfrac{1}{2}x - 2$

y-intercept $= -2$

slope $= \dfrac{1 \text{ (for every 1 up)}}{2 \text{ (go 2 to the right)}}$

or $\dfrac{-1 \text{ (for every 1 down)}}{-2 \text{ (go 2 to the left)}}$

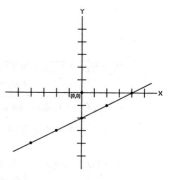

4. $2x - 3y = 0$
$ -3y = -2x + (0)$
$ 3y = 2x - (0)$
$ y = \tfrac{2}{3}x - (0)$

y-intercept $= 0$

slope $= \dfrac{2 \text{ (for every 2 up)}}{3 \text{ (go 3 to the right)}}$

or $\dfrac{-2 \text{ (for every 2 down)}}{-3 \text{ (go 3 to the left)}}$

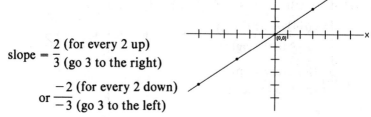

Finding the Distance Between Two Points in a Plane

● To find the distance between two points in a plane, the Pythagorean theorem could be used, but a special distance formula allows the computation of the distance between two points more easily.

Given two points on a plane, P_1 and P_2, the distance between P_1 and P_2 can be found by the following formula:

$$d = \sqrt{(x_1 - x_2)^2 + (y_1 - y_2)^2}$$

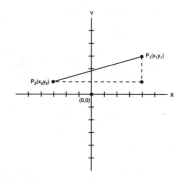

Examples:

Find the distance between the given points.

1. $(-2, -1)(4, 7)$

$$d = \sqrt{(x_1 - x_2)^2 + (y_1 - y_2)^2}$$
$$d = \sqrt{[(-2) - (4)]^2 + [(-1) - (7)]^2}$$
$$d = \sqrt{(-6)^2 + (-8)^2}$$
$$d = \sqrt{36 + 64}$$
$$d = \sqrt{100}$$
$$d = 10$$

2. $(0, -2)(-4, -5)$

$$d = \sqrt{(x_1 - x_2)^2 + (y_1 - y_2)^2}$$
$$d = \sqrt{[(0) - (-4)]^2 + [(-2) - (-5)]^2}$$
$$d = \sqrt{(4)^2 + (3)^2}$$
$$d = \sqrt{16 + 9}$$
$$d = \sqrt{25}$$
$$d = 5$$

3. $(-4,1)(1,-3)$

$d = \sqrt{(x_1 - x_2)^2 + (y_1 - y_2)^2}$
$d = \sqrt{[(-4) - (1)]^2 + [(1) - (-3)]^2}$
$d = \sqrt{(-5)^2 + (4)^2}$
$d = \sqrt{25 + 16}$
$d = \sqrt{41}$

Practice: Finding the Distance Between Two Points in a Plane Problems

Find the distance between the given points.

1. $(-1,-3)(3,0)$ 3. $(-1,5)(-1,-1)$
2. $(-3,-5)(2,7)$ 4. $(-3,-2)(1,6)$

Answers: Finding the Distance Between Two Points in a Plane Problems

1. $(-1,-3)(3,0)$

$d = \sqrt{(x_1 - x_2)^2 + (y_1 - y_2)^2}$
$d = \sqrt{[(-1) - (3)]^2 + [(-3) - (0)]^2}$
$d = \sqrt{(-4)^2 + (-3)^2}$
$d = \sqrt{16 + 9}$
$d = \sqrt{25}$
$d = 5$

2. $(-3,-5)(2,7)$

$d = \sqrt{(x_1 - x_2)^2 + (y_1 - y_2)^2}$
$d = \sqrt{[(-3) - (2)]^2 + [(-5) - (7)]^2}$
$d = \sqrt{(-5)^2 + (-12)^2}$
$d = \sqrt{25 + 144}$
$d = \sqrt{169}$
$d = 13$

3. $(-1,5)(-1,-1)$

$d = \sqrt{(x_1 - x_2)^2 + (y_1 - y_2)^2}$
$d = \sqrt{[(-1) - (-1)]^2 + [(5) - (-1)]^2}$
$d = \sqrt{(0)^2 + (6)^2}$
$d = \sqrt{0 + 36}$
$d = \sqrt{36}$
$d = 6$

4. $(-3,-2)(1,6)$

$d = \sqrt{(x_1 - x_2)^2 + (y_1 - y_2)^2}$
$d = \sqrt{[(-3) - (1)]^2 + [(-2) - (-6)]^2}$
$d = \sqrt{(-4)^2 + (-8)^2}$
$d = \sqrt{16 + 64}$
$d = \sqrt{80}$
$d = 4\sqrt{5}$

Finding the Midpoint of a Line Segment in a Plane

- From the drawing at the right, it should be obvious that the coordinates of the midpoint of $\overline{P_1P_2}$ would be the average of the coordinates of P_1 and P_2. The following formula states that fact.

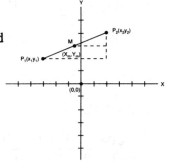

$$x_m = \frac{x_1 + x_2}{2} \qquad y_m = \frac{y_1 + y_2}{2}$$

Examples:

Given $\overline{P_1P_2}$ with endpoints given, find the midpoint M.

1. $(0,4)(-3,-2)$

$$x_m = \frac{x_1 + x_2}{2} \qquad\qquad y_m = \frac{y_1 + y_2}{2}$$

$$x_m = \frac{(0) + (-3)}{2} \qquad\qquad y_m = \frac{(4) + (-2)}{2}$$

$$x_m = \frac{0 - 3}{2} \qquad\qquad y_m = \frac{2}{2}$$

$$x_m = -\frac{3}{2} \qquad\qquad y_m = 1 \qquad M = \left(-\frac{3}{2}, 1\right)$$

2. $(2,5)(6,-1)$

$$x_m = \frac{x_1 + x_2}{2} \qquad\qquad y_m = \frac{y_1 + y_2}{2}$$

$$x_m = \frac{(2) + (6)}{2} \qquad\qquad y_m = \frac{(5) + (-1)}{2}$$

$$x_m = \frac{8}{2} \qquad\qquad y_m = \frac{4}{2}$$

$$x_m = 4 \qquad\qquad y_m = 2 \qquad M = (4,2)$$

3. $(-1, 1/2)(-4, 3 1/2)$

$$x_m = \frac{x_1 + x_2}{2} \qquad\qquad y_m = \frac{y_1 + y_2}{2}$$

$$x_m = \frac{(-1) + (-4)}{2} \qquad\qquad y_m = \frac{(1/2) + (3 1/2)}{2}$$

$$x_m = -\frac{5}{2} \qquad\qquad y_m = \frac{4}{2}$$

$$x_m = -2 1/2 \qquad\qquad y_m = 2$$

4. Given $\overline{P_1P_2}$ with P_1 and the midpoint M given, find P_2.

   $P_1 (-3,3), M (-1,0), P_2 (\ , \ )$

$$x_m = \frac{x_1 + x_2}{2} \qquad\qquad y_m = \frac{y_1 + y_2}{2}$$

$$(-1) = \frac{(-3) + x}{2} \qquad\qquad (0) = \frac{(3) + y}{2}$$

$$-1 = \frac{-3 + x}{2} \qquad\qquad 0 = \frac{3 + y}{2}$$

$$-2 = -3 + x \qquad\qquad 0 = 3 + y$$
$$1 = x \qquad\qquad\qquad -3 = y \qquad\qquad P_2 (1,-3)$$

5. Given $\overline{P_1P_2}$ with $P_1 (-a,4)$, $P_2 (3,-2a)$, and midpoint M (a,a), find a.

$$x_m = \frac{x_1 + x_2}{2} \qquad \text{or} \qquad y_m = \frac{y_1 + y_2}{2}$$

$$(a) = \frac{(-a) + 3}{2} \qquad\qquad (a) = \frac{(4) + (-2a)}{2}$$

$$a = \frac{-a + 3}{2} \qquad\qquad a = \frac{4 - 2a}{2}$$

$$2a = -a + 3 \qquad\qquad 2a = 4 - 2a$$
$$3a = 3 \qquad\qquad\qquad 4a = 4$$
$$a = 1 \qquad\qquad\qquad a = 1$$

Practice: Finding the Midpoint of a Line Segment in a Plane Problems

Given $\overline{AB}$ with midpoint M, find the missing coordinate.

1. A $(-1,-1)$, B $(3,5)$, M $(\ , \ )$
2. A $(-1,2)$, B $(3,-3)$, M $(\ , \ )$
3. A $(-2,4)$, B $(\ , \ )$, M $(-\frac{1}{2},1)$
4. A $(\ , \ )$, B $(-2,-3)$, M $(-1\frac{1}{2}, \frac{1}{2})$
5. Find a if the endpoints of a line segment are $(1 - 2a, -2)$ and $(5,a)$ with the midpoint at $(\frac{a}{2},0)$.

Answers: Finding the Midpoint of a Line Segment in a Plane Problems

1. A $(-1,-1)$, B $(3,5)$, M (,)

$$x_m = \frac{x_A + x_B}{2} \qquad\qquad y_m = \frac{y_A + y_B}{2}$$

$$x_m = \frac{(-1) + (3)}{2} \qquad\qquad y_m = \frac{(-1) + (5)}{2}$$

$$x_m = \frac{-1 + 3}{2} \qquad\qquad y_m = \frac{-1 + 5}{2}$$

$$x_m = \frac{2}{2} \qquad\qquad y_m = \frac{4}{2}$$

$$x_m = 1 \qquad\qquad y_m = 2 \qquad\qquad M\,(1,2)$$

2. A $(-1,2)$, B $(3,-3)$, M (,)

$$x_m = \frac{x_A + x_B}{2} \qquad\qquad y_m = \frac{y_A + y_B}{2}$$

$$x_m = \frac{(-1) + (3)}{2} \qquad\qquad y_m = \frac{(2) + (-3)}{2}$$

$$x_m = \frac{-1 + 3}{2} \qquad\qquad y_m = \frac{2 - 3}{2}$$

$$x_m = \frac{2}{2} \qquad\qquad y_m = -\frac{1}{2}$$

$$x_m = 1 \qquad\qquad\qquad M\,(1,-\tfrac{1}{2})$$

3. A $(-2,4)$, B (,), M $(-\tfrac{1}{2},1)$

$$x_m = \frac{x_A + x_B}{2} \qquad\qquad y_m = \frac{y_A + y_B}{2}$$

$$-\frac{1}{2} = \frac{(-2) + x}{2} \qquad\qquad (1) = \frac{(4) + y}{2}$$

$$-\frac{1}{2} = \frac{-2 + x}{2} \qquad\qquad 1 = \frac{4 + y}{2}$$

$$-1 = -2 + x \qquad\qquad 2 = 4 + y$$
$$1 = x \qquad\qquad\qquad -2 = y \qquad\qquad B\,(1,-2)$$

4. A (,), B $(-2,-3)$, M $(-1\frac{1}{2},\frac{1}{2})$

$$x_m = \frac{x_A + x_B}{2} \qquad\qquad y_m = \frac{y_A + y_B}{2}$$

$$(-1\frac{1}{2}) = \frac{x + (-3)}{2} \qquad\qquad \left(\frac{1}{2}\right) = \frac{y + (-3)}{2}$$

$$-\frac{3}{2} = \frac{x-2}{2} \qquad\qquad \frac{1}{2} = \frac{y-3}{2}$$

$$-3 = x - 2 \qquad\qquad 1 = y - 3$$
$$-1 = x \qquad\qquad\qquad 4 = y \qquad\qquad A\,(-1,4)$$

5. Find a if the endpoints of a line segment are $(1 - 2a, -2)$ and $(5,a)$, with the midpoint at $(\frac{a}{2},0)$.

$$x_m = \frac{x_1 + x_2}{2} \qquad \text{or} \qquad y_m = \frac{y_1 + y_2}{2}$$

$$\left(\frac{a}{2}\right) = \frac{(1 - 2a) + (5)}{2} \qquad\qquad (0) = \frac{(-2) + (a)}{2}$$

$$\frac{a}{2} = \frac{1 - 2a + 5}{2} \qquad\qquad 0 = \frac{-2 + a}{2}$$

$$a = 1 - 2a + 5 \qquad\qquad 0 = -2 + a$$
$$a = 6 - 2a \qquad\qquad\qquad 2 = a$$
$$3a = 6$$
$$a = 2$$

Roots and Radicals

Note: This subject is introduced in the Arithmetic Review.

● The symbol $\sqrt{}$ is called a *radical sign* and is used to designate *square root*. To designate *cube root,* a small three is placed above the radical sign, $\sqrt[3]{}$; a fourth root is designated as $\sqrt[4]{}$ and a fifth root as $\sqrt[5]{}$, etc. When two radical signs are next to each other, they automatically mean that the two are multiplied. The multiplication sign may be omitted. Note that the square root of a negative number is not possible within the real number system. A completely different system of imaginary numbers is used. The (so-called) imaginary numbers are multiples of the imaginary unit i. $\sqrt{-1} = i$, $\sqrt{-4} = 2i$, $\sqrt{-9} = 3i$, etc.

Simplifying Square Roots

Examples:

1. $\sqrt{9} = 3$ ⎫ Reminder: this notation is used on
   most standardized exams and will
2. $-\sqrt{9} = -3$ ⎭ be adhered to in this book.

3. $\sqrt{18} = \sqrt{9 \cdot 2} = \sqrt{9} \cdot \sqrt{2} = 3\sqrt{2}$

4. If each variable is nonnegative (not a negative number), $\sqrt{x^2} = x$

5. If each variable is nonnegative, $\sqrt{x^4} = x^2$

6. If each variable is nonnegative, $\sqrt{x^6 y^8} = \sqrt{x^6} \sqrt{y^8} = x^3 y^4$

7. If each variable is nonnegative, $\sqrt{25a^4 b^6} = \sqrt{25} \sqrt{a^4} \sqrt{b^6} = 5a^2 b^3$

8. If each variable is nonnegative, $\sqrt{x^7} = \sqrt{x^6(x)} = \sqrt{x^6} \sqrt{x} = x^3 \sqrt{x}$

9. If each variable is nonnegative, $\sqrt{x^9 y^8} = \sqrt{x^9} \sqrt{y^8} = \sqrt{x^8(x)} \sqrt{y^8} = x^4 \sqrt{x} \cdot y^4 = x^4 y^4 \sqrt{x}$

10. If each variable is nonnegative, $\sqrt{16x^5} = \sqrt{16} \sqrt{x^5} = \sqrt{16} \sqrt{x^4(x)} = 4x^2 \sqrt{x}$

Practice: Simplifying Square Root Problems

Simplify each of the following. All variables are nonnegative.

1. $\sqrt{36} =$

2. $-\sqrt{49} =$

3. $\sqrt{121} =$

4. $\sqrt{50} =$

5. $\sqrt{72x^4} =$

6. $\sqrt{y^6} =$

7. $\sqrt{x^6 y^{10}} =$

8. $\sqrt{36a^2 b^8} =$

9. $\sqrt{a^9} =$

10. $\sqrt{49a^5 b^4} =$

Answers: Simplifying Square Root Problems

1. 6

2. -7

3. 11

4. $\sqrt{50} = \sqrt{25 \cdot 2} = \sqrt{25} \cdot \sqrt{2} = 5\sqrt{2}$

5. $\sqrt{72x^4} = x^2\sqrt{36 \cdot 2} = x^2\sqrt{36} \cdot \sqrt{2} = 6x^2\sqrt{2}$

6. y^3

7. $\sqrt{x^6y^{10}} = \sqrt{x^6}\sqrt{y^{10}} = x^3y^5$

8. $\sqrt{36a^2b^8} = \sqrt{36}\sqrt{a^2}\sqrt{b^8} = 6ab^4$

9. $\sqrt{a^9} = \sqrt{a^8(a)} = a^4\sqrt{a}$

10. $\sqrt{49a^5b^4} = \sqrt{49}\sqrt{a^5}\sqrt{b^4} = \sqrt{49}\sqrt{a^4(a)}\sqrt{b^4} = 7a^2\sqrt{a}\,(b^2) = 7a^2b^2\sqrt{a}$

Operations with Square Roots

● You may perform *operations under a single radical sign.*

Examples:

1. $\sqrt{(5)(20)} = \sqrt{100} = 10$

2. $\sqrt{30 + 6} = \sqrt{36} = 6$

3. $\sqrt{\dfrac{32}{2}} = \sqrt{16} = 4 \left(\text{Note: } \sqrt{\dfrac{32}{2}} = \dfrac{\sqrt{32}}{\sqrt{2}}\right)$

4. $\sqrt{30 - 5} = \sqrt{25} = 5$

5. $\sqrt{2 + 5} = \sqrt{7}$

● You can *add or subtract square roots themselves only if the values under the radical sign are equal.* Then simply add or subtract the coefficients (numbers in front of the radical sign) and keep the original number in the radical sign.

Examples:

1. $2\sqrt{3} + 3\sqrt{3} = (2 + 3)\sqrt{3} = 5\sqrt{3}$

2. $4\sqrt{6} - 2\sqrt{6} = (4 - 2)\sqrt{6} = 2\sqrt{6}$

3. $5\sqrt{2} + \sqrt{2} = 5\sqrt{2} + 1\sqrt{2} = (5 + 1)\sqrt{2} = 6\sqrt{2}$

Note that 1 is understood in $\sqrt{2}$. $(1\sqrt{2})$

● You *may not add or subtract different square roots.*

Examples:

1. $\sqrt{28} - \sqrt{3} \neq \sqrt{25}$
2. $\sqrt{16} + \sqrt{9} \neq \sqrt{25}$

Practice: Operations under the Radical and Adding and Subtracting Square Roots Problems

All variables are nonnegative.

1. $\sqrt{(18)(2)} =$

2. $\sqrt{\dfrac{200}{8}} =$

3. $\sqrt{17 + 32} =$

4. $\sqrt{31 - 16} =$

5. $4\sqrt{3} + 2\sqrt{3} =$

6. $12\sqrt{7} - 6\sqrt{7} =$

7. $8\sqrt{11} - \sqrt{11} =$

8. $3\sqrt{5} - 7\sqrt{5} =$

9. $\sqrt{(20x^2)(5x^4)} =$

10. $\sqrt{8x^2 + 28x^2} =$

Answers: Operations under the Radical and Adding and Subtracting Square Roots Problems

1. $\sqrt{(18)(2)} = \sqrt{36} = 6$

2. $\sqrt{\dfrac{200}{8}} = \sqrt{25} = 5$

3. $\sqrt{17 + 32} = \sqrt{49} = 7$

4. $\sqrt{31 - 16} = \sqrt{15}$

5. $6\sqrt{3}$

6. $6\sqrt{7}$

7. $7\sqrt{11}$ derived from $8\sqrt{11} - 1\sqrt{11}$

8. $-4\sqrt{5}$ derived from $3\sqrt{5} - 7\sqrt{5} = (3 - 7)\sqrt{5} = -4\sqrt{5}$

9. $\sqrt{(20x^2)(5x^4)} = \sqrt{100x^6} = 10x^3$

10. $\sqrt{8x^2 + 28x^2} = \sqrt{36x^2} = 6x$

Addition and Subtraction of Square Roots after Simplifying

● Sometimes after *simplifying the square root(s), addition or subtraction becomes possible.* Always simplify if possible.

Examples:

1. $\sqrt{50} + 3\sqrt{2} =$

These cannot be added until $\sqrt{50}$ is simplified.

$$\sqrt{50} = \sqrt{25 \cdot 2} = \sqrt{25} \cdot \sqrt{2} = 5\sqrt{2}$$

Now, since both are alike under the radical sign

$$5\sqrt{2} + 3\sqrt{2} = (5 + 3)\sqrt{2} = 8\sqrt{2}$$

2. $\sqrt{300} + \sqrt{12} =$

Try to simplify each one.

$$\sqrt{300} = \sqrt{100 \cdot 3} = \sqrt{100} \cdot \sqrt{3} = 10\sqrt{3}$$
$$\sqrt{12} = \sqrt{4 \cdot 3} = \sqrt{4} \cdot \sqrt{3} = 2\sqrt{3}$$

Now, since both are alike under the radical sign

$$10\sqrt{3} + 2\sqrt{3} = (10 + 2)\sqrt{3} = 12\sqrt{3}$$

3. If $y > 0$, then $\sqrt{9y} + \sqrt{y^5} =$

Simplify each one.

$$\sqrt{9y} = 3\sqrt{y}$$
$$\sqrt{y^5} = \sqrt{y^4 \cdot y} = y^2\sqrt{y}$$

Now, since both are alike under the radical sign,

$$3\sqrt{y} + y^2\sqrt{y} = (3 + y^2)\sqrt{y} \text{ or } \sqrt{y}(3 + y^2)$$

Practice: Addition and Subtraction of Square Roots after Simplifying Problems

1. $4\sqrt{5} - \sqrt{20} =$ 4. $\sqrt{40} + \sqrt{27} =$

2. $\sqrt{18} + \sqrt{32} =$ 5. If $x > 0$, then $\sqrt{x^3} + \sqrt{25x} =$

3. $9\sqrt{7} - \sqrt{28} =$

Answers: Addition and Subtraction of Square Roots after Simplifying Problems

1. $4\sqrt{5} - \sqrt{20} =$

   $(\sqrt{20} = \sqrt{4 \cdot 5} = \sqrt{4} \cdot \sqrt{5} = \underline{2\sqrt{5}})$

   $4\sqrt{5} - 2\sqrt{5} = 2\sqrt{5}$

2. $\sqrt{18} + \sqrt{32} =$

   $(\sqrt{18} = \sqrt{9 \cdot 2} = \sqrt{9} \cdot \sqrt{2} = \underline{3\sqrt{2}})$

   $(\sqrt{32} = \sqrt{16 \cdot 2} = \sqrt{16} \cdot \sqrt{2} = \underline{4\sqrt{2}})$

   $3\sqrt{2} + 4\sqrt{2} = 7\sqrt{2}$

3. $9\sqrt{7} - \sqrt{28} =$

   $(\sqrt{28} = \sqrt{4 \cdot 7} = \sqrt{4} \cdot \sqrt{7} = \underline{2\sqrt{7}})$

   $9\sqrt{7} - 2\sqrt{7} = 7\sqrt{7}$

4. $\sqrt{40} + \sqrt{27} =$

   $(\sqrt{40} = \sqrt{4 \cdot 10} = \sqrt{4} \cdot \sqrt{10} = \underline{2\sqrt{10}})$

   $(\sqrt{27} = \sqrt{9 \cdot 3} = \sqrt{9} \cdot \sqrt{3} = \underline{3\sqrt{3}})$

   $2\sqrt{10} + 3\sqrt{3}$ cannot be added

5. $\sqrt{x^3} + \sqrt{25x} =$

   $(\sqrt{x^3} = \sqrt{x^2 \cdot x} = \underline{x\sqrt{x}})$

   $(\sqrt{25x} = \underline{5\sqrt{x}})$

   $x\sqrt{x} + 5\sqrt{x} = (x + 5)\sqrt{x}$ or $\sqrt{x}(x + 5)$

Products of Nonnegative Roots

Remember that in multiplication of roots, the multiplication sign may be omitted. Always simplify the answer when possible.

Examples:

1. $\sqrt{2} \cdot \sqrt{8} = \sqrt{16} = 4$

2. If each variable is nonnegative,

$$\sqrt{x^3} \cdot \sqrt{x^5} = \sqrt{x^8} = x^4$$

3. If each variable is nonnegative.

$$\sqrt{ab} \cdot \sqrt{ab^3c} = \sqrt{a^2b^4c} = \sqrt{a^2} \sqrt{b^4} \sqrt{c} = ab^2 \sqrt{c}$$

4. If each variable is nonnegative,

$$\sqrt{3x} \cdot \sqrt{6xy^2} \cdot \sqrt{2xy} = \sqrt{36x^3y^3} = \sqrt{36} \sqrt{x^3} \sqrt{y^3} =$$
$$\sqrt{36} \sqrt{x^2(x)} \sqrt{y^2(y)} = 6xy \sqrt{xy}$$

5. $2\sqrt{5} \cdot 7\sqrt{3} = (2 \cdot 7) \sqrt{5 \cdot 3} = 14\sqrt{15}$

6. If each variable is nonnegative,

$$(\sqrt{x} + 1)^2 = (\sqrt{x} + 1)(\sqrt{x} + 1)$$

$$
\begin{array}{r}
\sqrt{x} + 1 \\
\times\ \sqrt{x} + 1 \\
\hline
\sqrt{x} + 1 \\
x + \sqrt{x} \\
\hline
x + 2\sqrt{x} + 1
\end{array}
$$

7. If each variable is nonnegative,

$$\sqrt{2x}(\sqrt{2} + \sqrt{x}) = (\sqrt{2x} \cdot \sqrt{2}) + (\sqrt{2x} \cdot \sqrt{x}) =$$
$$(\sqrt{2x \cdot 2}) + (\sqrt{2x \cdot x}) = (\sqrt{4x}) + (\sqrt{2x^2}) =$$
$$2\sqrt{x} + x\sqrt{2}$$

Practice: Products of Nonnegative Roots Problems

In the following, all variables are nonnegative.

1. $\sqrt{12} \cdot \sqrt{3} =$ 2. $\sqrt{6} \cdot \sqrt{8} =$

3. $\sqrt{y^5} \cdot \sqrt{y^7} =$ 7. $3\sqrt{2} \cdot 2\sqrt{5} =$

4. $\sqrt{x^2 y} \cdot \sqrt{xy^2} =$ 8. $4\sqrt{2} \cdot 5\sqrt{8} =$

5. $\sqrt{abc} \cdot \sqrt{bc} \cdot \sqrt{ac^2} =$ 9. $(3 - \sqrt{x})^2 =$

6. $\sqrt{5a^2} \cdot \sqrt{2ab} \cdot \sqrt{10b^2} =$ 10. $\sqrt{5x}(\sqrt{x} + \sqrt{5}) =$

Answers: Products of Nonnegative Roots Problems

1. $\sqrt{12} \cdot \sqrt{3} = \sqrt{36} = 6$

2. $\sqrt{6} \cdot \sqrt{8} = \sqrt{48} = \sqrt{16 \cdot 3} = \sqrt{16} \cdot \sqrt{3} = 4\sqrt{3}$

3. $\sqrt{y^5} \cdot \sqrt{y^7} = \sqrt{y^{12}} = y^6$

4. $\sqrt{x^2 y} \cdot \sqrt{xy^2} = \sqrt{x^3 y^3} = \sqrt{x^2(x)y^2(y)} = xy\sqrt{xy}$

   or

   $\sqrt{x^2 y} \cdot \sqrt{xy^2} = x\sqrt{y} \cdot y\sqrt{x} = xy\sqrt{xy}$

5. $\sqrt{abc} \cdot \sqrt{bc} \cdot \sqrt{ac^2} = \sqrt{a^2 b^2 c^4} = abc^2$

6. $\sqrt{5a^2} \cdot \sqrt{2ab} \cdot \sqrt{10b^2} = \sqrt{100a^3 b^3} = \sqrt{100}\sqrt{a^3}\sqrt{b^3} =$
   $\sqrt{100}\sqrt{a^2(a)}\sqrt{b^2(b)} = 10ab\sqrt{ab}$

7. $3\sqrt{2} \cdot 2\sqrt{5} = (3 \cdot 2)\sqrt{2 \cdot 5} = 6\sqrt{10}$

8. $4\sqrt{2} \cdot 5\sqrt{8} = (4 \cdot 5)\sqrt{2 \cdot 8} = 20\sqrt{16} = 20(4) = 80$

9. $(3 - \sqrt{x})^2 = (3 - \sqrt{x})(3 - \sqrt{x}) =$

$$
\begin{array}{r}
3 - \sqrt{x} \\
\times\, 3 - \sqrt{x} \\
\hline
-3\sqrt{x} + x \\
9 - 3\sqrt{x} \\
\hline
9 - 6\sqrt{x} + x
\end{array}
$$

10. $\sqrt{5x}(\sqrt{x} + \sqrt{5}) = (\sqrt{5x} \cdot \sqrt{x}) + (\sqrt{5x} \cdot \sqrt{5}) =$
    $(\sqrt{5x \cdot x}) + (\sqrt{5x \cdot 5}) = (\sqrt{5x^2}) + (\sqrt{25x}) =$
    $x\sqrt{5} + 5\sqrt{x}$

Quotients of Nonnegative Roots

● For all positive real numbers, $\dfrac{\sqrt{x}}{\sqrt{y}} = \sqrt{\dfrac{x}{y}}$

Leave all fractions with rational denominators.

Examples:

1. $\dfrac{\sqrt{10}}{\sqrt{2}} = \sqrt{\dfrac{10}{2}} = \sqrt{5}$

2. $\dfrac{\sqrt{24}}{\sqrt{3}} = \sqrt{\dfrac{24}{3}} = \sqrt{8} = 2\sqrt{2}$

3. $\dfrac{\sqrt{28x^6}}{\sqrt{7x^2}} = \sqrt{\dfrac{28x^6}{7x^2}} = \sqrt{4x^4} = 2x^2$

4. $\dfrac{\sqrt{15}}{\sqrt{6}} = \sqrt{\dfrac{15}{6}} = \sqrt{\dfrac{5}{2}} \text{ or } \dfrac{\sqrt{5}}{\sqrt{2}}$

Note: The denominator of this fraction is irrational. In order to rationalize the denominator of this fraction, multiply it by 1 in the form of

$$\dfrac{\sqrt{2}}{\sqrt{2}}$$

$$\dfrac{\sqrt{5}}{\sqrt{2}} \cdot 1 = \dfrac{\sqrt{5}}{\sqrt{2}} \cdot \dfrac{\sqrt{2}}{\sqrt{2}} = \dfrac{\sqrt{10}}{2}$$

5. $\dfrac{5\sqrt{7}}{\sqrt{12}}$

First simplify $\sqrt{12}$:

$$\dfrac{5\sqrt{7}}{\sqrt{12}} = \dfrac{5\sqrt{7}}{2\sqrt{3}} \cdot 1 = \dfrac{5\sqrt{7}}{2\sqrt{3}} \cdot \dfrac{\sqrt{3}}{\sqrt{3}} = \dfrac{5\sqrt{21}}{2 \cdot 3} = \dfrac{5\sqrt{21}}{6}$$

6. $\dfrac{9\sqrt{2x}}{\sqrt{24x^3}} = 9\sqrt{\dfrac{2x}{24x^3}} = \dfrac{9}{\sqrt{12x^2}} = \dfrac{9}{2x\sqrt{3}} \cdot 1 = \dfrac{9}{2x\sqrt{3}} \cdot \dfrac{\sqrt{3}}{\sqrt{3}} =$

$\dfrac{9\sqrt{3}}{2x \cdot 3} = \dfrac{9\sqrt{3}}{6x} = \dfrac{3\sqrt{3}}{2x}$

7. $\dfrac{3}{2 + \sqrt{3}} \cdot 1 = \dfrac{3}{(2 + \sqrt{3})} \cdot \dfrac{(2 - \sqrt{3})}{(2 - \sqrt{3})} = \dfrac{3(2 - \sqrt{3})}{4 - 3} = \dfrac{6 - 3\sqrt{3}}{1} =$

$6 - 3\sqrt{3}$

Note: In order not to leave an irrational term in the denominator, it is necessary to multiply both the numerator and denominator by the conjugate of the denominator. The conjugate of a binomial contains the same terms but the opposite sign. Thus, $(x + y)$ and $(x - y)$ are conjugates.

8. $\dfrac{1 + \sqrt{5}}{2 - \sqrt{5}} \cdot 1 = \dfrac{(1 + \sqrt{5})}{(2 - \sqrt{5})} \cdot \dfrac{(2 + \sqrt{5})}{(2 + \sqrt{5})} = \dfrac{2 + 3\sqrt{5} + 5}{4 - 5} =$

$\dfrac{7 + 3\sqrt{5}}{-1} = -7 - 3\sqrt{5}$

Practice: Quotients of Nonnegative Roots Problems

1. $\dfrac{\sqrt{15}}{\sqrt{3}}$

2. $\dfrac{\sqrt{48}}{\sqrt{6}}$

3. $\dfrac{\sqrt{45a^7}}{\sqrt{5a}}$

4. $\dfrac{8}{\sqrt{8}}$

5. $\dfrac{3\sqrt{3}}{\sqrt{18}}$

6. $\dfrac{\sqrt{27x^2}}{\sqrt{32x^5}}$

7. $\dfrac{5}{\sqrt{3} + 1}$

8. $\dfrac{\sqrt{2} - 3}{\sqrt{2} + 5}$

Answers: Quotients of Nonnegative Roots Problems

1. $\dfrac{\sqrt{15}}{\sqrt{3}} = \sqrt{\dfrac{15}{3}} = \sqrt{5}$

2. $\dfrac{\sqrt{48}}{\sqrt{6}} = \sqrt{\dfrac{48}{6}} = \sqrt{8} = 2\sqrt{2}$

3. $\dfrac{\sqrt{45a^7}}{\sqrt{5a}} = \sqrt{\dfrac{45a^7}{5a}} = \sqrt{9a^6} = 3a^3$

4. $\dfrac{8}{\sqrt{8}} = \dfrac{8}{\sqrt{4}\sqrt{2}} = \dfrac{8}{2\sqrt{2}} \cdot 1 = \dfrac{8}{2\sqrt{2}} \cdot \dfrac{\sqrt{2}}{\sqrt{2}} = \dfrac{8\sqrt{2}}{2 \cdot 2} = \dfrac{8\sqrt{2}}{4} = 2\sqrt{2}$

5. $\dfrac{3\sqrt{3}}{\sqrt{18}} = \dfrac{3\sqrt{3}}{\sqrt{9}\sqrt{2}} = \dfrac{3\sqrt{3}}{3\sqrt{2}} = \dfrac{\sqrt{3}}{\sqrt{2}} \cdot 1 = \dfrac{\sqrt{3}}{\sqrt{2}} \cdot \dfrac{\sqrt{2}}{\sqrt{2}} = \dfrac{\sqrt{6}}{2}$

6. $\dfrac{\sqrt{27x^2}}{\sqrt{32x^5}} = \dfrac{\sqrt{9x^2}\sqrt{3}}{\sqrt{16x^4}\sqrt{2x}} = \dfrac{3x\sqrt{3}}{4x^2\sqrt{2x}} = \dfrac{3\sqrt{3}}{4x\sqrt{2x}} \cdot 1 =$

$\dfrac{3\sqrt{3}}{4x\sqrt{2x}} \cdot \dfrac{\sqrt{2x}}{\sqrt{2x}} = \dfrac{3\sqrt{6x}}{4x \cdot 2x} = \dfrac{3\sqrt{6x}}{8x^2}$

7. $\dfrac{5}{\sqrt{3}+1} \cdot 1 = \dfrac{5}{(\sqrt{3}+1)} \cdot \dfrac{(\sqrt{3}-1)}{(\sqrt{3}-1)} = \dfrac{5(\sqrt{3}-1)}{3-1} = \dfrac{5\sqrt{3}-5}{2}$

8. $\dfrac{\sqrt{2}-3}{\sqrt{2}+5} \cdot 1 = \dfrac{(\sqrt{2}-3)}{(\sqrt{2}+5)} \cdot \dfrac{(\sqrt{2}-5)}{(\sqrt{2}-5)} = \dfrac{2-8\sqrt{2}+15}{2-25} =$

$\dfrac{17-8\sqrt{2}}{-23} = \dfrac{8\sqrt{2}-17}{23}$

Solving Simple Radical Equations

● To solve a simple radical equation, you must get the radical by itself on one side. Then square both sides to remove the radical sign and solve as usual.

Examples:

1. If $\sqrt{x} + 3 = 7$, then x =

   First subtract 3 from each side.

   $$\sqrt{x} + 3 = 7$$
   $$\underline{\quad - 3 \;\; -3}$$
   $$\sqrt{x} \quad\;\; = 4$$

   Now square both sides

   $$(\sqrt{x})^2 = (4)^2$$
   $$x = 16$$

2. If $5\sqrt{x} - 3 = 7$, then x =

   First add 3 to each side.

   $$5\sqrt{x} - 3 = 7$$
   $$\underline{\quad + 3 \;\; +3}$$
   $$5\sqrt{x} \quad\;\; = 10$$

   Now divide each side by 5.

   $$\frac{5\sqrt{x}}{5} = \frac{10}{5}$$

   $$\sqrt{x} = 2$$

   Finally square each side.

   $$(\sqrt{x})^2 = (2)^2$$
   $$x = 4$$

Practice: Solving Simple Radical Equations Problems

1. If $\sqrt{y} + 4 = 6$, then y =

2. If $\sqrt{x} - 3 = 2$, then x =

3. If $2\sqrt{x} - 4 = 8$, then x =

4. If $3\sqrt{y} + 6 = 15$, then y =

Answers: Solving Simple Radical Equations Problems

1. $\sqrt{y} + 4 = 6$

$$\begin{array}{r} \sqrt{y} + 4 \quad 6 \\ -4 \quad -4 \\ \hline \sqrt{y} \quad\quad 2 \end{array}$$

$(\sqrt{y})^2 = (2)^2$
$y = 4$

2. $\sqrt{x} - 3 = 2$

$$\begin{array}{r} \sqrt{x} - 3 = 2 \\ +3 \quad +3 \\ \hline \sqrt{x} \quad\quad = 5 \end{array}$$

$(\sqrt{x})^2 = (5)^2$
$x = 25$

3. $2\sqrt{x} - 4 = 8$

$$\begin{array}{r} 2\sqrt{x} - 4 = 8 \\ +4 \quad +4 \\ \hline 2\sqrt{x} \quad\quad = 12 \end{array}$$

$$\frac{2\sqrt{x}}{2} \quad \frac{12}{2}$$

$\sqrt{x} = 6$
$(\sqrt{x})^2 = (6)^2$
$x = 36$

4. $3\sqrt{y} + 6 = 15$

$$\begin{array}{r} 3\sqrt{y} + 6 = 15 \\ -6 \quad -6 \\ \hline 3\sqrt{y} \quad\quad = 9 \end{array}$$

$$\frac{3\sqrt{y}}{3} \quad \frac{9}{3}$$

$\sqrt{y} = 3$
$(\sqrt{y})^2 = (3)^2$
$y = 9$

Changing Expressions Between Radical Form and Exponential Form

● There is another way of representing irrational expressions besides the use of the radical sign ($\sqrt{}$). This method involves the use of fractional exponents. A fractional exponent is simply an exponent written as a fraction (for example, $2^{\frac{1}{3}}$) where the numerator of the fraction is the power and the denominator is the root.

$$\text{So } \sqrt{2} = 2^{\frac{1}{2}}$$

$$\sqrt{x^3} = x^{\frac{3}{2}}$$

In general, $\sqrt[b]{x^a} = x^{\frac{a}{b}}$ where $\dfrac{a \text{ is the power}}{b \text{ is the root}}$

Examples:

1. $\sqrt[3]{x} = x^{\frac{1}{3}}$

2. $\sqrt{5} = 5^{\frac{1}{2}}$

3. $\sqrt[5]{x^2} = x^{\frac{2}{5}}$

4. $4\sqrt[7]{4y^3} = 4y^{\frac{3}{7}}$

5. $a^{\frac{2}{3}} = \sqrt{a^3}$

6. $3^{\frac{1}{2}} = \sqrt{3}$

7. $y^{\frac{3}{5}} = \sqrt[5]{y^3}$

8. $(3x)^{\frac{1}{2}} = \sqrt{3x}$

These fractional exponents can be used in the same way as integral exponents.

$$2^5 \cdot 2^6 = 2^{11}$$

$$3^{\frac{1}{2}} \cdot 3^{\frac{1}{2}} = 3^1 \qquad \text{etc.}$$

Practice: Changing Expressions Between Radical Form and Exponential Form Problems

1. $\sqrt[4]{a^3} =$

2. $\sqrt{x^5} =$

3. $\sqrt[3]{7} =$

4. $3\sqrt[5]{x^4} =$

5. $5^{\frac{2}{3}} =$

6. $x^{\frac{4}{9}} =$

7. $2x^{\frac{1}{2}} =$

8. $(2x)^{\frac{1}{3}} =$

Answers: Changing Expressions Between Radical Form and Exponential Form Problems

1. $\sqrt[4]{a^3} = a^{\frac{3}{4}}$

2. $\sqrt{x^5} = x^{\frac{5}{2}}$

3. $\sqrt[3]{7} = 7^{\frac{1}{3}}$

4. $3\sqrt[5]{x^4} = 3x^{\frac{4}{5}}$

5. $5^{\frac{2}{3}} = \sqrt[3]{5^2}$

6. $x^{\frac{4}{9}} = \sqrt[9]{x^4}$

7. $2x^{\frac{1}{2}} = 2\sqrt{x}$

8. $(2x)^{\frac{1}{3}} = \sqrt[3]{2x}$

Evaluating Numerical Expressions with Fractional Exponents

● Change the expression from exponential form to radical form and simplify.

Examples:

1. $25^{\frac{1}{2}} = \sqrt{25} = 5$

2. $8^{\frac{1}{3}} = \sqrt[3]{8} = 2$

3. $5 \cdot 16^{\frac{1}{4}} = 5 \sqrt[4]{16} = 5 \cdot 2 = 10$

4. $27^{\frac{2}{3}} = \sqrt[3]{27^2} = (\sqrt[3]{27})^2 = (3)^2 = 9$

5. $32^{-\frac{1}{5}} = \dfrac{1}{32^{\frac{1}{5}}} = \dfrac{1}{\sqrt[5]{32}} = \dfrac{1}{2}$

6. $16^{\frac{5}{4}} = \sqrt[4]{16^5} = (\sqrt[4]{16})^5 = (2)^5 = 32$

Practice: Evaluating Numerical Expressions with Fractional Exponents Problems

1. $27^{\frac{1}{3}}$

2. $81^{\frac{1}{4}}$

3. $-2 \cdot 25^{\frac{1}{2}}$

4. $8^{\frac{2}{3}}$

5. $9^{-\frac{1}{2}}$

6. $5 \cdot 81^{\frac{3}{4}}$

7. $4^{-\frac{5}{2}}$

8. $9 \cdot 100^{\frac{3}{2}}$

Answers: Evaluating Numerical Expressions with Fractional Exponents Problems

1. $27^{\frac{1}{3}} = \sqrt[3]{27} = 3$

2. $81^{\frac{1}{4}} = \sqrt[4]{81} = 3$

3. $-2 \cdot 25^{\frac{1}{2}} = -2\sqrt{25} = -2 \cdot 5 = -10$

4. $8^{\frac{2}{3}} = \sqrt[3]{8^2} = (\sqrt[3]{8})^2 = (2)^2 = 4$

5. $9^{-\frac{1}{2}} = \dfrac{1}{9^{\frac{1}{2}}} = \dfrac{1}{\sqrt{9}} = \dfrac{1}{3}$

6. $5 \cdot 81^{\frac{3}{4}} = 5 \cdot \sqrt[4]{81^3} = 5(\sqrt[4]{81})^3 = 5(3)^3 = 5 \cdot 27 = 135$

7. $4^{-\frac{5}{2}} = \dfrac{1}{4^{\frac{5}{2}}} = \dfrac{1}{\sqrt{4^5}} = \dfrac{1}{(\sqrt{4})^5} = \dfrac{1}{(2)^5} = \dfrac{1}{32}$

8. $9 \cdot 100^{\frac{3}{2}} = 9\sqrt{100^3} = 9(\sqrt{100})^3 = 9(10)^3 = 9(1000) = 9000$

Evaluating Literal Expressions with Fractional Exponents

● There is really no difference between using fractional exponents and integral exponents. Some operations can be performed with fractional exponents more easily than by using radical forms.

Examples:

1. $(x^{\frac{1}{2}})^4 = x^2$

2. $m^{\frac{1}{3}} \cdot m^{\frac{2}{3}} = m^{\frac{3}{3}} = m$

3. $(a^{\frac{1}{2}}b^{\frac{1}{3}})^6 = a^3b^2$

4. $\dfrac{t^{\frac{2}{3}}}{t^{\frac{1}{3}}} = t^{\frac{1}{3}}$

5. $y^{-\frac{2}{3}} \cdot y = y^{(-\frac{2}{3}+\frac{3}{3})} = y^{\frac{1}{3}}$

Note: The following examples would be difficult to do in their original form. By changing the expressions from radical form to exponential form, the operation is easy. Be sure to change answers back to radical forms.

6. $\sqrt{x} \cdot \sqrt[3]{x}$

$x^{\frac{1}{2}} \cdot x^{\frac{1}{3}}$

$x^{\frac{3}{6}} \cdot x^{\frac{2}{6}}$

$x^{\frac{5}{6}}$ or $\sqrt[6]{x^5}$

7. $\sqrt[3]{y^2} \cdot \sqrt{y^3}$

$y^{\frac{2}{3}} \cdot y^{\frac{3}{2}}$

$y^{\frac{4}{6}} \cdot y^{\frac{9}{6}}$

$y^{\frac{13}{6}} = \sqrt[6]{y^{13}} = y^2\sqrt[6]{y}$

Practice: Evaluating Literal Expressions with Fractional Exponents Problems

1. $(y^{\frac{3}{5}})^{10} =$

2. $a^{\frac{2}{3}} \cdot a^{\frac{2}{3}} \cdot a^{\frac{2}{3}} =$

3. $(x^{\frac{3}{4}}y^{\frac{1}{4}})^8 =$

4. $\left(\dfrac{25a^8}{9b^6}\right)^{\frac{1}{2}} =$

5. $m^{-\frac{1}{2}} \cdot m^{-4} =$

6. $\sqrt{x} \cdot \sqrt[4]{x} =$

7. $\sqrt[5]{y^2} \cdot \sqrt{y} =$

Answers: Evaluating Literal Expressions with Fractional Exponents Problems

1. $(y^{\frac{3}{5}})^{10} = y^{\frac{30}{5}} = y^6$

2. $a^{\frac{2}{3}} \cdot a^{\frac{2}{3}} \cdot a^{\frac{2}{3}} = a^{\frac{6}{3}} = a^2$

3. $(x^{\frac{3}{4}}y^{\frac{1}{4}})^8 = x^{\frac{24}{4}}y^{\frac{8}{4}} = x^6y^2$

4. $\left(\dfrac{25a^8}{9b^6}\right)^{\frac{1}{2}} = \dfrac{25^{\frac{1}{2}}a^{\frac{8}{2}}}{9^{\frac{1}{2}}b^{\frac{6}{2}}} = \dfrac{5a^4}{3b^3}$

5. $m^{-\frac{1}{2}} \cdot m^{-4} = m^{-\frac{4}{2}} = m^2$

6. $\sqrt{x} \cdot \sqrt[4]{x} = x^{\frac{1}{2}} \cdot x^{\frac{1}{4}} = x^{\frac{2}{4}} \cdot x^{\frac{1}{4}} = x^{\frac{3}{4}} = \sqrt[4]{x^3}$

7. $\sqrt[5]{y^2} \cdot \sqrt{y} = y^{\frac{2}{5}} \cdot y^{\frac{1}{2}} = y^{\frac{4}{10}} \cdot y^{\frac{5}{10}} = y^{\frac{9}{10}} = \sqrt[10]{y^9}$

Expanding the Number Concept

● Up to this point, the idea of "number" has been limited to two specific sets of numbers, rational and irrational. The union of these two sets of numbers is a set of numbers called real numbers. Real numbers have been likened to points on a number line.

In reality, "all numbers" would more nearly be likened to the points of a plane than to a single line. The plane might be envisioned as being divided by a set of coordinate axes, one of which is the real number line. There is another set of numbers that might be represented by the other axis in our plane. These numbers are called imaginary numbers, and they all have one thing in common. They all contain the factor $\sqrt{-1}$. Thus $\sqrt{-2}$, $\sqrt{-5}$, $\sqrt{-4}$, and $-\sqrt{-3}$ are all imaginary numbers. The $\sqrt{-1}$ factor is usually represented by the lower case i in mathematical writing. The examples above would become $i\sqrt{2}$, $i\sqrt{5}$, $2i$, and $-i\sqrt{3}$.

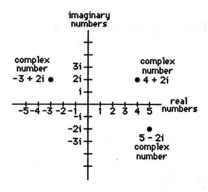

The points not on either of these axes are called complex numbers. Complex numbers are a combination of one real term and one imaginary term. Complex numbers are written as a + bi where a is the rational component and bi is the imaginary component. The set of complex numbers contains all numbers having both a real element and an imaginary element. Along the real number line, all of the numbers would be in the form of a + 0i and hence have only the real component. Along the imaginary number line, all of the numbers would be in the form of 0 + bi, and they are usually referred to as pure imaginary numbers. All complex numbers in the form of a + bi where b $\neq$ 0 are considered as being imaginary.

Simplifying Imaginary Numbers

- Remember, $\sqrt{-1} = i$

Examples:

1. $\sqrt{-25} = \sqrt{25} \cdot \sqrt{-1} = 5i$
2. $\sqrt{-12} = \sqrt{4} \cdot \sqrt{3} \cdot \sqrt{-1} = 2i\sqrt{3}$
3. $-\sqrt{-36} = -\sqrt{36} \cdot \sqrt{-1} = -6i$
4. $2\sqrt{-20} = 2\sqrt{4} \cdot \sqrt{5} \cdot \sqrt{-1} = 2 \cdot 2i\sqrt{5} = 4i\sqrt{5}$
5. $(3 + 2i) + (6 - i) = 9 + i$
6. $(-1 - 4i) - (3 + 7i) = -4 - 11i$

Practice: Simplifying Imaginary Numbers Problems

1. $\sqrt{-9} =$
2. $\sqrt{-8} =$
3. $-\sqrt{-18} =$
4. $3\sqrt{-24} =$
5. $(-1 + 2i) + (5 - 4i) =$
6. $(7 - 3i) - (2 - i) =$

Answers: Simplifying Imaginary Numbers Problems

1. $\sqrt{-9} = \sqrt{9} \cdot \sqrt{-1} = 3i$
2. $\sqrt{-8} = \sqrt{4} \cdot \sqrt{2} \cdot \sqrt{-1}$
   $= 2i\sqrt{2}$
3. $-\sqrt{-18} = -\sqrt{9} \cdot \sqrt{2} \cdot \sqrt{-1}$
   $= -3i\sqrt{2}$

4. $3\sqrt{-24} = 3\sqrt{4} \cdot \sqrt{6} \cdot \sqrt{-1}$
   $= 3 \cdot 2i\sqrt{6} = 6i\sqrt{6}$
5. $(-1 + 2i) + (5 - 4i)$
   $= 4 - 2i$
6. $(7 - 3i) - (2 - i) = 5 - 2i$

Raising i to a Power

- There is a pattern to i^{nth} as n increases in value.

$$i = \sqrt{-1}$$
$$i^2 = \sqrt{-1} \cdot \sqrt{-1} = -1$$
$$i^3 = \sqrt{-1} \cdot \sqrt{-1} \cdot \sqrt{-1} = -\sqrt{-1}$$
$$i^4 = \sqrt{-1} \cdot \sqrt{-1} \cdot \sqrt{-1} \cdot \sqrt{-1} = (-1)(-1) = 1$$

From here on, the pattern just repeats itself as n increases.

$i^5 = i^4 \cdot i = 1 \cdot \sqrt{-1} = \sqrt{-1}$

$i^6 = i^4 \cdot i^2 = 1(-1) = -1$ etc.

A good way to find the value of i^{nth} is to factor it into

$i^2 \cdot i^2 \cdot i^2 \ldots (i)$

$(-1)(-1)(-1) \ldots$

Examples:

1. $i^9 =$
   $i^9 = i^2 \cdot i^2 \cdot i^2 \cdot i^2 \cdot i$
   $(-1)(-1)(-1)(-1) \sqrt{-1}$
   $(1)(1) \sqrt{-1}$
   $\sqrt{-1}$

2. $i^6 =$
   $i^6 = i^2 \cdot i^2 \cdot i^2$
   $(-1)(-1)(-1)$
   $(1)(-1)$
   -1

Practice: Raising i to a Power Problems

1. i^7 2. i^8 3. i^{10} 4. i^{11}

Answers: Raising i to a Power Problems

1. $i^7 =$
   $i^7 = i^2 \cdot i^2 \cdot i^2 \cdot i$
   $(-1)(-1)(-1) \sqrt{-1}$
   $(1)(-1) \sqrt{-1}$
   $- \sqrt{-1}$

3. $i^{10} =$
   $i^{10} = i^2 \cdot i^2 \cdot i^2 \cdot i^2 \cdot i^2$
   $(-1)(-1)(-1)(-1)(-1)$
   $(1)(1)(-1)$
   -1

2. $i^8 =$
   $i^8 = i^2 \cdot i^2 \cdot i^2 \cdot i^2$
   $(-1)(-1)(-1)(-1)$
   $(1)(1)$
   1

4. $i^{11} =$
   $i^{11} = i^2 \cdot i^2 \cdot i^2 \cdot i^2 \cdot i^2 \cdot i$
   $(-1)(-1)(-1)(-1)(-1)$
   $\cdot \sqrt{-1}$
   $(1)(1)(-1) \sqrt{-1}$
   $- \sqrt{-1}$

Multiplying Imaginary Numbers

● Before multiplying imaginary numbers, it is necessary to make sure that they are written in "i" form. Multiplication is then typical.

Examples:

1. $\sqrt{-2} \cdot \sqrt{-3} =$
   $i\sqrt{2} \cdot i\sqrt{3}$
   $i^2\sqrt{6}$
   $-\sqrt{6}$

2. $3\sqrt{-2} \cdot \sqrt{-5} \cdot \sqrt{3} =$
   $3i\sqrt{2} \cdot i\sqrt{5} \cdot \sqrt{3}$
   $3i^2\sqrt{30}$
   $3(-1)\sqrt{30}$
   $-3\sqrt{30}$

3. $6i \cdot 7i =$
   $42i^2$
   $42(-1)$
   -42

4. $(-4i)^3 =$
   $(-4i)(-4i)(-4i)$
   $-64i^3$
   $-64 \cdot i^2 \cdot i$
   $-64(-1) \cdot i$
   $64i$

5. $\sqrt{-3}(\sqrt{-5} + \sqrt{2}) =$
   $i\sqrt{3}(i\sqrt{5} + \sqrt{2})$
   $i^2\sqrt{15} + i\sqrt{6}$
   $(-1)\sqrt{15} + i\sqrt{6}$
   $-\sqrt{15} + i\sqrt{6}$

6. $(3 - 2i)(4 + 5i) =$
   $12 + 7i - 10i^2$
   $12 + 7i - 10(-1)$
   $12 + 7i + 10$
   $22 + 7i$

7. $(1 - 2i)^2 =$
   $(1 - 2i)(1 - 2i)$
   $1 - 4i + 4i^2$
   $1 - 4i + 4(-1)$
   $1 - 4i - 4$
   $-3 - 4i$

Practice: Multiplying Imaginary Numbers Problems

1. $\sqrt{-5} \cdot \sqrt{-6} =$
2. $3\sqrt{-3} \cdot \sqrt{-2} \cdot \sqrt{5} =$
3. $4i \cdot 3i =$
4. $(-2i)^5 =$

5. $\sqrt{-2}(\sqrt{-3} + \sqrt{7}) =$
6. $(2 - 3i)(4 + 5i) =$
7. $(2 - 3i)^2 =$

Answers: Multiplying Imaginary Numbers Problems

1. $\sqrt{-5} \cdot \sqrt{-6} =$
   $i\sqrt{5} \cdot i\sqrt{6}$
   $i^2\sqrt{30}$
   $-1\sqrt{30}$
   $-\sqrt{30}$

2. $3\sqrt{-3} \cdot \sqrt{-2} \cdot \sqrt{5} =$
   $3i\sqrt{3} \cdot i\sqrt{2} \cdot \sqrt{5}$
   $3i^2\sqrt{30}$
   $3(-1)\sqrt{30}$
   $-3\sqrt{30}$

3. $4i \cdot 3i =$
   $12i^2 = 12(-1) = -12$

4. $(-2i)^5 =$
   $(-2)^5(i)^5$
   $-32 \cdot i^2 \cdot i^2 \cdot i$
   $-32 \cdot (-1)(-1) \cdot i$
   $-32i$

5. $\sqrt{-2}(\sqrt{-3} + \sqrt{7}) =$
   $i\sqrt{2}(i\sqrt{3} + \sqrt{7})$
   $i^2\sqrt{6} + i\sqrt{14}$
   $(-1)\sqrt{6} + i\sqrt{14}$
   $-\sqrt{6} + i\sqrt{14}$ or $i\sqrt{14} - \sqrt{6}$

6. $(2 - 3i)(4 + 5i) =$
   $6 - 2i - 15i^2$
   $6 - 2i - 15(-1)$
   $6 - 2i + 15$
   $21 - 2i$

7. $(2 - 3i)^2 =$
   $(2 - 3i)(2 - 3i)$
   $4 - 12i + 9i^2$
   $4 - 12i + 9(-1)$
   $4 - 12i - 9$
   $-5 - 12i$

Rationalizing the Denominator in Fractions with Imaginary Terms

- As you learned when working with irrational expressions, the denominator of any fraction must be left rational. To rationalize the denominator of a fraction, multiply the fraction by 1 in any form necessary to make the denominator rational.

Examples:

1. $\dfrac{7}{2i} =$

   $\dfrac{7}{2i} \cdot 1 = \dfrac{7}{2i} \cdot \dfrac{i}{i} = \dfrac{7i}{2i^2} = \dfrac{7i}{2(-1)} = -\dfrac{7i}{2}$

2. $\dfrac{1}{-9i} =$

$$\dfrac{1}{-9i} \cdot 1 = \dfrac{1}{-9i} \cdot \dfrac{i}{i} = \dfrac{i}{-9i^2} = \dfrac{i}{-9(-1)} = \dfrac{i}{9}$$

3. $\dfrac{3}{1-i} =$

$$\dfrac{3}{1-i} \cdot 1 = \dfrac{3}{(1-i)} \cdot \dfrac{(1+i)}{(1+i)} = \dfrac{3(1+i)}{1-i^2} = \dfrac{3+3i}{1-(-1)} =$$

$$\dfrac{3+3i}{1+1} = \dfrac{3+3i}{2}$$

Note: In order not to leave an imaginary term in the denominator, it was necessary to multiply both the numerator and denominator by the conjugate of the denominator.

4. $\dfrac{5-2i}{2+3i} =$

$$\dfrac{5-2i}{2+3i} \cdot 1 = \dfrac{(5-2i)}{(2+3i)} \cdot \dfrac{(2-3i)}{(2-3i)} = \dfrac{10-19i+6i^2}{4-9i^2} =$$

$$\dfrac{10-19i+6(-1)}{4-9(-1)} = \dfrac{10-19i-6}{4+9} = \dfrac{4-19i}{13}$$

Practice: Rationalizing the Denominator in Fractions with Imaginary Terms Problems

1. $\dfrac{5}{2i} =$

2. $\dfrac{-7}{i} =$

3. $\dfrac{-8}{10i} =$

4. $\dfrac{4}{2-3i} =$

5. $\dfrac{i}{1-i} =$

6. $\dfrac{2+3i}{3-2i} =$

Answers: Rationalizing the Denominator in Fractions with Imaginary Terms Problems

1. $\dfrac{5}{2i} =$

$$\frac{5}{2i} \cdot 1 = \frac{5}{2i} \cdot \frac{i}{i} = \frac{5i}{2i^2} = \frac{5i}{2(-1)} = \frac{5i}{-2} = \frac{5i}{2}$$

2. $\dfrac{-7}{i} =$

$$\frac{-7}{i} \cdot 1 = \frac{-7}{i} \cdot \frac{i}{i} = \frac{-7i}{i^2} = \frac{-7i}{(-1)} = 7i$$

3. $\dfrac{-8}{10i} =$

$$\frac{-8}{10i} = \frac{-4}{5i} \cdot 1 = \frac{-4}{5i} \cdot \frac{i}{i} = \frac{-4i}{5i^2} = \frac{-4i}{5(-1)} = \frac{-4i}{-5} = \frac{4i}{5}$$

4. $\dfrac{4}{2 - 3i} =$

$$\frac{4}{2 - 3i} \cdot 1 = \frac{4}{(2 - 3i)} \cdot \frac{(2 + 3i)}{(2 + 3i)} = \frac{4(2 + 3i)}{4 - 9i^2} = \frac{8 + 12i}{4 - 9(-1)} =$$

$$\frac{8 + 12i}{4 + 9} = \frac{8 + 12i}{13}$$

5. $\dfrac{i}{1 - i} =$

$$\frac{i}{1 - i} \cdot 1 = \frac{i}{(1 - i)} \cdot \frac{(1 + i)}{(1 + i)} = \frac{i(1 + i)}{1 - i^2} = \frac{i + i^2}{1 - i^2} = \frac{i + (-1)}{1 - (-1)} =$$

$$\frac{i - 1}{1 + 1} = \frac{i - 1}{2}$$

6. $\dfrac{2 + 3i}{3 - 2i} =$

$$\dfrac{2 + 3i}{3 - 2i} \cdot 1 = \dfrac{(2 + 3i)}{(3 - 2i)} \cdot \dfrac{(3 + 2i)}{(3 + 2i)} = \dfrac{6 + 13i + 6i^2}{9 - 4i^2} =$$

$$\dfrac{6 + 13i + 6(-1)}{9 - 4(-1)} = \dfrac{6 + 13i - 6}{9 + 4} = \dfrac{13i}{13} = i$$

Different Methods for Solving Quadratic Equations

The Quadratic Formula

● Many quadratic equations cannot be solved by factoring. This is generally true when the roots, or answers, are not rational numbers. A second method of solving quadratic equations involves the use of the formula

$$x = \dfrac{-b \pm \sqrt{b^2 - 4ac}}{2a}$$

where a, b, and c are taken from the quadratic equation written in its general form of $ax^2 + bx + c = 0$, where a is the numeral that goes in front of x^2, b is the numeral that goes in front of x, and c is the numeral with no variable next to it.

Examples:

1. Solve for x: $x^2 - 5x = -6$

Setting all terms equal to 0,

$$x^2 - 5x + 6 = 0$$

Then substitute 1 (which is understood to be in front of the x^2), -5, and 6 for a, b, and c in the quadratic formula and simplify.

$$x = \dfrac{-b \pm \sqrt{b^2 - 4ac}}{2a}$$

$$x = \dfrac{-(-5) \pm \sqrt{(-5)^2 - 4(1)(6)}}{2(1)}$$

$$x = \frac{5 \pm \sqrt{25 - 24}}{2}$$

$$x = \frac{5 \pm \sqrt{1}}{2}$$

$$x = \frac{5 \pm 1}{2}$$

$$x = \frac{5 + 1}{2} \qquad\qquad x = \frac{5 - 1}{2}$$

$$x = \frac{6}{2} \qquad\qquad x = \frac{4}{2}$$

$$x = 3 \qquad\qquad x = 2$$

● The first example produces rational roots. Following, the quadratic formula is used to solve an equation whose roots are not rational.

2. Solve for y: $y^2 = -2y + 2$

Setting all terms equal to 0,

$$y^2 + 2y - 2 = 0$$

Then substitute 1, 2, and -2 for a, b, and c in the quadratic formula and simplify.

$$y = \frac{-b \pm \sqrt{b^2 - 4ac}}{2a}$$

$$y = \frac{-(2) \pm \sqrt{(2)^2 - 4(1)(-2)}}{2(1)}$$

$$y = \frac{-2 \pm \sqrt{4 + 8}}{2}$$

$$y = \frac{-2 \pm \sqrt{12}}{2}$$

$$y = \frac{-2 \pm \sqrt{4}\,\sqrt{3}}{2}$$

$$y = \frac{-2 \pm 2\sqrt{3}}{2}$$

$$y = \frac{\cancel{2}(-1 \pm \sqrt{3})}{\cancel{2}}$$

$$y = -1 + \sqrt{3} \qquad\qquad y = -1 - \sqrt{3}$$

Note that the two roots are irrational.

- The quadratic formula can also be used to solve quadratic equations whose roots are not real but imaginary.

3. Solve for x: x(x + 2) + 2 = 0
   or: $x^2 + 2x + 2 = 0$)

Substituting in the quadratic formula,

$$x = \frac{-b \pm \sqrt{b^2 - 4ac}}{2a}$$

$$x = \frac{-(2) \pm \sqrt{(2)^2 - 4(1)(2)}}{2(1)}$$

$$x = \frac{-2 \pm \sqrt{4 - 8}}{2}$$

$$x = \frac{-2 \pm \sqrt{-4}}{2}$$

$$x = \frac{-2 \pm \sqrt{4}\sqrt{-1}}{2}$$

$$x = \frac{-2 \pm 2i}{2}$$

$$x = \frac{\cancel{2}(-1 \pm i)}{\cancel{2}}$$

$$x = -1 + i \qquad\qquad x = -1 - i$$

Completing the Square

● A third method of solving quadratic equations that works with both real and imaginary roots is called completing the square.

  a. Put the equation in the form of $ax^2 + bx = -c$.

  b. Make sure that $a = 1$ (if $a \neq 1$, multiply through the equation by $1/a$ before proceeding).

  c. Using the value of b from this new equation, add $(b/2)^2$ to both sides of the equation to form a perfect square on the left side of the equation.

  d. Find the square root of both sides of the equation.

  e. Solve the resulting equation.

Examples:

1. Solve for x: $x^2 - 6x + 5 = 0$

Arrange in the form of $ax^2 + bx \quad = -c$

$$x^2 - 6x \quad = -5$$

$a = 1$, so add $(6/2)^2$, or 9, to both sides to complete the square.

$$x^2 - 6x + 9 = -5 + 9$$
$$x^2 - 6x + 9 = 4$$

or $$(x - 3)^2 = 4$$

Take the square root of both sides.

$$x - 3 = \pm 2$$

Solve. $$x = \pm 2 + 3$$

$$x = +2 + 3 \qquad\qquad x = -2 + 3$$
$$x = 5 \qquad\qquad\qquad x = 1$$

2. Solve for y: $y^2 + 2y - 4 = 0$

Arrange in the form of $ay^2 + by = -c$
$$y^2 + 2y = \quad 4$$

$a = 1$, so add $(2/2)^2$, or 1, to both sides to complete the square.

$$y^2 + 2y + 1 = 4 + 1$$
$$y^2 + 2y + 1 = 5$$

or $$(y + 1)^2 = 5$$

Take the square root of both sides.

$$y + 1 = \pm \sqrt{5}$$

Solve. $$y = -1 \pm \sqrt{5}$$

$$y = -1 + \sqrt{5} \qquad\qquad y = -1 - \sqrt{5}$$

3. Solve for x: $2x^2 + 3x + 2 = 0$

Arrange in the form of $ax^2 + bx = -c$.

$$2x^2 + 3x = -2$$

$a \neq$, so multiply through the equation by $1/2$.

$$x^2 + \frac{3}{2}x = -1$$

Add $[(1/2)(3/2)]^2$, or $9/16$, to both sides.

$$x^2 + \frac{3}{2}x + \frac{9}{16} = -1 + \frac{9}{16}$$

$$x^2 + \frac{3}{2}x + \frac{9}{16} = -\frac{7}{16}$$

$$\left(x + \frac{3}{4}\right)^2 = -\frac{7}{16}$$

Take the square root of both sides.

$$x + \frac{3}{4} = \pm\sqrt{\frac{-7}{16}}$$

$$x + \frac{3}{4} = \frac{\pm\sqrt{-7}}{4}$$

$$x = \frac{-3}{4} \pm \frac{\sqrt{-7}}{4}$$

$$x = \frac{-3 \pm i\sqrt{7}}{4}$$

$$x = \frac{-3 + i\sqrt{7}}{4} \qquad\qquad x = \frac{-3 - i\sqrt{7}}{4}$$

Practice: Solving Quadratic Equations Problems
Using the Quadratic Formula and Completing the Square

Solve each problem using both methods.

1. $x^2 - 3x = 4$ 3. $y^2 + 2y + 3 = 0$
2. $x^2 + 4x + 1 = 0$ 4. $9x^2 + 12x - 8 = 0$

Answers: Solving Quadratic Equations Problems
Using the Quadratic Formula and Completing the Square

Quadratic Formula | *Completing the Square*

1.
$$x^2 - 3x = 4$$
$$x^2 - 3x - 4 = 0$$

$$x = \frac{-b \pm \sqrt{b^2 - 4ac}}{2a}$$

$$x =$$

$$\frac{-(-3) \pm \sqrt{(-3)^2 - 4(1)(-4)}}{2(1)}$$

$$x = \frac{3 \pm \sqrt{9 + 16}}{2}$$

$$x = \frac{3 \pm \sqrt{25}}{2}$$

$$x = \frac{3 \pm 5}{2}$$

$$x = \frac{3 + 5}{2} \quad x = \frac{3 - 5}{2}$$

$$x = 4 \qquad x = -1$$

Completing the Square:

$$x^2 - 3x = 4$$

$$x^2 - 3x + \frac{9}{4} = 4 + \frac{9}{4}$$

$$x^2 - 3x + \frac{9}{4} = \frac{25}{4}$$

$$\left(x - \frac{3}{2}\right)^2 = \frac{25}{4}$$

$$x - \frac{3}{2} = \pm\frac{5}{2}$$

$$x = \frac{3}{2} \pm \frac{5}{2}$$

$$x = \frac{3 \pm 5}{2}$$

$$x = \frac{3 + 5}{2} \quad x = \frac{3 - 5}{2}$$

$$x = 4 \qquad x = -1$$

2. $x^2 + 4x + 1 = 0$

$$x = \frac{-b \pm \sqrt{b^2 - 4ac}}{2a}$$

$$x = \frac{-(4) \pm \sqrt{(4)^2 - 4(1)(1)}}{2(1)}$$

$$x = \frac{-4 \pm \sqrt{16 - 4}}{2}$$

$$x = \frac{-4 \pm \sqrt{12}}{2}$$

$$x = \frac{-4 \pm 2\sqrt{3}}{2}$$

$$x = \frac{\cancel{2}(-2 \pm \sqrt{3})}{\cancel{2}}$$

$$x = -2 + \sqrt{3}$$

$$x = -2 - \sqrt{3}$$

$x^2 + 4x + 1 = 0$
$x^2 + 4x + 4 = -1 + 4$
$x^2 + 4x + 4 = 3$
$(x + 2)^2 = 3$
$x + 2 = \pm \sqrt{3}$
$x = -2 \pm \sqrt{3}$
$x - 2 + \sqrt{3} \quad x = -2 - \sqrt{3}$

3. $y^2 + 2y + 3 = 0$

$$y = \frac{-b \pm \sqrt{b^2 - 4ac}}{2a}$$

$$y - \frac{-(2) \pm \sqrt{(2)^2 - 4(1)(3)}}{2(1)}$$

$$y = \frac{-2 \pm \sqrt{4 - 12}}{2}$$

$$y = \frac{-2 \pm \sqrt{-8}}{2}$$

$$y = \frac{-2 \pm 2i\sqrt{2}}{2}$$

$y^2 + 2y + 3 = 0$
$y^2 + 2y + 1 = -3 + 1$
$y^2 + 2y + 1 = -2$
$(y + 1)^2 = -2$
$y + 1 = +\sqrt{-2}$
$y = -1 \pm i\sqrt{2}$
$y = -1 + i\sqrt{2} \quad y = -1 - i\sqrt{2}$

$$y = -1 \pm i\sqrt{2}$$

$$y = -1 + i\sqrt{2}$$

$$y = -1 - i\sqrt{2}$$

4. $9x^2 + 12x - 8 = 0$

$$x = \frac{-b \pm \sqrt{b^2 - 4ac}}{2a}$$

$$x =$$

$$\frac{-(12) \pm \sqrt{(12)^2 - 4(9)(-8)}}{2(9)}$$

$$x = \frac{-12 \pm \sqrt{144 + 288}}{18}$$

$$x = \frac{-12 \pm \sqrt{432}}{18}$$

$$x = \frac{-12 \pm \sqrt{144}\sqrt{3}}{18}$$

$$x = \frac{-12 \pm 12\sqrt{3}}{18}$$

$$x = \frac{-2 \pm 2\sqrt{3}}{3}$$

$$x = \frac{-2 + 2\sqrt{3}}{3}$$

$$x = \frac{-2 - 2\sqrt{3}}{3}$$

$9x^2 + 12x - 8 = 0$

$$\frac{9}{9}x^2 + \frac{12}{9}x = \frac{8}{9}$$

$$x^2 + \frac{4}{3}x + \frac{4}{9} = \frac{8}{9} + \frac{4}{9}$$

$$x^2 + \frac{4}{3}x + \frac{4}{9} = \frac{12}{9}$$

$$\left(x + \frac{2}{3}\right)^2 = \frac{12}{9}$$

$$x + \frac{2}{3} = \pm\sqrt{\frac{12}{9}}$$

$$x + \frac{2}{3} = \pm\frac{2\sqrt{3}}{3}$$

$$x = \frac{-2 \pm 2\sqrt{3}}{3}$$

$$x = \frac{-2 + 2\sqrt{3}}{3}$$

$$x = \frac{-2 - 2\sqrt{3}}{3}$$

Solving Quadratic Inequalities

- a. Change the inequality into a quadratic equation.
  b. Solve the equation.
  c. Draw a number line and use the roots of the equation to separate the number line into three sets of numbers.
  d. Select one of the numbers in each set and substitute it in the original inequality.
  e. If the substitution makes the statement true, then that set of numbers is part of the solution set.
  f. Repeat for all three sets.

Examples:

1. Solve $x^2 - x - 6 < 0$

Change $x^2 - x - 6 < 0$ into $x^2 - x - 6 = 0$

Solve $x^2 - x - 6 = 0$ $\qquad x^2 - x - 6 = 0$

$$(x - 3)(x + 2) = 0$$

$$x - 3 = 0 \qquad x + 2 = 0$$
$$x = 3 \qquad x = -2$$

Draw a number line and use the two roots of the equation (3 and -2) to separate the number line into three sets of numbers.

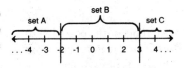

Select a number from set A and substitute it in the inequality.

$$x^2 - x - 6 < 0$$
$$(-3)^2 - (-3) - 6 < 0$$
$$9 + 3 - 6 < 0$$
$$6 < 0$$

Since this is *not* true, the numbers in set A are *not* part of the solution set.

Select a number from set B and substitute it in the inequality.

$$x^2 - x - 6 < 0$$
$$(0)^2 - (0) - 6 < 0$$
$$0 - 0 - 6 < 0$$

This is *true,* so all the numbers in set B are part of the solution set.

Select a number from set C and substitute it in the inequality.

$$x^2 - x - 6 < 0$$
$$(4)^2 - (4) - 6 < 0$$
$$16 - 4 - 6 < 0$$
$$6 < 0$$

This is *not* true, so the only numbers that satisfy the original quadratic inequality are the numbers in set **B**.

The answer is $\{x: -2 < x < 3\}$
or if graphed,

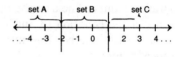

...-4 -3 -2 -1 0 1 2 3 4...

2. Solve $x^2 - x - 2 \geq 0$

Change $x^2 + x - 2 \geq 0$ into $x^2 + x - 2 = 0$

Solve $x^2 + x - 2 = 0$
$$x^2 + x - 2 = 0$$
$$(x - 1)(x + 2) = 0$$
$$x - 1 = 0 \qquad\qquad x + 2 = 0$$
$$x = 1 \qquad\qquad x = -2$$

Draw a number line and use the two roots of the equation to separate the number line into three sets of numbers.

set A   set B   set C
...-4 -3 -2 -1 0 1 2 3 4...

Select a number from set A and substitute it in the inequality.

$$x^2 + x - 2 \geq 0$$
$$(-3)^2 + (-3) - 2 \geq 0$$
$$9 - 3 - 2 \geq 0$$
$$4 \geq 0$$

This is true, so all the numbers in set A are part of the solution set.

Select a number from set B and substitute it in the inequality.

$$x^2 + x - 2 \geq 0$$
$$(0)^2 + (0) - 2 \geq 0$$
$$0 + 0 - 2 \geq 0$$
$$-2 \geq 0$$

This is not true, so the numbers in set B are not part of the solution set.

Select a number from set C and substitute it in the inequality.

$$x^2 + x - 2 \geq 0$$
$$(3)^2 + (3) - 2 \geq 0$$
$$9 + 3 - 2 \geq 0$$
$$10 \geq 0$$

This is true, so all the numbers in set C are part of the solution set.

The answer is $\{x: x \leq -2 \text{ or } x \geq 1\}$
or if graphed,

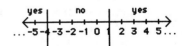

Practice: A Different Method for Solving Quadratic Inequality Problems

Solve each of the following.

1. $x^2 + 3x - 4 > 0$
2. $x^2 - 2x - 3 \leq 0$

3. $x^2 - 3x \geq 0$
4. $x^2 - 3x + 2 < 0$

Answers: A Different Method for Solving Quadratic Inequality Problems

1. $x^2 + 3x - 4 > 0$ Solve: $x^2 + 3x - 4 = 0$
$$(x - 1)(x + 4) = 0$$

$$x - 1 = 0 \qquad x + 4 = 0$$
$$x = 1 \qquad x = -4$$

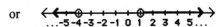

yes | no | yes

$$x^2 + 3x - 4 > 0 \qquad x^2 + 3x - 4 > 0 \qquad x^2 + 3x - 4 > 0$$
$$(5)^2 + 3(-5) - 4 > 0 \quad (0)^2 + 3(0) - 4 > 0 \quad (2)^2 + 3(2) - 4 > 0$$
$$25 - 15 - 4 > 0 \qquad 0 + 0 - 4 > 0 \qquad 4 + 6 - 4 > 0$$
$$6 > 0 \qquad -4 > 0 \qquad 6 > 0$$

$\{x: x < -4 \text{ or } x > 1\}$ or

2. $x^2 - 2x - 3 \leq 0$ Solve: $x^2 - 2x - 3 = 0$

$$(x + 1)(x - 3) = 0$$

$$x + 1 = 0 \qquad x - 3 = 0$$
$$x = -1 \qquad x = 3$$

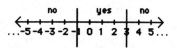

$x^2 - 2x - 3 \leq 0$	$x^2 - 2x - 3 \leq 0$	$x^2 - 2x - 3 \leq 0$
$(-2)^2 - 2(-2) - 3 \leq 0$	$(0)^2 - 2(0) - 3 \leq 0$	$(4)^2 - 2(4) - 3 \leq 0$
$4 + 4 - 3 \leq 0$	$0 - 0 - 3 \leq 0$	$16 - 8 - 3 \leq 0$
$5 \leq 0$	$-3 \leq 0$	$5 \leq 0$

$\{x: -1 \leq x \leq 3\}$ or   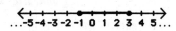

3. $x^2 - 3x \geq 0$ Solve: $x^2 - 3x = 0$

$$x(x - 3) = 0$$

$$x = 0 \qquad x - 3 = 0$$
$$x = 3$$

$x^2 - 3x \geq 0$	$x^2 - 3x \geq 0$	$x^2 - 3x \geq 0$
$(-2)^2 - 3(-2) \geq 0$	$(1)^2 - 3(1) \geq 0$	$(4)^2 - 3(4) \geq 0$
$4 + 6 \geq 0$	$1 - 3 \geq 0$	$16 - 12 \geq 0$
$10 \geq 0$	$-2 \geq 0$	$4 \geq 0$

$\{x: x \leq 0 \text{ or } x \geq 3\}$ or

4. $x^2 - 3x + 2 < 0$ Solve: $x^2 - 3x + 2 = 0$

$$(x - 1)(x - 2) = 0$$

$$x - 1 = 0 \qquad x - 2 = 0$$
$$x = 1 \qquad x = 2$$

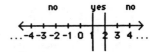

$x^2 - 3x + 2 < 0$	$x^2 - 3x + 2 < 0$	$x^2 - 3x + 2 < 0$
$(0)^2 - 3(0) + 2 < 0$	$(3/2)^2 - 3(3/2) + 2 < 0$	$(3)^2 - 3(3) + 2 < 0$
$0 - 0 + 2 < 0$	$9/4 - 9/2 + 2 < 0$	$9 - 9 + 2 < 0$
	$2\frac{1}{4} - 4\frac{1}{2} + 2 < 0$	$2 < 0$
	$-\frac{1}{2} < 0$	

$\{x: 1 < x < 2\}$ or

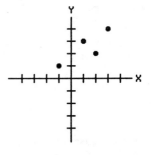

Functions

● Any set of ordered pairs is called a relation. The graph at the right shows a set of ordered pairs.

$A = \{(-1,1)(1,3)(2,2)(3,4)\}$

In the example, the set of all x's is called the domain of the relation. The set of all y's is called the range of the relation. The domain of set A is $\{-1,1,2,3\}$, while the range of set A is $\{1,3,2,4\}$.

Before going on, find the domain and range of this set of graphed points.

The domain is the set $\{-2,-1,1,3\}$.
The range is the set $\{3,-1,2,-1\}$.

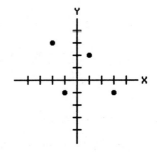

Both of these relations have pairs of coordinates with unique first terms. The x value of each pair of coordinates is different. When this happens, the relation is called a function.

A good example of a functional relation can be seen in the linear equation $y = x + 1$ graphed at the right. The domain and range of this function are both the set of real numbers, and the relation is a function because for any value of x there is a unique value of y.

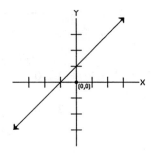

Some other examples of functions are:

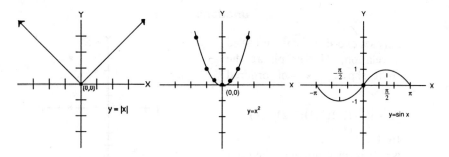

$y = |x|$

$y = x^2$

$y = \sin x$

In each case above, for any value of x there is only one value for y. Contrast this with the graphs below.

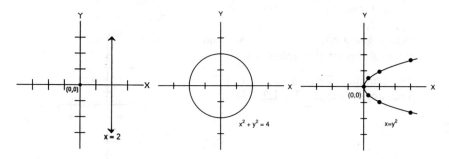

$x = 2$

$x^2 + y^2 = 4$

$x = y^2$

In each of these relations, a single value of x is associated with two or more values of y. These relations are **not** functions.

Determining Domain, Range, and if the Relation Is a Function

Examples:

1. $B = \{(-2,3)(-1,4)(0,5)(1,-3)\}$

    domain: $\{-2,-1,0,1\}$
    range: $\{3,4,5,-3\}$
    function: yes

2.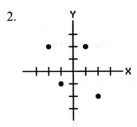

    domain: $\{-2,-1,1,2\}$
    range: $\{-2,-1,2\}$
    function: yes

3.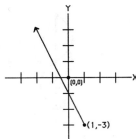

    domain: $\{x: x \le 1\}$
    range: $\{y: y \ge -3\}$
    function: yes

4.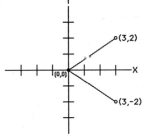

    domain: $\{x: 0 \le x < 3\}$
    range: $\{y: -2 < y < 2\}$
    function: no

5. $y = x^2$

    domain: $\{$all real numbers$\}$
    range: $\{y: y \ge 0\}$
    function: yes

6. $x = y^2$ domain: $\{x: x \geq 0\}$
                                        range: $\{$all real numbers$\}$
                                        function: no

Note: Problems 5 and 6 are examples of inverse relations: relations where the domain and the range have been interchanged. Notice that while the relation in problem 5 is a function, the inverse relation in problem 6 is not.

Practice: Determining Domain, Range, and if the Relation Is a Function Problems

For each of the following, determine the domain, the range, and if the relation is a function.

1. $C = \{(3,3)(-3,4)(0,3)(2,1)\}$ 5.

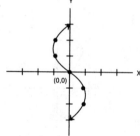

2. The inverse of set C in problem 1

3.
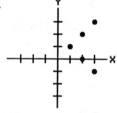

6. $xy = 4$

4.

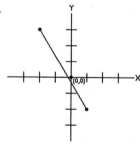

7. $y + \dfrac{x}{y} = 0$

Answers: Determining Domain, Range, and if the Relation Is a Function Problems

1. domain: $\{3,-3,0,2\}$
   range: $\{3,4,-1\}$
   function: yes

2. domain: $\{3,4,-1\}$
   range: $\{3,-3,0,2\}$
   function: no

3. domain: $\{1,2,3\}$
   range: $\{-1,0,1,2,3\}$
   function: no

4. domain: $\{x: -2 \le x \le 1\}$
   range: $\{y: -2 \le y \le 3\}$
   function: yes

5. domain: $\{x: -1 \le x \le 1\}$
   range: $\{$all real numbers$\}$
   function: no

6. domain: $\{$all real numbers$\}$
   range: $\{$all real numbers$\}$
   function: yes

7. $y + \dfrac{x}{y} = 0$

   $y^2 + x = 0$

   $x = -y^2$

   domain: $\{x: x \le 0\}$
   range: $\{$all real numbers$\}$
   function: no

Finding the Values of Functions

● The value of a function is really the value of the range of the relation.

Given the function, $f = \{(1,-3)(2,4)(-1,5)(3,-2)\}$, the value of the function at 1 is -3, at 2 is 4, etc. This is written $f(1) = -3$ and $f(2) = 4$ and is usually read f of 1 = -3 and f of 2 = 4. The lower case letter "f" has been used here to indicate the concept of function, but any lower case letter might have been used.

Examples:

1. Let $h = \{(3,1)(2,2)(1,-2)(-2,3)\}$

   Find $h(3) = \qquad h(2) = \qquad h(1) = \qquad h(-2) =$
   $\quad h(3) = 1 \qquad h(2) = 2 \qquad h(1) = -2 \qquad h(-2) = 3$

2. If $g(x) = 2x + 1$

   Find $g(-1) = \qquad\qquad g(2) = \qquad\qquad g(a) =$
   $\quad g(x) = 2x + 1 \qquad g(x) = 2x + 1 \qquad g(x) = 2x + 1$
   $\quad g(-1) = 2(-1) + 1 \quad g(2) = 2(2) + 1 \quad g(a) = 2(a) + 1$
   $\quad g(-1) = -2 + 1 \qquad g(2) = 4 + 1 \qquad g(a) = 2a + 1$
   $\quad g(-1) = -1 \qquad\quad g(2) = 5$

3. If $f(x) = 3x^2 + x - 1$, find the range of f for the domain $\{1, -2, -1\}$.

$f(x) = 3x^2 + x - 1$ $f(x) = 3x^2 + x - 1$
$f(1) = 3(1)^2 + (1) - 1$ $f(-2) = 3(-2)^2 + (-2) - 1$
$f(1) = 3(1) + 1 - 1$ $f(-2) = 3(4) - 2 - 1$
$f(1) = 3$ $f(-2) = 12 - 3$
                             $f(-2) = 9$

   $f(x) = 3x^2 + x - 1$
$f(-1) = 3(-1)^2 + (-1) - 1$
$f(-1) = 3(1) - 1 - 1$
$f(-1) = 3 - 2$
$f(-1) = 1$

range: $\{3, 9, 1\}$

Practice: Finding the Values of Functions Problems

1. Let $j = \{(-5, 2)(4, 1)(-3, 3)(2, -1)\}$

   Find $j(-5) = $ $j(4) = $ $j(-3) = $ $j(2) = $

2. Let $f(x) = x^2 + 1$

   Find $f(2) = $ $f(-1) = $ $f(a) = $ $f(a - 1) = $

3. Given $f(x) = x - 2$, domain = $\{1, 5, 0\}$, find the range.

Answers: Finding the Values of Functions Problems

1. $j(-5) = 2$ $j(4) = 1$ $j(-3) = 3$ $j(2) = -1$

2. $f(2) = $ $f(-1) = $
   $f(x) = x^2 + 1$ $f(x) = x^2 + 1$
   $f(2) = (2)^2 + 1$ $f(-1) = (-1)^2 + 1$
   $f(2) = 4 + 1$ $f(-1) = 1 + 1$
   $f(2) = 5$ $f(-1) = 2$

   $f(a) = $ $f(a - 1) = $
   $f(x) = x^2 + 1$ $f(x) = x^2 + 1$
   $f(a) = (a)^2 + 1$ $f(a - 1) = (a - 1)^2 + 1$
   $f(a) = a^2 + 1$ $f(a - 1) = (a^2 - 2a + 1) + 1$
                                          $f(a - 1) = a^2 - 2a + 2$

3. $f(x) = x - 2$ $f(x) = x - 2$ $f(x) = x - 2$
   $f(1) = (1) - 2$ $f(5) = (5) - 2$ $f(0) = (0) - 2$
   $f(1) = 1 - 2$ $f(5) = 5 - 2$ $f(0) = 0 - 2$
   $f(1) = -1$ $f(5) = 3$ $f(0) = -2$

$$\text{range} = \{-1, 3, -2\}$$

Logarithms

Logarithmic Form

● A logarithm (log) of a number is the exponent to which a base must be raised to produce the number. The logarithm of the number 100 is the exponent 2 to which the base 10 must be raised to give the number 100. This is written $\log_{10} 100 = 2$ and read "log, base 10, of 100 is 2."

Examples:

problem	solution	answer
1. $\log_{10} 1000 = x$	$10^x = 1000$ $10^x = 10^3$ $x = 3$	$\log_{10} 1000 = 3$
2. $\log_2 8 = x$	$2^x = 8$ $2^x = 2^3$ $x = 3$	$\log_2 8 = 3$
3. $\log_3 81 = y$	$3^y = 81$ $3^y = 3^4$ $y = 4$	$\log_3 81 = 4$
4. $\log_5 x = 3$	$5^3 = x$ $125 = x$	$\log_5 125 = 3$
5. $\log_x 64 = 3$	$x^3 = 64$ $x^3 = 4^3$ $x = 4$	$\log_4 64 = 3$

Practice: Logarithmic Form Problems

Find the value of the unknown.

1. $\log_3 27 = x$
2. $\log_7 49 = y$
3. $\log_{10} x = 3$
4. $\log_6 1 = x$

5. $\log_x 16 = 2$
6. $\log_5 y = 2$
7. $\log_x 32 = 5$
8. $\log_{10} \frac{1}{10} = x$

Answers: Logarithmic Form Problems

1. $\log_3 27 = x$ $3^x = 27$
$3^x = 3^3$
$x = 3$ $\log_3 27 = 3$

2. $\log_7 49 = y$ $7^y = 49$
$7^y = 7^2$
$y = 2$ $\log_7 49 = 2$

3. $\log_{10} x = 3$ $10^3 = x$
$1000 = x$ $\log_{10} 1000 = 3$

4. $\log_6 1 = x$ $6^x = 1$
$6^0 = 1$ $\log_6 1 = 0$

5. $\log_x 16 = 2$ $x^2 = 16$
$x^2 = 4^2$
$x = 4$ $\log_4 16 = 2$

6. $\log_5 y = 2$ $5^2 = y$
$25 = y$ $\log_5 25 = 2$

7. $\log_x 32 = 5$ $x^5 = 32$
$x = 2$ $\log_2 32 = 5$

8. $\log_{10} \frac{1}{10} = x$ $10^x = \frac{1}{10}$
$10^{-1} = \frac{1}{10}$ $\log_{10} \frac{1}{10} = -1$

Graphing Logarithmic and Exponential Equations

● Graphing a logarithmic equation can best be done by first changing it into an exponential equation. The procedure for graphing an exponential equation is basically the same as graphing any equation. Substitute a value for one variable and determine the value of the other variable. One possible difference is that the magnitude of the units for each axis is frequently not the same.

Examples:

1. Graph $\log_2 y = x$

    First change $\log_2 y = x$
    to $2^x = y$.

    Then substitute values
    for x and find y.

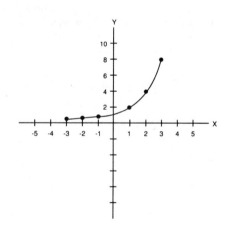

x	y
3	8
2	4
1	2
0	1
-1	$\frac{1}{2}$
-2	$\frac{1}{4}$
-3	$\frac{1}{8}$

2. Graph $\log_{1/2} y = x$

    First change $\log_{1/2} y = x$
    to $(\frac{1}{2})^x = y$

    $$\frac{1^x}{2^x} = y$$

    $$\frac{1}{2^x} = y$$

    $$2^{-x} = y$$

Then substitute values
for x and find y.

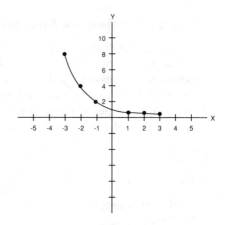

x	y
3	$\frac{1}{8}$
2	$\frac{1}{4}$
1	$\frac{1}{2}$
0	1
−1	2
−2	4
−3	8

Practice: Graphing Logarithmic and Exponential Equations Problems

Graph the following equations.

1. $y = \log_3 x$ 2. $y = 3 \cdot 2^x$

Answers: Graphing Logarithmic and Exponential Equations Problems

1. $y = \log_3 x$

    $3^y = x$

x	y
27	3
9	2
3	1
1	0
$\frac{1}{3}$	−1
$\frac{1}{9}$	−2
$\frac{1}{27}$	−3

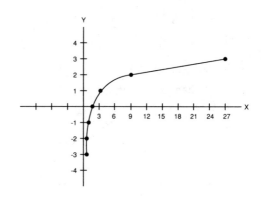

2. $y = 3 \cdot 2^x$

x	y
3	24
2	12
1	6
0	3
−1	1½
−2	¾
−3	⅜

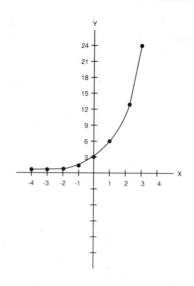

Arithmetic and Geometric Progressions

- An ordered list of numbers formed according to a pattern is called a progression. The numbers in the progression are called terms of the progression. Two kinds of progressions are arithmetic progressions and geometric progressions.

Arithmetic Progressions

- An arithmetic progression is a progression where there is a common difference between terms. Subtracting any term from the next term results in the same value. In the progression 4, 7, 10, 13, ..., the common difference is 3.

$$7 - 4 = 3 \qquad\qquad 10 - 7 = 3 \qquad\qquad 13 - 10 = 3$$

This progression is an arithmetic progression. Other examples of A.P.'s (arithmetic progressions) are:

−4, 1, 6, 11, ...   (common difference is 5)
.26, .56, .86, 1.16, ...   (common difference is .3)
½, ¼, 0, −¼, ...   (common difference is −¼)

To find the next term of an A.P., add the common difference to the previous term, or if the tenth term is desired, proceed as follows:

Given: 1, 5, 9, 13, . . . , find the tenth term in this progression.

The solution to the problem is in knowing that in order to reach the tenth term, there must be 6 more 4's (or 24) added to the fourth term, 13.

$$6 \times 4 = 24$$

So 1, 5, 9, 13, . . . , **37** (the tenth term). In this manner, any term of an A.P. may be found.

The terms between two given terms of an A.P. are called arithmetic means of the given terms. The two arithmetic means of 2 and 17 would be the two terms betwen 2 and 17 that make the four terms into an A.P.

$$2, \underline{\quad}, \underline{\quad}, 17$$

Finding the sum of the terms in an A.P. is a problem only if there are a great many terms. A helpful hint will make this easier to do.

Given: 1, 2, 3, . . . , 10, find the sum of the first 10 terms of this A.P.

$$
\begin{array}{r}
1, \quad 2, \quad 3, \ldots, 10 \\
+ \ 10, \quad 9, \quad 8, \ldots, \ 1 \\
\hline
11, 11, 11, \ldots, 11
\end{array}
$$

Add the same terms but in reverse order.

Each column adds up to 11, so 11 × 10 (the number of columns) = 110. By dividing 110 by 2, the sum of the original terms is 55.

Practice: Arithmetic Progression Problems

1. Find the twelfth term in the A.P. $-7, -3, 2, 5, \ldots$

2. Find the fortieth term in the A.P. 5, 10, 15, 20, . . .

3. Find the sum of the first 12 terms in problem 1 above.

4. Find 3 arithmetic means between -2 and 10.

5. Find the arithmetic mean between .6 and 3.

Answers: Arithmetic Progression Problems

1. Common difference is $5 - 1 = 4$. The twelfth term is 8 terms beyond the fourth term, 5.

$$4 \times 8 = 32$$

$$-7, -3, 1, 5, \ldots, \overset{+32}{37}$$

2. Common difference is $10 - 5 = 5$. The fortieth term is 36 terms beyond the fourth term, 20.

$$5 \times 36 = 180$$

$$5, 10, 15, 20, \ldots, \overset{+180}{\mathbf{200}}$$

3.
$$
\begin{array}{l}
\,-7, \quad -3, \quad 1, \quad 5, \quad \ldots, \quad 37 \\
+\ 37, \quad 33, \quad 29, \quad 25, \quad \ldots, \quad -7 \\
\hline
\,30 \quad\ \ 30 \quad\ 30 \quad 30 30 \quad 30 \times 12 = 360 \div 2 = 180
\end{array}
$$

The sum of the terms is 180.

4. $-2, \underline{}, \underline{}, \underline{}, 10 \qquad \dfrac{10 - (-2)}{4} = \dfrac{12}{4} = 3$ (common difference)

   $-2, \mathbf{1}, \mathbf{4}, \mathbf{7}, 10$

5. $.6, \underline{}, 3 \qquad \dfrac{3 - .6}{2} = \dfrac{2.4}{2} = 1.2$ (common difference)

   $.6, \mathbf{1.8}, 3$

Geometric Progressions

● A geometric progression (G.P.) is a progression where there is a constant ratio between terms. The ratio found by dividing any term by the preceding term is constant. In the progression $1, 2, 4, 8, \ldots$, the ratio of $^2/_1 = {}^4/_2 = {}^8/_4$, making this a G.P.

Other examples of G.P.'s are:

$$27, 9, 3, 1, \ldots \qquad \text{(constant ratio} = {}^1/_3)$$
$$^1/_5, 1, 5, 25, \ldots \qquad \text{(constant ratio} = 5)$$
$$-4, 2, -1, {}^1/_2, \ldots \qquad \text{(constant ratio} = -{}^1/_2)$$

To find the next term of a G.P., multiply the previous term by the constant ratio. In each of the 4 examples above, the next term would be:

1, 2, 4, 8, **16**	$2 \times 8 = 16$
27, 9, 3, 1, $\frac{1}{3}$	$\frac{1}{3} \times 1 = \frac{1}{3}$
$\frac{1}{5}$, 1, 5, 25, **125**	$5 \times 25 = 125$
$-4, 2, -1, \frac{1}{2}, -\frac{1}{4}$	$-\frac{1}{2} \times \frac{1}{2} = -\frac{1}{4}$

The geometric mean of two numbers is that number which may be inserted between the given numbers to produce a G.P.

Example: Find the geometric mean between 3 and 27.

$$3, \underline{}x, 27 \qquad \text{The ratio of } \frac{x}{3} = \frac{27}{x}$$

$$\text{so} \qquad x^2 = 81$$

$$x = \pm 9$$

There are two geometric means between 3 and 27, $+9$ and -9.

Practice: Geometric Progressions Problems

1. Find the next 2 terms in the G.P. $\frac{1}{9}$, $\frac{1}{3}$, 1, 3.

2. Find the next 2 terms in the G.P. 64, -16, 4, -1.

3. Find the geometric mean(s) between 3 and 12.

4. Find the positive geometric mean between 5 and 10.

Answers: Geometric Progressions Problems

1. Constant ratio $\frac{3}{1}$ or 3.

    $\frac{1}{9}$, $\frac{1}{3}$, 1, 3, **9, 27** $3 \times 3 = 9$ $3 \times 9 = 27$

2. Constant ratio $-\frac{1}{4}$ or $-\frac{1}{4}$.

    64, -16, 4, -1, **$\frac{1}{4}$, $-\frac{1}{16}$** $-\frac{1}{4} \times -1 = \frac{1}{4}$
    $-\frac{1}{4} \times \frac{1}{4} = -\frac{1}{16}$

3. $\frac{x}{3} = \frac{12}{x}$

$$x^2 = 36$$
$$x = \pm 6$$ Both $+6$ and -6 are geometric means between 3 and 12.

4. $\dfrac{x}{5} = \dfrac{10}{x}$

$$x^2 = 50$$
$$x = \pm \sqrt{50}$$
$$x = \pm 5\sqrt{2}$$ The positive geometric mean between 5 and 10 is $5\sqrt{2}$.

Binomial Expansion

● Raising a binomial to a power by the normal process of multiplication is a time-consuming operation. By observing the inherent patterns, binomials may be expanded to any power without resorting to repeated multiplication.

Some examples of expanding the binomial $(a + b)^n$ are:

$$(a + b)^0 = 1$$
$$(a + b)^1 = a + b$$
$$(a + b)^2 = a^2 + 2ab + b^2$$
$$(a + b)^3 = a^3 + 3a^2b + 3ab^2 + b^3$$
$$(a + b)^4 = a^4 + 4a^3b + 6a^2b^2 + 4ab^3 + b^4$$

Patterns to be noted are:

1. The number of terms is $n + 1$.
2. The exponent of the first and last term is n.
3. The exponent of a decreases by 1 in each term, while the exponent of b increases by 1 in each term.
4. The sum of the exponents in each term is n.
5. All of the signs are positive except when the second term of the binomial is being raised to an odd power.
6. The numerical coefficients follow the pattern in Pascal's triangle, namely:

Each new row is formed by adding elements of the previous row.

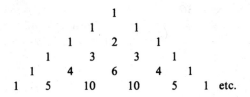

```
                    1
                1       1
            1       2       1
        1       3       3       1
    1       4       6       4       1
1       5      10      10       5       1   etc.
```

Examples:

1. $(x + y)^5$

   Step 1: x^5 x^4 x^3 x^2 x _____

   There should be $5 + 1$, or 6, terms with decreasing powers of x.

   Step 2: x^5 x^4y x^3y^2 x^2y^3 xy^4 y^5

   The y factors are the reverse of the x. Check to make sure that the exponents of each term add up to 5.

   Step 3: $x^5 + 5x^4y + 10x^3y^2 + 10x^2y^3 + 5xy^4 + y^5$

Insert the numerical coefficients using Pascal's triangle.

```
                          1
                      1       1
                  1       2       1
              1       3       3       1
          1       4       6       4       1
  6 terms ——→  1    5      10      10       5       1
          1       6      15      20      15       6       1
```

2. $(p - q)^4$

   Note: a negative sign is used for the second and fourth terms because q is raised to an odd power.

   p^4 p^3 p^2 p _____
   p^4 p^3q p^2q^2 pq^3 q^4
   $p^4 - 4p^3q + 6p^2q^2 - 4pq^3 + q^4$

3. $(r + t)^6$

r^6	r^5	r^4	r^3	r^2	r	
r^6	$r^5 t$	$r^4 t^2$	$r^3 t^3$	$r^2 t^4$	rt^5	t^6

$r^6 + 6r^5 t + 15r^4 t^2 + 20r^3 t^3 + 15r^2 t^4 + 6rt^5 + t^6$

4. $(x - 2y)^3$

$[x + (-2y)]^3$ ⟵——— think

x^3	x^2	x	
x^3	$x^2(-2y)$	$x(-2y)^2$	$(-2y)^3$

$x^3 + 3x^2(-2y) + 3x(-2y)^2 + (-2y)^3$

$x^3 + 3x^2(-2y) + 3x(4y^2) + (-8y^3)$

$x^3 - 6x^2 y + 12xy^2 - 8y^3$

Practice: Binomial Expansion Problems

1. $(x + y)^4 =$ 2. $(a - b)^5 =$ 3. $(p - 2q)^4 =$ 4. $(c + d)^7 =$

Answers: Binomial Expansion Problems

1. $(x + y)^4 = x^4 + 4x^3 y + 6x^2 y^2 + 4xy^3 + y^4$

2. $(a - b)^5 = a^5 - 5a^4 b + 10a^3 b^2 - 10a^2 b^3 + 5ab^4 - b^5$

3. $(p - 2q)^4 = [p + (-2q)]^4 =$

$p^4 + 4p^3(-2q) + 6p^2(-2q)^2 + 4p(-2q)^3 + (-2q)^4$

$p^4 + 4p^3(-2q) + 6p^2(4q^2) + 4p(-8q^3) + (16q^4)$

$p^4 - 8p^3 q + 24p^2 q^2 - 32pq^3 + 16q^4$

4. $(c + d)^7 = c^7 + 7c^6 d + 21c^5 d^2 + 35c^4 d^3 + 35c^3 d^4 + 21c^2 d^5$
$+ 7cd^6 + d^7$

ALGEBRA REVIEW TEST

Questions

1. Express each of the following algebraically.
   a. four more than twice a number
   b. a number decreased by six
   c. a number increased by ten
   d. a number x decreased by four times y

2. Evaluate: $p^2 + 7p - 5$ if $p = 6$

3. Evaluate: $4x^2y^3z^2$ if $x = 2$, $y = 3$, and $z = 4$

4. Evaluate: $\dfrac{xy}{4} - \dfrac{x + yz}{z}$ if $x = 3$, $y = 4$, and $z = 6$

5. Solve for x: $x + 18 = 64$

6. Solve for x: $4x - 8 = 32$

7. Solve for y: $\dfrac{y}{8} - 3 = 9$

8. Solve for z: $\dfrac{2}{5}z + 4 = 13$

9. Solve for x: $7x = 4x - 9$

10. Solve for n: $5n + 7 = 3n - 9$

11. Solve for y: $\dfrac{3y}{4} = 2 - y$

12. Solve for x: $\dfrac{x + 2}{x - 2} = 4$

13. Solve for x: $\dfrac{7}{6x} - \dfrac{3}{x} = 1 - \dfrac{5}{2x}$

14. Solve for y: $\dfrac{2}{y - 3} + \dfrac{2}{y} = 1$

15. Solve for y: $my - n = x$

16. Solve for m: $\dfrac{m}{n} = a$

17. Solve for x: $\dfrac{r}{x} = \dfrac{s}{t}$

18. Solve for x: x is to y as z is to a

19. Solve for x: $\dfrac{x}{6} = \dfrac{1}{2}$

20. Solve for c: $\dfrac{7}{2} = \dfrac{12}{c}$

21. x is inversely proportional to y, and x = 8 when y = 3. If y = 6, then x =

22. Solve this system for x and y:
    $x - 2y = 8$
    $3x + 2y = 4$

23. Solve this system for a and b:
    $3a + 2b = 1$
    $2a - 3b = -8$

24. Solve this system for x and y:
    $y = x + 3$
    $2x + y = 8$

25. Solve this system for x, y, and z:
    $x + y + z = 2$
    $2x + y + 2z = 3$
    $3x - y + z = 4$

26. $12xy$
    $\underline{- 15xy}$

27. $6qt^2 - 2qt^2 + 6qt^2 =$

28. Simplify: $a \cdot a \cdot a \cdot x \cdot x \cdot y$

29. Simplify: $3(x)(y)(2)(z)$

30. $(y^3)(y^5) =$

31. $(a^2b)(a^3b^4) =$

32. $(-2x^2y)(3x^3y^4) =$

33. $-3(m^3n^3)(-2m^4n^2) =$

34. $(4a^2b^3c^3)(b^3c^2d) =$

35. $(x^7)^4 =$

36. $(a^2b^3)^3 =$

37. $(3x^3y^5)^2 =$

38. $x^5 \div x^2 =$

39. $\dfrac{a^6b^2}{a^4b} =$

40. $\dfrac{14\,x^6y^4}{2xy} =$

41. $3p^6q^4 \div 15p^4q^8 =$

42. $\dfrac{a^{-5}}{b^6} =$

43. $(a^3b^{-5})(a^{-2}b^6) =$

44. $\dfrac{a^4}{a^{-7}} =$

45. $(4x^{-2})^{-3} =$

46. $\left(\dfrac{1}{5}\right)^{-2} =$

47. $\dfrac{x^2y^{-5}}{x^{-5}y^3} =$

48. $4y^0 + (4y)^0 =$

49. $\dfrac{x^2y^{-2}}{x^0y^4} =$

50. $\sqrt[3]{x^2} = x^?$

51. $8^{-2/3} =$

52. $x^2 + xy + 2y^2$
   $\underline{+3x^2 + 5xy + 3y^2}$

53. $(3x + 7y) + (6x - 2y) =$

54. $(3s^2 + 4st + 13t^2) - (2s^2 + 2st + 3t^2) =$

55. $2a^2b + 3ab^2 + 7a^2b - 5ab^2 =$

56. $(2x + 4)(3x - 1) =$

57. $(a + 3ab + 4)(2a + b) =$

58. $(2 + 3i)(1 - 2i) =$

59. $(12a^8 - 8a^7) \div 2a^3 =$

60. $\dfrac{-3(x^2y^3)(-4xy^4)}{2xy^2} =$

61. $(x^2 + 2x + 1) \div (x + 1) =$

62. $(5x^2 + 6x + 1) \div (x + 1) =$

63. $(a^3 - 27) \div (a - 3) =$

64. Factor: $9a - 6$

65. Factor completely: $5x^3 + 10x^2$

66. Factor: $n^2 - 9$

67. Factor: $36a^2 - b^2$

68. Factor completely: $2a^2 - 32$

69. Factor: $x^2 + 3x + 2$

70. Factor: $x^2 - 5x - 6$

71. Factor: $3x^2 - 20x - 7$

72. Factor completely: $x^3 - 4x^2 + 3x$

73. Factor: $24 - 10r + r^2$

74. Factor: $x^2 - 2xy + y^2$

75. Factor: $x^3 + 8$

76. Factor: $y^2 + cy - 3y - 3c$

77. Solve for y: $y^2 = 5y - 4$

78. Solve for x: $x^2 - 25 = 0$

79. Solve for x: $x^2 - 5x = 0$

80. Solve for t: $3t^2 + 21t = 2t^2 - 3t + 81$

81. Solve for x: $3x^2 - 3x + 1 = 0$

82. Reduce: $\dfrac{9x^5}{12x^3}$

83. Reduce: $\dfrac{5x - 15}{4x - 12}$

84. Reduce: $\dfrac{x^2 - 9x + 20}{x^2 - x - 12}$

85. $\dfrac{8x^5}{9y^2} \cdot \dfrac{3y^4}{2x^3} =$

86. $\dfrac{x - 1}{x} \cdot \dfrac{x + 3}{x^2 - 7x + 6} =$

87. $\dfrac{4x^3}{7} \div \dfrac{2x}{9} =$

88. $\dfrac{10y + 5}{4} \div \dfrac{2y + 1}{2} =$

89. $\dfrac{\dfrac{xy^2}{z}}{\dfrac{x^2y^3}{z^3}} =$

90. $\dfrac{x + \dfrac{1}{2}}{x + \dfrac{1}{4}} =$

91. $\dfrac{y + 3}{y} + \dfrac{2y + 5}{y} =$

92. $\dfrac{4x - 5}{x - 1} - \dfrac{3x + 6}{x - 1} =$

93. $\dfrac{7}{x} - \dfrac{6}{y} =$

94. $\dfrac{x - 3}{2x} + \dfrac{x + 1}{4x} =$

95. $\dfrac{7x}{x^4 y^7} + \dfrac{3}{x^6 y^2} =$

96. $\dfrac{3x}{x - 3} - \dfrac{2x}{x + 1} =$

97. $\dfrac{x}{x^2 - 16} + \dfrac{4x}{x^2 + 5x + 4} =$

98. $\dfrac{x^2}{x - 1} + \dfrac{1}{1 - x} =$

99. Solve for x: $5x + 2 > 17$

100. Solve for y: $-4y - 8 \le 12$

101. Solve for x: $5x + 6 \ge 2x + 2$

102. Solve for x and graph answer: $x(x - 4) < -3$

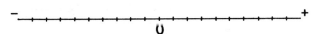

103. Graph: $\{x: 5 \ge x \ge 3\}$

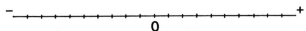

104. Graph: $\{x: -2 \le x < 8, x \text{ is an integer}\}$

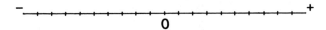

105. Graph: $\{x: x > 1\}$

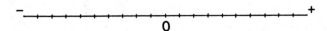

106. Graph: $\{x: x \leq -2\}$

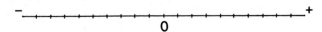

107. $|-6| =$

108. $|3 - 7| =$

109. $5 - |-3| =$

110. Solve for y: $3|y| + 2 = 8$

111. Solve for x and graph answer: $|2x - 5| < 7$

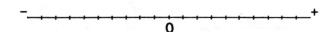

112. Give the coordinates represented by points

    A.
    B.
    C.
    D.

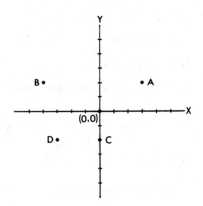

113. Is $x + \dfrac{3}{y} = 5$ linear or nonlinear?

114. Graph: $x + y = 9$

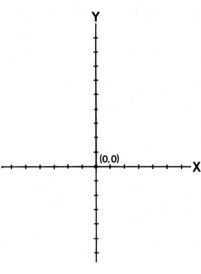

115. Find the slope and y-intercept of the line $x + 2y = 4$

116. Graph: $x - 2y > 2$

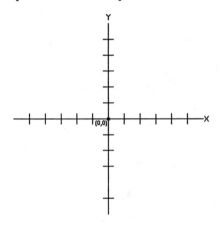

117. Graph: $y = x^2 + 3$

118. $-\sqrt{64} =$

119. $\sqrt{144} =$

120. Simplify: $\sqrt{75}$

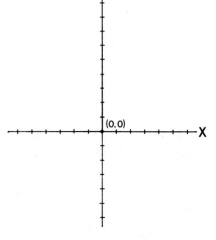

In problems 121 through 142, each variable is nonnegative.

121. $\sqrt{x^8} =$

122. $\sqrt{x^2y^8} =$

123. $\sqrt{9x^6y^{10}} =$

124. $\sqrt{y^9} =$

125. $\sqrt{a^3b^3} =$

126. $\sqrt{27a^3b^6} =$

127. $\sqrt{(2x)(8x^3)} =$

128. $\sqrt{4x^4 + 5x^4} =$

129. $\sqrt{(18)(2)} =$

130. $\sqrt{25 + 4} =$

131. $7\sqrt{5} + 3\sqrt{5} =$

132. $\sqrt{60} + 2\sqrt{15} =$

133. $\sqrt{27} + \sqrt{48} =$

134. $\sqrt{x^5} + \sqrt{9x} =$

135. $\sqrt{6} \cdot \sqrt{10} =$

136. $\sqrt{x^3y} \cdot \sqrt{x^2yz} =$

137. $\sqrt{2xy} \cdot \sqrt{32x^3y^2} =$

138. $6\sqrt{6} \cdot 2\sqrt{3} =$

139. $(2\sqrt{2} - 1)^2 =$

140. $\sqrt{3x}(\sqrt{3} + \sqrt{x}) =$

141. If $\sqrt{x} - 8 = 1$, then $x =$

142. If $2\sqrt{x} - 4 = 6$, then $x =$

143. If $f(x) = x^2 + 1$, then $f(x + 1) =$

Questions 144 through 147 refer to the graph.

144. Is the relation a function?

145. What is the domain?

146. What is the range?

147. Would the inverse
     be a function?

148. If $\log_x 16 = 2$, then $x =$

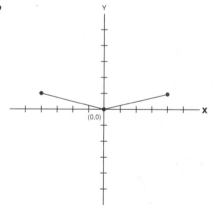

149. What is the next term in the geometric progression 80, -16, 3.2, _____ ?

150. The midpoint of a line segment is $(-\frac{1}{2}, -1)$. If one end point is $(-3, -7)$, what are the coordinates of the other end point?

151. $\dfrac{3i}{3i - 1} =$

152. $(x - y)^5 =$

Answers

Page numbers following each answer refer to the review section applicable to this problem type.

1. a. $2x + 4$ (p. 102)
   b. $x - 6$ (p. 102)
   c. $x + 10$ (p. 102)
   d. $x - 4y$ (p. 102)

2. 73 (p. 104)

3. 6,912 (p. 104)

4. $-\dfrac{3}{2}$ or $-1\frac{1}{2}$ (p. 104)

5. $x = 46$ (p. 107)

6. $x = 10$ (p. 107)

7. $y = 96$ (p. 107)

8. $z = \dfrac{45}{2}$ or $22\frac{1}{2}$ (p. 107)

9. $x = -3$ (p. 107)

10. $n = -8$ (p. 107)

11. $y = -\frac{8}{7}$ or $1\frac{1}{7}$ (p. 107)

12. $x = \dfrac{10}{3}$ or $3\frac{1}{3}$ (p. 107)

13. $\frac{2}{3}$ (p. 172)

14. $(1, 6)$ (p. 155, p. 172)

15. $y = \dfrac{x + n}{m}$ (p. 114)

16. m = an (p. 114)

17. $x = \dfrac{rt}{s}$ (p. 114)

18. $x = \dfrac{zy}{a}$ (p. 117)

19. x = 3 (p. 118)

20. $c = \dfrac{24}{7}$ or $3\dfrac{3}{7}$ (p. 118)

21. x = 4 (p. 118)

22. $x = 3, y = \dfrac{-5}{2}$ or $-2\frac{1}{2}$ (p. 121)

23. $a = -1, b = 2$ (p. 121)

24. $x = \dfrac{5}{3}$ or $1\dfrac{2}{3}$, $y = \dfrac{14}{3}$ or $4\dfrac{2}{3}$ (p. 121)

25. $(2, 1, -1)$ (p. 127)

26. $-3xy$ (p.132)

27. $10qt^2$ (p. 132)

28. a^3x^2y (p. 133)

29. $6xyz$ (p. 133)

30. y^8 (p. 133)

31. a^5b^5 (p. 133)

32. $-6x^5y^5$ (p. 133)

33. $6m^7n^5$ (p. 133)

34. $4a^2b^6c^5d$ (p. 133)

35. x^{28} (p. 133)

36. a^6b^9 (p. 133)

37. $9x^6y^{10}$ (p. 133)

38. x^3 (p. 134)

39. a^2b (p. 134)

40. $7x^5y^3$ (p. 134)

41. $\dfrac{p^2}{5q^4}$ or $.2p^2q^{-4}$ (p. 134)

42. $\dfrac{1}{a^5b^6}$ (p. 136)

43. ab (p. 136)

44. a^{11} (p. 136)

45. $\dfrac{x^6}{64}$ (p. 136)

46. 25 (p. 136)

47. $\dfrac{x^7}{y^8}$ (p. 136)

48. 5 (p. 136)

49. $\dfrac{x^2}{y^6}$ (p. 136)

50. $x^{2/3}$ (p. 217)

51. $\frac{1}{4}$ (p. 219)

52. $4x^2 + 6xy + 5y^2$ (p. 138)

53. $9x + 5y$ (p. 138)

54. $s^2 + 2st + 10t^2$ (p. 138)

55. $9a^2b - 2ab^2$ (p. 138)

56. $6x^2 + 10x - 4$ (p. 140)

57. $2a^2 + 6a^2b + 8a + ab + 3ab^2 + 4b$ (p. 140)

58. $8 - i$ (p. 225)

59. $6a^5 - 4a^4$ (p. 142)

60. $6x^2y^5$ (p. 142)

61. $(x + 1)$ (p. 143)

62. $(5x + 1)$ (p. 143)

63. $(a^2 + 3a + 9)$ (p. 143)

64. $3(3a - 2)$ (p. 147)

65. $5x^2 (x + 2)$ (p. 147)

66. $(n - 3)(n + 3)$ (p. 147)

67. $(6a - b)(6a + b)$ (p. 147)

68. $2(a - 4)(a + 4)$ (p. 147)

69. $(x + 1)(x + 2)$ (p. 148)

70. $(x - 6)(x + 1)$ (p. 148)

71. $(3x + 1) (x - 7)$ (p. 148)

72. $x(x - 3)(x - 1)$ (p. 148)

73. $(6 - r)(4 - r)$ (p. 148)

74. $(x - y)(x - y)$ (p. 148)

75. $(x + 2)(x^2 + 2x + 4)$ (p. 152)

76. $(y + c)(y - 3)$ (p. 153)

77. $y = 1, 4$ (p. 155)

78. $x = 5, -5$ (p. 155)

79. $x = 0, 5$ (p. 155)

80. $t = 3, -27,$ (p. 155)

81. $\dfrac{3 + i\sqrt{3}}{6}, \dfrac{3 - i\sqrt{3}}{6}$ (p. 229)

82. $\dfrac{3x^2}{4}$ (p.160)

83. $\dfrac{5}{4}$ or $1\frac{1}{4}$ (p. 160)

84. $\dfrac{x - 5}{x + 3}$ (p. 160)

85. $\dfrac{4x^2y^2}{3}$ (p. 162)

86. $\dfrac{x + 3}{x(x - 6)}$ or $\dfrac{x + 3}{x^2 - 6x}$ (p. 162)

87. $\dfrac{18x^2}{7}$ (p. 164)

88. $\dfrac{5}{2}$ or $2\frac{1}{2}$ (p. 164)

89. $\dfrac{z^2}{xy}$ (p. 164)

90. $\dfrac{2(2x + 1)}{4x + 1}$ or $\dfrac{4x + 2}{4x + 1}$ (p. 164)

91. $\dfrac{3y + 8}{y}$ (p. 166)

92. $\dfrac{x - 11}{x - 1}$ (p. 166)

93. $\dfrac{7y - 6x}{xy}$ (p. 166)

94. $\dfrac{3x - 5}{4x}$ (p. 166)

95. $\dfrac{7x^3 + 3y^5}{x^6y^7}$ (p. 166)

96. $\dfrac{x^2 + 9x}{(x - 3)(x + 1)}$ (p. 166)

97. $\dfrac{5x^2 - 15x}{(x + 4)(x - 4)(x + 1)}$ (p. 166)

98. $x - 1$ (p. 166)

99. {x: x > 3}(p. 176)

100. {y: y ≥ − 5}(p. 176)

101. $\left\{x: x \ge \dfrac{-4}{3}\right\}$ (p. 176)

102.
... −6 −5 −4 −3 −2 −1 0 1 2 3 4 5 6 ... (p. 237)

103.
... −1 0 1 2 3 4 5 ... (p. 178)

104.
... −2 −1 0 1 2 3 4 5 6 7 8 ... (p. 178)

105.
... −1 0 1 2 3 ... (p. 178)

106.
... −4 −3 −2 −1 0 1 ... (p. 178)

107. 6 (p. 180)

108. 4 (p. 180)

109. 2 (p. 180)

110. {2, −2} (p. 181)

111.
... −6 −5 −4 −3 −2 −1 0 1 2 3 4 5 6 ... (p. 183)

112. A. (3,2) (p. 186)
    B. (−4,2) (p. 186)
    C. (0,−2) (p. 186)
    D. (−3,−2) (p. 186)

113. nonlinear (p. 189)

114.

x	y
0	9
1	8
2	7

(p. 189)

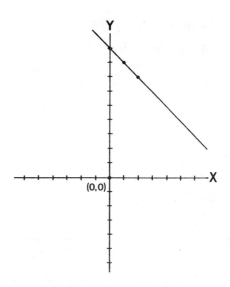

115. slope $= -\frac{1}{2}$, y-intercept $= 2$ (p. 193)

116.   (p. 189)

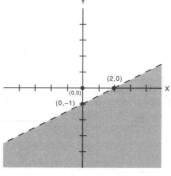

117.

x	y
0	3
1	4
2	7
-1	4
-2	7

(p. 190)

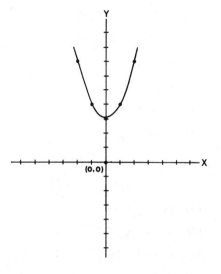

118. -8 (p. 206)

119. 12 (p. 206)

120. $5\sqrt{3}$ (p. 206)

121. x^4 (p. 206)

122. xy^4 (p. 206)

123. $3x^3y^5$ (p. 206)

124. $y^4\sqrt{y}$ (p. 206)

125. $ab\sqrt{ab}$ (p. 206)

126. $3ab^3\sqrt{3a}$ (p. 206)

127. $4x^2$ (p. 206)

128. $3x^2$ (p. 206)

129. 6 (p. 206)

130. $\sqrt{29}$ (p. 206)

131. $10\sqrt{5}$ (p. 207)

132. $4\sqrt{15}$ (p. 209)

133. $7\sqrt{3}$ (p. 209)

134. $\sqrt{x}(x^2 + 3)$ (p. 209)

135. $2\sqrt{15}$ (p. 211)

136. $x^2y\sqrt{xz}$ (p. 211)

137. $8x^2y\sqrt{y}$ (p. 211)

138. $12\sqrt{18} = 36\sqrt{2}$ (p. 211)

139. $9 - 4\sqrt{2}$ (p. 215)

140. $3\sqrt{x} + x\sqrt{3}$ (p. 215)

141. $x = 81$ (p. 215)

142. $x = 25$ (p. 215)

143. $x^2 + 2x + 2$ (p. 245)

144. yes (p. 241)

145. $\{x: -4 \le x \le 4\}$ (p. 241)

146. $\{y: 0 \le y \le 2\}$ (p. 241)

147. no (p. 241)

148. $x = 4$ (p. 247)

149. $-.64$ (p. 251)

150. $(2,5)$ (p. 201)

151. $\dfrac{9 - 3i}{10}$ (p. 226)

152. $x^5 - 5x^4y + 10x^3y^2 - 10x^2y^3 + 5xy^4 - y^5$ (p. 255)

ALGEBRA GLOSSARY OF TERMS

ABSCISSA: The distance along the horizontal axis in a coordinate graph.

ABSOLUTE VALUE: The numerical value when direction or sign is not considered.

ALGEBRA: Arithmetic operations using letters and/or symbols in place of numbers.

ALGEBRAIC FRACTIONS: Fractions using a variable in the numerator and/or denominator.

ASCENDING ORDER: Basically, when the power of a term increases for each succeeding term.

BINOMIAL: An algebraic expression consisting of two terms.

CARTESIAN COORDINATES: A system of assigning ordered number pairs to points on a plane.

CLOSED INTERVAL: An interval which includes both endpoints or fixed boundaries.

COEFFICIENT: The number in front of a variable. For example, in 9x, 9 is the coefficient.

COORDINATE AXES: Two perpendicular number lines used in a coordinate graph.

COORDINATE GRAPH: Two perpendicular number lines, the x axis and the y axis, creating a plane on which each point is assigned a pair of numbers.

CUBE: The result when a number is multiplied by itself twice. Designated by the exponent 3. (x^3)

CUBE ROOT: The number that when multiplied by itself twice gives you the original number. For example, 5 is the cube root of 125. Its symbol is $\sqrt[3]{}$. $\sqrt[3]{125} = 5$

DENOMINATOR: Everything below the fraction bar in a fraction.

DESCENDING ORDER: Basically, when the power of a term decreases for each succeeding term.

EQUATION: A balanced relationship between numbers and/or symbols. A mathematical sentence.

EVALUATE: To determine the value, or numerical amount.

EXPONENT: A numeral used to indicate the power of a number.

EXTREMES: Outer terms.

FACTOR: To find two or more quantities whose product equals the original quantity.

FINITE: Countable. Having a definite ending.

F.O.I.L. METHOD: A method of multiplying binomials in which first terms, outside terms, inside terms, and last terms are multiplied.

HALF-OPEN INTERVAL: An interval that includes one endpoint, or one boundary.

IMAGINARY NUMBERS: Square roots of negative numbers. The imaginary unit is i.

INCOMPLETE QUADRATIC EQUATION: A quadratic equation with a term missing.

INEQUALITY: A statement in which the relationships are not equal. The opposite of an equation.

INFINITE: Uncountable. Continues forever.

INTERVAL: All the numbers that lie within two certain boundaries.

LINEAR EQUATION: An equation whose solution set forms a straight line when plotted on a coordinate graph.

LITERAL EQUATION: An equation having mostly variables.

MEANS: Inner terms.

MONOMIAL: An algebraic expression consisting of only one term.

NONLINEAR EQUATION: An equation whose solution set does not form a straight line when plotted on a coordinate graph.

NUMBER LINE: A graphic representation of integers and real numbers. The point on this line associated with each number is called the graph of the number.

NUMERATOR: Everything above the fraction bar in a fraction.

OPEN INTERVAL: An interval that does not include endpoints or fixed boundaries.

OPEN RAY: A ray that does include its endpoint (half line).

ORDERED PAIR: Any pair of elements (x, y) having a first element x and a second element y. Used to identify or plot points on a coordinate grid.

ORDINATE: The distance along the vertical axis on a coordinate graph.

ORIGIN: The point of intersection of the two number lines on a coordinate graph. Represented by the coordinates (0,0).

POLYNOMIAL: An algebraic expression consisting of two or more terms.

PROPORTION: Two ratios equal to each other. For example, a is to c as b is to d.

QUADRANTS: Four quarters or divisions of a coordinate graph.

QUADRATIC EQUATION: An equation that could be written $Ax^2 + Bx + C = 0$.

RADICAL SIGN: The symbol used to designate square root.

RATIO: A method of comparing two or more numbers. For example, a:b. Often written as a fraction.

REAL NUMBERS: The set consisting of all rational and irrational numbers.

SIMPLIFY: To combine several or many terms into fewer terms.

SOLUTION SET or SOLUTION: All the answers that satisfy the equation.

SQUARE: The result when a number is multiplied by itself. Designated by the exponent 2. (x^2)

SQUARE ROOT: The number that when multiplied by itself gives you the original number. For example, 5 is the square root of 25. Its symbol is $\sqrt{}$. $\sqrt{25} = 5$

SYSTEM OF EQUATIONS: Simultaneous equations.

TERM: A numerical or literal expression with its own sign.

TRINOMIAL: An algebraic expression consisting of three terms.

UNKNOWN: A letter or symbol whose value is not known.

VALUE: Numerical amount.

VARIABLE: A symbol used to stand for a number.

X-AXIS: The horizontal axis in a coordinate graph.

X-COORDINATE: The first number in the ordered pair. Refers to the distance on the x-axis. Abscissa.

Y-AXIS: The vertical axis in a coordinate graph.

Y-COORDINATE: The second number in the ordered pair. Refers to the distance on the y-axis. Ordinate.

GEOMETRY

GEOMETRY DIAGNOSTIC TEST

Questions

1. Name any angle of this triangle three different ways.

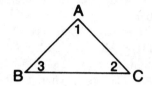

2. A(n) _____ angle measures less than 90 degrees.

3. A(n) _____ angle measures 90 degrees.

4. A(n) _____ angle measures more than 90 degrees but less than 180 degrees.

5. A(n) _____ angle measures 180 degrees.

6. Two angles are complementary when the sum of their measures is _____.

7. Two angles are supplementary when the sum of their measures is _____.

8. In the diagram, find the measure of ∠a, ∠b, and ∠c.

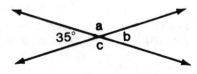

9. In the diagram, find the measure of all remaining angles. ℓ ∥ m

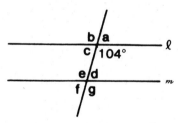

10. Lines that stay the same distance apart and never meet are called _____ lines.

11. Lines that meet to form right angles are called _____ lines.

12. A(n) _____ triangle has three equal sides. Therefore, each interior angle measures _____.

13. In the diagram, △ABC is isosceles: AB = AC. Find ∠A and ∠C.

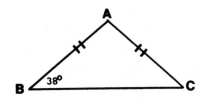

14. In the triangle, AC must be less than _____ inches.

15. In the triangle, which angle is smaller, ∠A or ∠C?

Questions 14 and 15

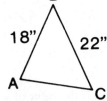

16. What is the measure of ∠ACD?

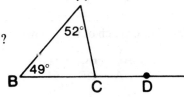

17. What is the length of AC?

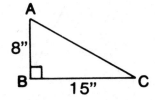

18. What is the length of BC?

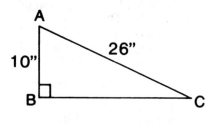

19. What is the value of x?

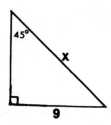

20. What is the value of a?

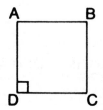

21. Name each of the following polygons.

(A) AB = BC = AC   (B) AB = BC = CD = AD
    ∠A = ∠B = ∠C = 60°   ∠A = ∠B = ∠C = ∠D = 90°

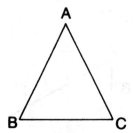

(C) AB ∥ DC
     AB = DC
     AD ∥ BC
     AD = BC
     ∠A = ∠C

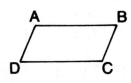

(D) AB = DC
     AD = BC
     ∠A = ∠B = ∠C = ∠D = 90°

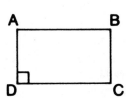

(E) AB ∥ DC

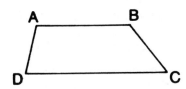

22. Fill in the blanks for
    circle R.
    (A) RS is called the _____.
    (B) AB is called the _____.
    (C) CD is called a _____.

23. In the circle, if B͡S = 62°,
    what is the measure of ∠BRS?

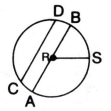

24. In this circle, if D͡S – 62°,
    what is the measure of
    ∠BCS?

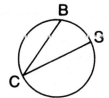

25. Find the area and circumference
    for the circle O (π ≈ ²²/₇).
    (A) area = _____
    (B) circumference = _____

26. Find the area and perimeter
of the trapezoid.
(A) area = _____
(B) perimeter = _____

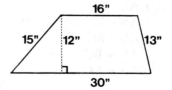

27. Find the area and perimeter
of the figure (ABCD is a
parallelogram).
(A) area = _____
(B) perimeter = _____

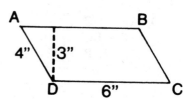

28. Find the volume of the
right circular cylinder
(use 3.14 for π).

29. What is the surface area
and volume of the cube?
(A) surface area = _____
(B) volume = _____

Answers

Page numbers following each answer refer to the review section applicable to this problem type.

1. $\angle 3$, $\angle CBA$, $\angle ABC$, $\angle B$ (p. 288)
   $\angle 1$, $\angle BAC$, $\angle CAB$, $\angle A$ (p. 288)
   $\angle 2$, $\angle ACB$, $\angle BCA$, $\angle C$ (p. 288)

2. acute (p. 289)

3. right (p. 289)

4. obtuse (p. 289)

5. straight (p. 289)

6. 90° (p. 291)

7. 180° (p. 291)

8. a = 145°
   b = 35°
   c = 145° (p. 291)

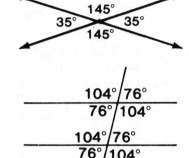

9. ∠a, ∠c, ∠d, ∠f = 76°
   ∠b, ∠e, ∠g = 104° (p. 295)

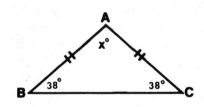

10. parallel (p. 295)

11. perpendicular (p. 295)

12. equilateral, 60° (p. 300)

13. 38° + 38° + x° = 180°
        76° + x° = 180°
             x° = 104°
           ∠A = 104°
          ∠C = 38°
    (p. 301)

14. 40 inches. Since AB + BC = 40 inches
    then AC < AB + BC
    and AC < 40 inches (p. 303)

15. ∠C must be the smaller angle, since it is opposite the shorter side AB. (p. 303)

16. ∠ACD = 101° (p. 304)

17. AC = 17 inches (p. 306)

18. BC = 24 inches. Since 5, 12, 13 is a Pythagorean triple, doubled is 10, <u>24</u>, 26. (p. 306)

19. x = 9 $\sqrt{2}$. Since this is an isosceles right triangle, the ratio of the sides is x, x, x $\sqrt{2}$. (p. 308)

20. a = 8. Since this is a 30-60-90 right triangle, the ratio of the sides is x, 2x, x $\sqrt{3}$. (p. 309)

21. (A) equilateral triangle or equilangular triangle (p. 300)
    (B) square (p. 312)
    (C) parallelogram (p. 312)
    (D) rectangle (p. 312)
    (E) trapezoid (p. 313)

22. (A) radius (p. 318)
    (B) diameter (p. 319)
    (C) chord (p. 319)

23. 62° (p. 321)

24. 31° (p. 322)

25. (A) area = πr^2
    $\quad\quad\quad = \pi(7^2)$
    $\quad\quad\quad = {}^{22}\!/_7(7)(7)$
    $\quad\quad\quad = 154$ square inches (p. 320)
    (B) circumference = πd
    $\quad\quad\quad\quad\quad\quad\quad = \pi(14)$ $\quad\quad$ d = 14″, since r = 7″
    $\quad\quad\quad\quad\quad\quad\quad = {}^{22}\!/_7(14)$
    $\quad\quad\quad\quad\quad\quad\quad = 22(2)$
    $\quad\quad\quad\quad\quad\quad\quad = 44$ inches (p. 320)

26. (A) area = ½(a + b)h
    $\quad\quad\quad\quad = ½(16 + 30)12$
    $\quad\quad\quad\quad = ½(46)12$
    $\quad\quad\quad\quad = 23(12)$
    $\quad\quad\quad\quad = 276$ square inches (p. 315)
    (B) perimeter = 16 + 13 + 30 + 15 = 74 inches (p. 315)

27. (A) area = bh
    $\quad\quad\quad = 6(3)$
    $\quad\quad\quad = 18$ square inches (p. 315)
    (B) perimeter = 6 + 4 + 6 + 4 = 20 inches (p. 315)

28. Volume = (area of base)(height)

$$= (\pi r^2)h$$
$$= (\pi \cdot 10^2)(12)$$
$$= 3.14(100)(12)$$
$$= 314(12)$$
$$= 3{,}768 \text{ cubic inches (p. 328)}$$

29. (A) All six surfaces have an area of 4 × 4, or 16 square inches, since each surface is a square. Therefore, 16(6) = 96 square inches in the surface area. (p. 329)

(B) Volume = side × side × side, or 4^3 = 64 cubic inches. (p. 328)

GEOMETRY REVIEW

- PLANE GEOMETRY is the study of shapes and figures in two dimensions (the plane). Plane figures have only length and width.
- SOLID GEOMETRY is the study of shapes and figures in three dimensions. Solid figures have length, width, and thickness.
- A POINT is the most fundamental idea in geometry. It is represented by a dot and named by a capital letter.

Angles

- An *angle* is formed by two rays that have the same endpoint. That point is called the *vertex;* the rays are called the *sides* of the angle. An angle is measured in degrees from 0 to 360. The number of degrees indicates the size of the angle or the difference in direction of the two rays.

In the diagram, the angle is formed by rays $\overrightarrow{AB}$ and $\overrightarrow{AC}$. A is the vertex. $\overrightarrow{AB}$ and $\overrightarrow{AC}$ are the sides of the angle.

The symbol ∠ is used to denote an angle.
The symbol m ∠ is sometimes used to denote the measure of an angle.

- An angle can be named in various ways:

  1. By the letter of the vertex—therefore, the angle above could be named ∠A.
  2. By the number (or small letter) in its interior—therefore, the angle above could be named ∠1.
  3. By the letters of the three points that formed it—therefore, the angle above could be named ∠BAC or ∠CAB. The center letter is always the letter of the vertex.

Types of Angles

Right Angle

● A *right angle* has a measure of 90°. The symbol ∟ in the interior of an angle designates the fact that a right angle is formed.

In the diagram, ∠ABC is
a right angle.

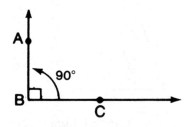

Acute Angle

● Any angle whose measure is less than 90° is called an *acute angle*.

In the diagram, ∠b is acute.

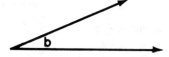

Obtuse Angle

● Any angle whose measure is larger than 90° but smaller than 180° is called an *obtuse angle*.

In the diagram,
∠4 is an obtuse angle.

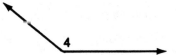

Straight Angle

● A *straight angle* has a measure of 180°.

In the diagram, ∠BAC is a
straight angle (often called a line).

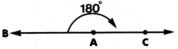

Practice: Angle Problems

Name the angles.

1.

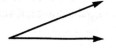

2.

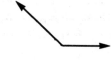

3.

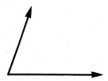

4.

What kind of angle is formed between the hands of a clock (measured clockwise) when it is

5. 6 o'clock   6. 2 o'clock   7. 3 o'clock   8. 8 o'clock

Answers: Angle Problems

1. an acute angle
2. an obtuse angle
3. an acute angle
4. an obtuse angle

5. a straight angle
6. an acute angle
7. a right angle
8. an obtuse angle

Pairs of Angles

Adjacent Angles

● *Adjacent angles* are any angles that share a common side and a common vertex.

In the diagram, ∠1 and ∠2 are adjacent angles.

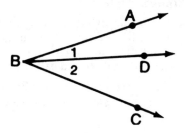

Vertical Angles

● If two straight lines intersect, they do so at a point. Four angles are formed. Those angles opposite each other are called *vertical angles*. Those angles sharing a common side and a common vertex are, again, *adjacent angles*. Vertical angles are always equal in measure.

In the diagram, line *l* and line *m* intersect at point Q. ∠1, ∠2, ∠3, and ∠4 are formed.

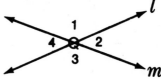

$$\left.\begin{matrix} \angle 1 \text{ and } \angle 3 \\ \angle 2 \text{ and } \angle 4 \end{matrix}\right\} \text{ are vertical angles}$$

$$\left.\begin{matrix} \angle 1 \text{ and } \angle 2 \\ \angle 2 \text{ and } \angle 3 \\ \angle 3 \text{ and } \angle 4 \\ \angle 1 \text{ and } \angle 4 \end{matrix}\right\} \text{ are adjacent angles}$$

Therefore,   ∠1 = ∠3
                        ∠2 = ∠4

Complementary Angles

● Two angles whose sum is 90° are called *complementary angles*.

In the diagram, since ∠ABC is a right triangle, ∠1 + ∠2 = 90°.

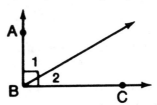

Therefore, ∠1 and ∠2 are complementary angles. If ∠1 = 55°, its complement, ∠2, would be: 90° − 55° = 35°.

Supplementary Angles

● Two angles whose sum is 180° are called *supplementary angles*. Two adjacent angles that form a straight line are supplementary.

In the diagram, since ∠ABC is a straight angle, ∠3 + ∠4 = 180°.

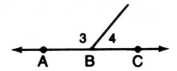

Therefore, ∠3 and ∠4 are supplementary angles. If ∠3 = 122°, its
supplement, ∠4, would have a measure of: 180° − 122° = 58°.

Angle Bisector

● A ray from the vertex of an angle that divides the angle into two
angles of equal measure is called an *angle bisector.*

In the diagram, $\overrightarrow{AB}$ is the angle
bisector of ∠CAD.

Therefore, ∠1 = ∠2.

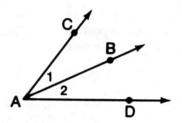

Practice: Angle Problems

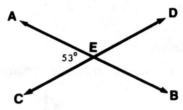

1. In the figure above, if lines AB and CD intersect at E, and if
   ∠AEC measures 53°, how many degrees are there in ∠BED?

2. Find the complement of the following angles.
   (a) 17°   (b) t°

3. Find the supplement of the following angles.
   (a) 124°   (b) (x + 9)°

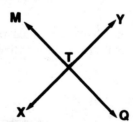

4. In the figure above, ∠XTM and ∠_____ are *vertical* angles.

5. Find the complement of an angle whose measure is
   (a) $74\frac{1}{2}°$ (b) $(q - 5)°$

6. Find the supplement of an angle whose measure is
   (a) $180°$ (b) $(m - 30)°$

Answers: Angle Problems

1. Since $\angle AEC$ and $\angle BED$ are vertical angles, $\angle BED$ contains $53°$.

2. (a) $90° - 17° = 73°$
   (b) $(90 - t)°$

3. (a) $180° - 124° = 56°$
   (b) $180° - (x + 9)° = 180° - x° - 9° = (171 - x)°$

4. YTQ

5. (a) $90° - 74\frac{1}{2}° = 15\frac{1}{2}°$
   (b) $90° - (q - 5)° = 90° - q° + 5° = (95 - q)°$

6. (a) $180° - 180° = 0°$
   (b) $180° - (m - 30)° = 180° - m° + 30° = (210 - m)°$

Lines

Straight Lines

- A *straight line* is often described as the shortest distance between
  two points. It continues forever in both directions. A line consists of
  an infinite number of points and is named by any two points on the
  line. (*Line* means *straight line)* The symbol ↔ written on top of the
  two letters is used to denote that line.

This is line AB.
It is written $\overleftrightarrow{AB}$.

A line may also be named by one small letter.

This is line *l*.

Line Segments

- A *line segment* is a piece of a line. It has two endpoints and is
  named by its two endpoints. Sometimes the symbol — written on

top of the two letters is used to denote that line segment.

This is line segment CD.
It is written $\overline{CD}$ or CD.
(Although there is a technical
difference, most standardized
exams use one form consistently
in context.)
Note that it is a piece of $\overleftrightarrow{AB}$.

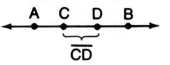

- A midpoint of a line segment is the halfway point, or the point equidistant from the endpoints.

Rays

- A *ray* has only one endpoint (or origin) and continues forever in one direction. A ray could be thought of as a half-line with an endpoint. It is named by the letter of its endpoint and any other point on the ray. The symbol → written on top of the two letters is used to denote that ray.

This is ray AB.
It is written $\overrightarrow{AB}$.

This is ray BC.
It is written $\overrightarrow{BC}$ or $\overleftarrow{CB}$.

Note that the direction of the symbol is the direction of the ray.

Types of Lines

Intersecting Lines

- Two or more lines that meet at a point are called *intersecting lines*. That point would be on each of those lines.

In the diagram, lines *l* and *m*
intersect at Q.

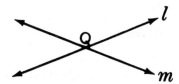

Perpendicular Lines

● Two lines that meet to form right angles (90°) are called *perpendicular lines*. The symbol ⊥ is used to denote perpendicular lines.

In the diagram, line *l* ⊥ line *m*.

Parallel Lines

● Two or more lines that remain the same distance apart at all times are called *parallel lines*. Parallel lines never meet. The symbol ‖ is used to denote parallel lines.

In the diagram, *l* ‖ *m*.

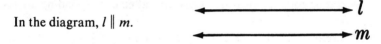

Parallel Lines Cut by Transversal

● When two parallel lines are both intersected by a third line, it is termed *parallel lines cut by a transversal*. In the diagram below, line *n* is the transversal, and lines *m* and *l* are parallel. Eight angles are formed. There are many facts and relationships about these angles.

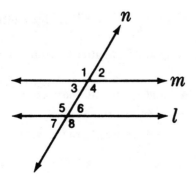

1. *Adjacent angles.* Angles 1 and 2 are adjacent and they form a straight line; therefore, they are supplementary. $\angle 1 + \angle 2 = 180°$.

Likewise: $\angle 2 + \angle 4 = 180°$ $\angle 7 + \angle 8 = 180°$
                $\angle 3 + \angle 4 = 180°$ $\angle 5 + \angle 7 = 180°$
                $\angle 1 + \angle 3 = 180°$ $\angle 6 + \angle 8 = 180°$
                $\angle 5 + \angle 6 = 180°$

2. *Vertical angles.* Angles 1 and 4 are vertical angles; therefore, they are equal. $\angle 1 = \angle 4$.

Likewise: $\angle 2 = \angle 3$
                $\angle 5 = \angle 8$
                $\angle 7 = \angle 6$

3. *Corresponding angles.* If we could physically pick up line *l* and place it on line *m*, the angles that would coincide with each other would be equal in measure. They are called corresponding angles.

Therefore: $\angle 1 = \angle 5$ $\angle 3 = \angle 7$
              $\angle 2 = \angle 6$ $\angle 4 = \angle 8$

4. *Alternate interior and exterior angles.* Alternate angles are on the opposite sides of the transversal. Interior angles are those contained within the parallel lines. Exterior angles are those on the outsides of the parallel lines.

Therefore: $\angle 3$ and $\angle 6$ are alternate interior angles.
              $\angle 3 = \angle 6$

              $\angle 4$ and $\angle 5$ are alternate interior angles.
              $\angle 4 = \angle 5$

              $\angle 2$ and $\angle 7$ are alternate exterior angles.
              $\angle 2 = \angle 7$

              $\angle 1$ and $\angle 8$ are alternate exterior angles.
              $\angle 1 = \angle 8$

5. *Consecutive interior angles.* Consecutive interior angles are on the same side of the transversal.

Therefore: $\angle 3$ and $\angle 5$ are consecutive interior angles.
$\angle 3 + \angle 5 = 180°$
$\angle 4$ and $\angle 6$ are consecutive interior angles.
$\angle 4 + \angle 6 = 180°$

The sum of the measures of each pair of consecutive angles = 180°.

Using all of these facts, if we are given the measure of one of the eight angles, the other angle measures can all be determined. *For example:*

$\angle a + 83° = 180°$

$\left.\begin{array}{l} \angle a = 97° \\ \angle b = 97° \end{array}\right\}$ vertical angles

$\left.\begin{array}{l} \angle c = 83° \\ \angle d = 83° \end{array}\right\}$ alternate interior angles

$\left.\begin{array}{l} \angle e = 97° \\ \angle f = 97° \end{array}\right\}$ vertical angles

$\left.\begin{array}{l} \angle g = 83° \end{array}\right\}$ alternate exterior angles

$\ell \parallel m$

Note that since the lines are parallel, you can *see* which angles are equal, even if you cannot remember the rules.

Practice: Parallel Lines Cut by Transversal Problems

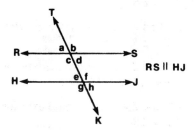

RS ∥ HJ

1. In the figure on the previous page, name all the pairs of the following types of angles.
   (a) vertical angles
   (b) consecutive interior angles
   (c) corresponding angles
   (d) alternate interior angles

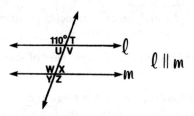

2. In the figure above, find the measure of the angles T, U, V, W, X, Y, and Z.

Answers: Parallel Lines Cut by Transversal Problems

1. (a) Vertical angles are a and d, b and c, e and h, f and g.
   (b) Consecutive interior angles are c and e, d and f.
   (c) Corresponding angles are a and e, c and g, b and f, d and h.
   (d) Alternate interior angles are c and f, d and e.

2. Angles V, W, and Z each have a measure of 110°.
   Angles T, U, X, and Y each have a measure of 70°.

Polygons

- Closed shapes, or figures in a plane, with three or more sides are called *polygons*. (*Poly* means *many*, and *gon* means *sides*. Thus, *polygon* means *many sides*. A plane is often described as a flat surface.) Examples of polygons are:

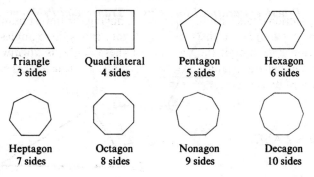

| Triangle | Quadrilateral | Pentagon | Hexagon |
| 3 sides | 4 sides | 5 sides | 6 sides |

| Heptagon | Octagon | Nonagon | Decagon |
| 7 sides | 8 sides | 9 sides | 10 sides |

Regular Polygons

- *Regular* means all sides have the same length and all angles have the same measure. A regular three-sided polygon is the equilateral triangle. A regular four-sided polygon is the square. There are no other special names. Other polygons will just be described as regular, if they are. For example, a regular five-sided polygon is called a regular pentagon. A regular six-sided polygon is called a regular hexagon.

Diagonals of Polygons

- A *diagonal of a polygon* is a line segment that connects one vertex with another vertex and is not itself a side. (AD and BC are both diagonals.)

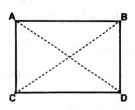

Convex Polygons

- A convex polygon has all diagonals within the figure.

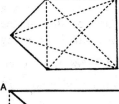

Concave Polygons

- A concave polygon (caves in) has at least one diagonal outside the figure. (AB is the diagonal.)

Triangles

- This section deals with those polygons having the fewest number of sides. A *triangle* is a three-sided polygon. It has three angles in its interior. The sum of the measure of these angles is *always* 180°. The symbol for triangle is △. A triangle is named by the three letters of its vertices.

This is △ABC.

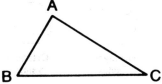

Types of Triangles by Sides

Equilateral Triangles

- A triangle having all three
  sides equal in measure
  is called an
  equilateral triangle.
  Note: by angles, this would
  be called an *equiangular
  triangle*—all angles are equal.

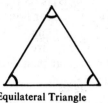

Equilateral Triangle
(or Equiangular Triangle)

Isosceles Triangles

- A triangle having two equal sides
  is called an
  isosceles triangle.

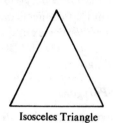

Isosceles Triangle

Scalene Triangles

- A triangle having no equal
  sides is called
  a *scalene triangle.*

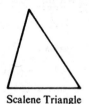

Scalene Triangle

Types of Triangles by Angles

Right Triangles

- A triangle having a right (90°)
  angle in its interior is
  called a *right triangle.*

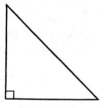

Right Triangle

Obtuse Triangles

● A triangle having an obtuse angle
(greater than 90° but less than
180°) in its interior is called
an *obtuse triangle.*

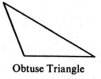

Obtuse Triangle

Acute Triangles

● A triangle having all acute
angles (less than 90°) in
its interior is called an
acute triangle.

Acute Triangle

Examples: Triangle Problems

1. Two angles of a triangle measure 45° and 85°. How many degrees
are there in the third angle?

Answer: The angles of a triangle add up to 180°. The sum of 45° and
85° is 130°. Therefore, the remaining angle must be 180° − 130° =
50°.

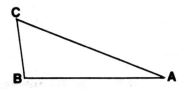

2. In △ABC above, ∠C is three times ∠A and ∠B is five times ∠A.
Find the number of degrees in each angle of the triangle.

Answer: Let y equal the number of degrees in ∠A. Then 3y equals the
number of degrees in ∠C, and 5y equals the number of degrees in ∠B.
Since the sum of the angles of the triangle is 180°, we can say

$$y + 3y + 5y = 180$$

$$\frac{9y}{9} = \frac{180}{9}$$

$$y = 20° (\angle A)$$
$$3y = 60° (\angle C)$$
$$5y = 100° (\angle B)$$

Notice that 20° + 60° + 100° = 180°.

Facts about Triangles

Base and Height

● Every triangle has three *bases* (bottom side) and three *heights* (altitude). Every height is the *perpendicular* (forms right angles) distance from a vertex to its opposite side (the base).

In this diagram of △ABC, BC is the base and AE is the height. AE ⊥ BC.

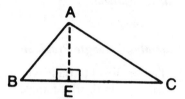

Median

● Every triangle has three medians. The median is the line segment drawn from a vertex to the midpoint of the opposite side.

In this diagram of △ABC, E is the midpoint of BC. Therefore, BE = EC. AE is the median of △ ABC.

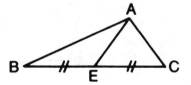

Angles Opposite Equal Sides

● *Angles* that are *opposite from equal sides* are also equal.

In the diagram of △ABC:
∠A is opposite from side BC.
∠B is opposite from side AC.
∠C is opposite from side AB.
Therefore, if side AB = side AC,
then ∠C = ∠B.

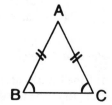

Angles of an Isosceles Triangle

- In an isosceles triangle, since two of the sides are equal, the angles opposite those sides are equal. There are always two equal sides in an isosceles triangle.

Angles of an Equilateral Triangle

- In an equilateral triangle, since all three sides are equal, all three angles will be equal; they are opposite equal sides. If all three angles are equal and their sum is 180°, the following must be true.

$$x + x + x = 180°$$
$$3x = 180°$$
$$x = 60°$$

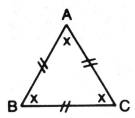

Every angle of an equilateral triangle always has a measure of 60°.

Unequal Angles

- In any triangle, the longest side is always opposite from the largest angle. Likewise, the shortest side is always opposite from the smallest angle. In a right triangle, the longest side will always be opposite from the right angle, as the right angle will be the largest angle in the triangle.

AC is the longest side of right △ABC.

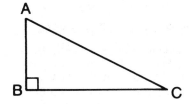

Adding Sides of a Triangle

- The sum of the lengths of any two sides of a triangle must be larger than the length of the third side.

In the diagram of △ABC:
AB + BC > AC
AB + AC > BC
AC + BC > AB

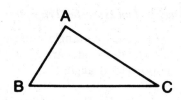

Exterior Angles

● If one side of a triangle is extended, the exterior angle formed by that extension is equal to the sum of the other two interior angles.

In the diagram of △ABC, side
BC is extended to D. ∠ACD is
the exterior angle formed.

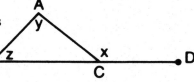

∠x = ∠y + ∠z
x = 82° + 41°
x = 123°

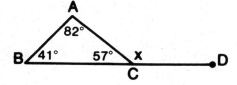

Practice: Triangle Problems

1. Two angles of a triangle measure 50° and 60°. How many degrees are there in the third angle?

2. One of the angles in a right triangle measures 35°. What is the measure of the other acute angle?

3. In an isosceles triangle, one of the angles opposite an equal side is 20°. What is the measure of each of the other two angles?

4. In △ABC, the measure of ∠A is twice the measure of ∠B. The measure of ∠C is three times the measure of ∠B. What is the measure of each of the three angles?

5. In the figure on the right, which side is the largest?

(Note: figure not drawn to scale.)

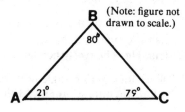

6. Which of the following measures could be the sides of a triangle?

   2, 3, 4   2, 2, 5   4, 3, 7
   3, 4, 5   3, 3, 6   1, 2, 3

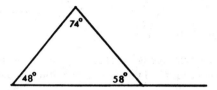

7. What is the measure of the exterior angle of the triangle above?

Answers: Triangle Problems

1. Since the measure of the three angles of a triangle must total 180°, there are 70° in the third angle.

2. Since in a right triangle one of the angles equals 90° and the total of the three angles equals 180°, there are 90° and 55° in the other two angles.

3. Since equal sides of a triangle have their opposite angles equal, the other two angles measure 20° and 140°.

4. Let the smallest angle equal x. Therefore, the larger angle equals 2x, and the largest angle equals 3x. Their total is 6x, which equals 180°.

$$6x = 180°$$
$$x = 30° \; (\angle B)$$
$$2x = 60° \; (\angle A)$$
$$3x = 90° \; (\angle C)$$

5. Side AC is largest, since in any triangle, the largest side is opposite the largest angle.

6. Since the sum of any two sides of a triangle must be greater than its third side, 2, 2, 5; 3, 3, 6; 1, 2, 3; and 4, 3, 7 cannot be sides of a triangle. The two other sets can.

7. Since an exterior angle of a triangle always equals the sum of the other two interior angles, the exterior angle measures 122°.

Pythagorean Theorem

- In any right triangle, the relationship between the lengths of the sides is stated by the *Pythagorean theorem*. The parts of a right triangle are:

∠C is the right angle.

The side opposite the right angle is called the *hypotenuse* (side c). (The hypotenuse will always be the longest side.)

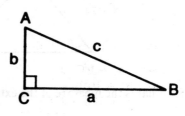

The other two sides are called the *legs* (sides a and b).

The three lengths a, b, and c will always be numbers such that

$$a^2 + b^2 = c^2$$

For example: If a = 3, b = 4, and c = 5,

$$a^2 + b^2 = c^2$$
$$3^2 + 4^2 = 5^2$$
$$9 + 16 = 25$$
$$25 = 25$$

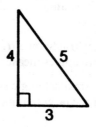

Therefore, 3-4-5 is called a *Pythagorean triple.* There are other values for a, b, and c that will always work. Some are: 5-12-13, and 8-15-17. Any multiple of one of these triples will also work. For example, using the 3-4-5: 6-8-10, 9-12-15, and 15-20-25 will also be Pythagorean triples.

- If perfect squares are known, the lengths of these sides can be determined easily. A knowledge of the use of algebraic equations can also be used to determine the lengths of the sides.

Examples: Pythagorean Theorem Problems

1. Find x in this right triangle.

Answer: $a^2 + b^2 = c^2$
$5^2 + 7^2 = x^2$
$25 + 49 = x^2$
$74 = x^2$
$\sqrt{74} = x$

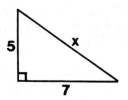

2. Find x in this right triangle.

Answer: $a^2 + b^2 = c^2$
$x^2 + 10^2 = 15^2$
$x^2 + 100 = 225$
$x^2 = 125$
$x = \sqrt{125}$
$= \sqrt{25} \times \sqrt{5}$
$= 5\sqrt{5}$

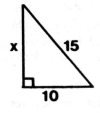

Practice: Pythagorean Theorem Problems

1. Find x in this right triangle.

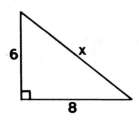

2. Find y in this right triangle.

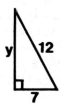

3. If the two legs of a right triangle measure 5 and 9, what is the length of the hypotenuse?

Answers: Pythagorean Theorem Problems

1. $6^2 + 8^2 = x^2$
   $36 + 64 = x^2$
   $100 = x^2$
   $10 = x$

2. $y^2 + 7^2 = 12^2$
   $y^2 + 49 = 144$
   $y^2 = 95$
   $y = \sqrt{95}$

3. $5^2 + 9^2 = x^2$
   $25 + 81 = x^2$
   $106 = x^2$
   $\sqrt{106} = x$

Special Triangles

Isosceles Right Triangles

- An *isosceles right triangle* has the characteristics of both the isosceles and the right triangles. It will have two equal sides, two equal angles, and one right angle. (The right angle cannot be one of the equal angles or the sum will be more than 180°.)

Therefore, in the diagram, $\triangle ABC$ is an isosceles right triangle. And the following must always be true:

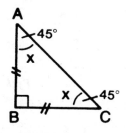

$x + x + 90° = 180°$
$2x = 90°$
$x = 45°$

$\triangle ABC$ is isosceles
$AB = BC$
$\angle A = \angle C$
$\angle B = 90°$

The ratio of the sides of an isosceles right triangle is always 1, 1, $\sqrt{2}$ or x, x, $x\sqrt{2}$.

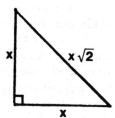

Example: Isosceles Right Triangle Problem

If one of the equal sides of an isosceles right triangle is 3, what is the measure of the other two sides?

Answer: Using the ratio x, x, x $\sqrt{2}$, the measure of the sides must be 3, 3, 3 $\sqrt{2}$.

Practice: Isosceles Right Triangle Problems

1. If one of the equal sides of an isosceles right triangle is 4, what is the measure of the other two sides?

2. If the longest side of an isosceles right triangle is 6 $\sqrt{2}$, what is the measure of each of the two equal sides?

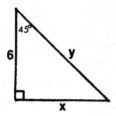

3. What is the measure of sides x and y in the triangle above?

Answers: Isosceles Right Triangle Problems

1. The sides of an isosceles right triangle are always in the ratio x, x, x $\sqrt{2}$. Therefore, the other two sides are 4 and 4 $\sqrt{2}$.

2. The two equal sides each equal 6.

3. Since one angle measures 90° and another measures 45°, the third angle must also measure 45°. 180 − (90 + 45) = 45. Therefore, we have an isosceles right triangle with the ratio of sides x, x, x $\sqrt{2}$. Since one equal side is 6, the other must be 6, and the longest side is then 6 $\sqrt{2}$.

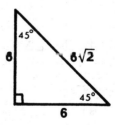

30°-60°-90° Right Triangles

● A *30°-60°-90° right triangle* has a unique ratio of its sides. It is a commonly referred to triangle. The ratio of the sides of a 30°-

60°-90° right triangle are 1, 2, $\sqrt{3}$, or x, 2x, x$\sqrt{3}$, placed as follows.

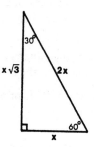

The side opposite 30° is 1 or x.
The side opposite 60° is 3 or x $\sqrt{3}$.
The side opposite 90° is the
longest side (hypotenuse), 2 or 2x.

Examples: 30°-60°-90° Right Triangle Problems

1. If the shortest side of a 30°-60°-90° right triangle is 4, what is the measure of the other sides?

Answer: Using the ratio x, 2x, x $\sqrt{3}$, the measure is 4, 8, 4 $\sqrt{3}$.

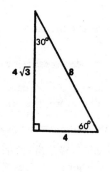

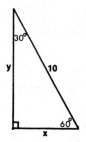

2. In the triangle above, find the remaining sides.

Answer: x is half of the hypotenuse, or 5. The side opposite 60° is x $\sqrt{3}$, or 5 $\sqrt{3}$.

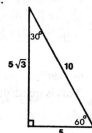

Practice: 30°-60°-90° Right Triangle Problems

1. If the longest side of a 30°-60°-90° right triangle is 12, what are the measures of the other sides?

2. If one angle of a right triangle is 30° and the measure of the shortest side is 7, what is the measure of the remaining two sides?

Answers: 30°-60°-90° Right Triangle Problems

1. Since the ratio of the sides of a 30°-60°-90° right triangle are x, 2x, x $\sqrt{3}$ and the longest side, 2x, is 12, then the shortest side, x, is 6, and the third side is 6 $\sqrt{3}$.

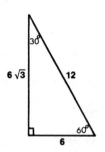

2. If one angle of a right triangle is 30°, then the other angle must be 60°. Hence we have a 30°-60°-90° right triangle. Using the ratio x, 2x, x $\sqrt{3}$, with x equaling 7, 2x = 14 and the third side is 7 $\sqrt{3}$.

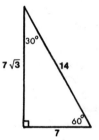

Quadrilaterals

● A polygon having four sides is called a *quadrilateral*. There are four angles in its interior. The sum of the measures of these interior angles will always be 360°. A quadrilateral is named by using the four letters of its vertices.

This is quadrilateral ABCD.

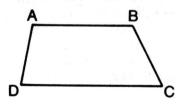

Types of Quadrilaterals

Square

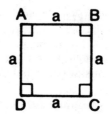

- The *square* has four equal sides and four right angles.
- Its opposite sides are parallel.
- Diagonals of a square are equal and bisect each other.

Rectangle

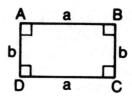

- The *rectangle* has opposite sides equal and parallel and four right angles.
- Diagonals of a rectangle are equal and bisect each other.

Parallelogram

- The *parallelogram* has opposite sides equal and parallel, opposite angles equal, and consecutive angles supplementary. Every parallelogram has a height.
- Diagonals of a parallelogram are not necessarily equal but do bisect each other.

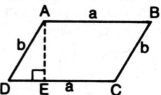

$\angle A = \angle C$
$\angle B = \angle D$
$\angle A + \angle B = 180°$
$\angle A + \angle D = 180°$
$\angle B + \angle C = 180°$
$\angle C + \angle D = 180°$

AE is the height of the parallelogram, AB ∥ DC, and AD ∥ BC.

Rhombus

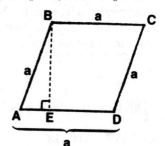

- The *rhombus* is a parallelogram with four equal sides. A rhombus has a height. BE is the height.
- Diagonals of a rhombus are not necessarily equal but do bisect each other.

Trapezoid

- The *trapezoid* has only one pair of parallel sides. A trapezoid has a height. AE is the height. AB ∥ DC.
- The parallel sides are called the *bases*. AB and DC are bases. The nonparallel sides are called the *legs*. AD and BC are legs.
- The *median* of a trapezoid is a line segment that is parallel to the bases and bisects the legs (connects the midpoints of the legs). FG is the median.

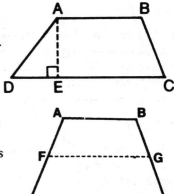

Comparing Quadrilaterals

- A *parallelogram* is a quadrilateral with opposite sides and angles equal.
- A *rectangle* is a parallelogram with right angles.
- A *rhombus* is a parallelogram with equal sides.
- A *square* is a rhombus with right angles.
- A *trapezoid* is a quadrilateral with only one pair of parallel sides.

Practice: Polygon Problems

Identify the following figures.

1.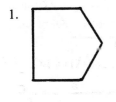

2.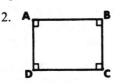
AB ∥ DC   AD ∥ BC

3.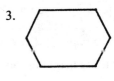

4.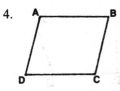
AB ∥ DC   AD ∥ BC

5.

6.
AB = BC = CD = DA

7.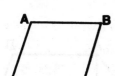
8.
9.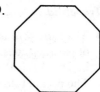

AB = BC = CD = DA

10.

All sides and angles are equal.

True or False:

11. A square must be a parallelogram.
12. A rhombus must be a rectangle.
13. A parallelogram must be a rectangle.

Answers: Polygon Problems

1. Pentagon	6. Square	11. True
2. Rectangle	7. Rhombus	12. False
3. Hexagon	8. Quadrilateral	13. False
4. Parallelogram	9. Octagon	
5. Triangle	10. Regular pentagon	

Sum of the Interior Angles of a Polygon

● The *sum of the interior angles* in any polygon can be determined by using this formula: $(n - 2)180°$, where n is the number of sides in the polygon. *For example:*

The triangle (3 sides):
$$(n - 2)180°$$
$$(3 - 2)180°$$
$$(1)180° = 180°$$

The quadrilateral (4 sides):
$$(n - 2)180°$$
$$(4 - 2)180°$$
$$(2)180° = 360°$$

The pentagon (5 sides)
$$(n - 2)180°$$
$$(5 - 2)180°$$
$$(3)180° = 540°$$

Practice: Sum of the Interior Angles of a Polygon Problems

1. Find the sum of the interior angles of a hexagon.
2. Find the degree measure of an angle of a regular nonagon.

Answers: Sum of the Interior Angles of a Polygon Problems

1. Since a hexagon has six sides, use n = 6.

$$(n - 2)180°$$
$$(6 - 2)180°$$
$$(4)180° = 720°$$

2. A regular nonagon has nine equal angles. First find the total degree measure.

$$(n - 2)180°$$
$$(9 - 2)180°$$
$$(7)180° = 1260°$$

Now to find one angle, divide the total by 9, the number of angles.

$$\frac{1260°}{9} = 140°$$

Perimeter and Area of Polygons

Perimeter of Polygons

- *Perimeter* means the total distance all the way around the outside of any polygon. The perimeter of any polygon can be determined by adding up the lengths of all the sides. The total distance around will be the sum of all sides of the polygon. No special formulas are really necessary, although two are commonly seen.

- Perimeter of a square = 4*s*. (*s* = length of side)

- Perimeter of a parallelogram (rectangle and rhombus) = 2*l* + 2*w* or 2(*l* + *w*). (*l* = length, *w* = width)

Area of Polygons

- *Area* (A) means the amount of space inside the polygon. The formulas for each area are as follows:

- Triangle: $A = \frac{1}{2}bh$

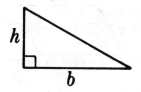 or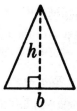

For example:

$A = \frac{1}{2}bh$
$A = \frac{1}{2}(24)(18) = 216$ sq in

- Square or rectangle: $A = lw$

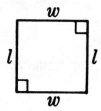 or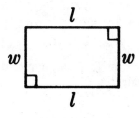

For example:

$A = l(w) = 4(4) = 16$ sq in

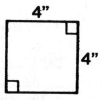

$A = l(w) = 12(5) = 60$ sq in

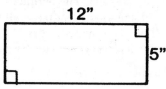

- Parallelogram: $A = bh$

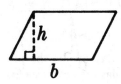

For example:

A = $b(h)$
A = $10(5)$ = 50 sq in

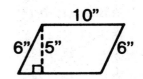

● Trapezoid: A = $\frac{1}{2}(b_1 + b_2)h$

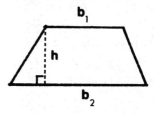

For example:

A = $\frac{1}{2}(b_1 + b_2)h$
A = $\frac{1}{2}(8 + 12)7$
   = $\frac{1}{2}(20)7$ = 70 sq in

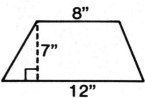

Practice: Perimeter and Area of Polygons Problems

1. P =
   A =

2. P =
   A =

3. P =
   A =

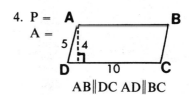

4. P =
   A =

AB∥DC AD∥BC

5. P =
   A =

6. P =
   A =

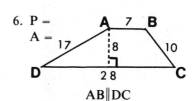

AB∥DC

Answers: Perimeter and Area of Polygons Problems

1. $P = 15 + 13 + 14 = 42$
   $A = \frac{1}{2}bh = \frac{1}{2}(14)(12) = 84$

2. $P = 6 + 8 + 10 = 24$
   $A = \frac{1}{2}bh = \frac{1}{2}(8)(6) = 24$

3. $P = 10 + 10 + 2 + 2 = 24$
   $A + bh = 10(2) = 20$

4. $P = 10 + 10 + 5 + 5 = 30$
   $A = bh = 10(4) = 40$

5. $P = 5 + 5 + 5 + 5 = 20$
   $A = bh = 4(5) = 20$

6. $P = 17 + 7 + 10 + 28 = 62$
   $A = \frac{1}{2}(b_1 + b_2)h = \frac{1}{2}(7 + 28)(8) = 4(35) = 140$

Circles

- In a plane the set of all points equidistant from a given point is called a *circle*. Circles are named by the letter of their center point.
  This is circle M.
  M is the center point, since it is the same distance away from any point on the circle.

Parts of a Circle

Radius

- The *radius* is a line segment whose endpoints lie one at the center of the circle and one on the circle. Also, the length of this segment.

MA is a radius.
MB is a radius.

In any circle, all radii (plural) are the same length.

Diameter

● The *diameter* of a circle is a
  line segment that contains the
  center and has its end points
  on the circle. Also, the length
  of this segment.

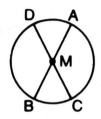

  AB is a diameter.
  CD is a diameter.

  In any circle, all diameters are
  the same length. Each diameter
  equals two radii in length.

Chord

● A *chord* of a circle is a line segment
  whose endpoints lie on the circle.

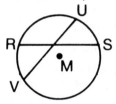

  RS is a chord.
  UV is a chord.

  The diameter is the longest chord
  in any circle.

Arc

● An *arc* is the distance between any two points *on* the circle itself.
  An arc is a piece of the circle. The symbol ⌢ is used to denote an
  arc. It is written on top of the two endpoints that form the arc. Arcs
  are measured in degrees (or radians). There are 360° around the
  circle.

  This is $\overarc{EF}$.
  Minor $\overarc{EF}$ is the shorter arc
  between E and F.
  Major $\overarc{EF}$ is the longer arc
  between E and F.
  When $\overarc{EF}$ is written, the minor arc
  is assumed.

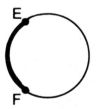

Practice: Parts of a Circle Problems

Match the parts of the following circle with center O.

1. Radius   2. Diameter   3. Chord   4. Name of circle

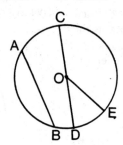

Answers: Parts of a Circle Problems

1. OE   2. CD   3. AB or CD   4. O

Circumference and Area of a Circle

Circumference

- *Circumference* is the distance around the circle. Since the circumference of any circle divided by its diameter yields the same value, the Greek letter π (pi) is used to represent that value. In fractional or decimal form, the commonly used approximations of π are $\pi \simeq$ 3.14 or $\pi \simeq 22/7$. Use either value in your calculations. The formula for circumference is: $C = \pi d$ or $C = 2\pi r$. *For example:*

In circle M, d = 8, since r = 4.
$C = \pi d$
$C = \pi(8)$
$C = 3.14(8)$
$C = 25.12$ inches

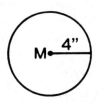

Area

- The *area* of a circle can be determined by: $A = \pi r^2$. *For example:*

In circle M, r = 5, since d = 10.
$A = \pi r^2$
$A = \pi(5^2)$
$A = 3.14(25)$
$A = 78.5$ sq in

Practice: Circumference and Area of a Circle Problems

Find the area and circumference (leave in terms of π) of each circle from the given radius or diameter.

1. A =
   C =

2. A =
   C =

Find the radius.

3. A = 49π sq in   4. C = 60π in

Answers: Circumference and Area of a Circle Problems

1. A = πr^2
   A = $\pi(3)^2$
   A = 9π sq in

   C = $2\pi r$
   C = $2\pi(3)$
   C = 6π in

2. A = πr^2
   A = $\pi(5)^2$
   A = 25π sq in

   C = $2\pi r$ *or* C = πd
   C = $2\pi(5)$ C = 10π in
   C = 10π in

3. A = πr^2
   $49\pi = \pi r^2$
   $49 = r^2$
   7 in = r

4. C = $2\pi r$ *or* C = πd
   $60\pi = 2\pi r$ $60\pi = \pi d$
   $60 = 2r$ $60 = d$
   30 in = r   30 in = r

Angles in a Circle

Central Angles

● *Central angles* are angles formed by any two radii in a circle. The vertex is the center of the circle. A central angle is equal to the measure of its intercepted arc. *For example:*

In circle O, AB = 75°.
Therefore, $\angle AOB = 75°$.
(m $\widehat{AB}$ is sometimes used to denote the measure of arc AB.)

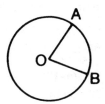

Inscribed Angles

- *Inscribed angles* are angles formed by any two chords of a circle that meet on the circle. (The vertex is on the circle.) An inscribed angle is equal to one-half the measure of its intercepted arc. *For example:*

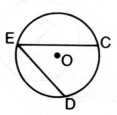

  In circle O, $\overset{\frown}{CD}$ = 90°.
  Therefore, ∠CED = 45°.

- In general as the vertex moves further away from the arc, the angle measure gets smaller. The closer the vertex to the arc, the larger the size of the angle. *For example:*

$$\overset{\frown}{AB} = 80°$$

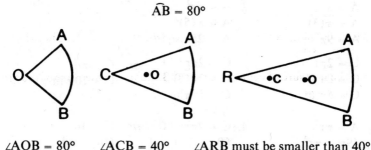

∠AOB = 80°   ∠ACB = 40°   ∠ARB must be smaller than 40°

Practice: Angles in a Circle Problems

1. Find the measure of ∠x in circle A.

2. Find the measure of ∠y in circle A.

3. Find the measure of ∠z.

4. Find the measure of ∠q.

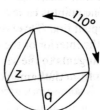

5. Find the measure of $\overset{\frown}{AB}$ of circle Q.

6. Find the measure of ∠AQB in circle Q.

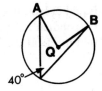

Answers: Angles in a Circle Problems

1. Since ∠x is a central angle, it equals the measure of the arc it intercepts, or 60°.

2. Since ∠y is an inscribed angle, it equals one-half the arc it intercepts, or 30°.

3. ∠z, an inscribed angle, equals one-half 110°, or 55°.

4. ∠q, an inscribed angle, equals one-half 110°, or 55°.

5. $\overset{\frown}{AB}$ is twice the inscribed angle which intercepts $\overset{\frown}{AB}$. Thus, 2 × 40° = 80°.

6. The measure of central angle AQB equals the measure of the arc it intercepts, or 80°.

Concentric Circles

● Circles with the same center are called *concentric circles*.

Tangents to a Circle

● A line that touches a circle at only one point is called a *tangent* or tangent line. This line cannot be in the interior of the circle. Two tangents to the same circle drawn from the same point are:

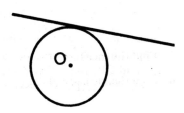

1. Equal in length. (AB = AC)
2. Perpendicular to a radius
   that meets at that point.

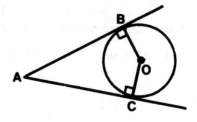

Congruence and Similarity

- Two plane geometric figures are said to be *congruent* if they are
  identical in size and shape. They are said to be *similar* if they have
  the same shape but are not identical in size. *For example:*

All squares are similar.

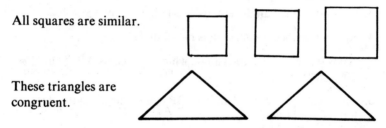

These triangles are
congruent.

A more precise working definition of similar figures follows:
- Similar figures have corresponding angles equal and corresponding
  sides that are in proportion. Corresponding sides are those sides
  which are across from the equal angles.

For example:

Triangles ADE and ACB are similar.
Side DE = 4 and corresponding
side CB = 6. If side AD = 6, then
side AC =

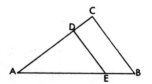

Since the triangles are similar, the corresponding sides are in
proportion. The corresponding sides in this case are AD and AC,
DE and CB, and AE and AB. The corresponding angles are ∠DAE
and ∠CAB, ∠ADE and ∠ACB, and ∠AED and ∠ABC. Because the

proportion of side DE to side CB is 4 to 6 or ⁴⁄₆, which reduces to ⅔, the same ratio holds for all corresponding sides. Therefore,

$$\frac{AD}{AC} = \frac{DE}{CB} \quad \text{or} \quad \frac{AD}{AC} = \frac{2}{3}$$

and since AD = 6, $\dfrac{6}{AC} = \dfrac{2}{3}$

Cross multiplying gives

$$6(3) = 2(AC)$$
$$18 = 2(AC)$$

Divide each side by 2.

$$\frac{18}{2} = \frac{2(AC)}{2}$$

$$9 = AC \quad \text{or} \quad AC = 9$$

Please note that this question could have been introduced as follows:

In the triangle shown, DE ∥ CB. If AD = 4, CB = 6, and AD = 6, . what is the length of AC?

A line parallel to one side within a triangle produces similar triangles. Therefore, triangles ADE and ACB are similar and the problem can be solved as above.

Practice: Similarity Problems

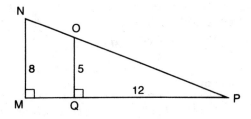

1. In the figure above, what is the length of PM?

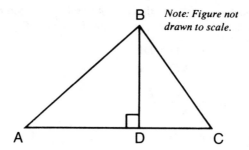

Note: Figure not drawn to scale.

2. In the figure above, triangles ADB and BDC are similar. ∠DAB = ∠DBC, and ∠ABD = ∠BCD. What is the length of DC?

Answers: Similarity Problems

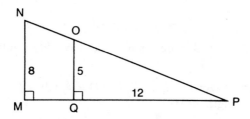

1. In the figure above, since MN and OQ are both perpendicular to AM, they are parallel to each other. Therefore, triangles OPQ and NPM are similar. Since OQ to NM is in the ratio 5 to 8, you can set up the following proportion to find PM.

$$\frac{OQ}{NM} = \frac{PQ}{PM} \quad \text{or} \quad \frac{5}{8} = \frac{12}{PM}$$

Cross multiplying gives

$$5(PM) = 8(12)$$
$$5(PM) = 96$$

Divide each side by 5.

$$\frac{5(PM)}{5} = \frac{96}{5}$$

$$PM = 19\tfrac{1}{5} \quad \text{or} \quad 19.2$$

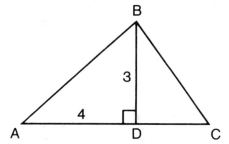

2. In the figure above, since triangles ADB and BDC are similar, the
   only real difficulty is matching the corresponding parts. Since
   ∠BAD = ∠CBD, they are corresponding and sides across from
   them, BD and DC, are corresponding. Since ∠DCB = ∠DBA, AD
   and BD are corresponding. (Note that BD is used twice, as it is
   part of both triangles.) Because BD to AD is in the ratio 3 to 4, you
   can set up the following proportion and solve accordingly.

$$\frac{BD}{AD} = \frac{DC}{BD} \quad \text{or} \quad \frac{3}{4} = \frac{DC}{3}$$

$$3(3) = 4(DC)$$

$$9 = 4(DC)$$

$$\frac{9}{4} = \frac{4(DC)}{4}$$

$$2\tfrac{1}{4} = DC \quad \text{or} \quad DC = 2\tfrac{1}{4} \text{ or } 2.25$$

Volumes of Solid Figures

- Three of the most common solid geometric figures are the cube, the
  rectangular solid, and the cylinder. Each of these figures may be
  thought of as the three-dimensional extensions of three flat two-
  dimensional figures, namely the square, the rectangle, and the
  circle.
- The *volume* of a solid is the number of cubic units of space the
  figure contains. Volume is always labeled *cubic* units. The formula
  for the volume of each shape is different, but in general, it is the
  area of the base times the height.

Volume of a Cube

- The formula for the
  volume of a cube is
  $V = s \times s \times s = s^3$

Volume of a Rectangular Solid

- The formula for the volume
  of a rectangular solid is
  $V = (lw)(h) = lwh$

Volume of a Right Circular Cylinder (Circular Bases)

- The formula for the volume of
  a right circular cylinder
  (circular bases) is
  $V = (\pi r^2)h = \pi r^2 h$

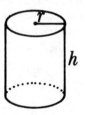

Practice: Volumes of Solid Figures Problems

Find the volumes of the solid figures below whose dimensions are indicated.

1. Rectangular Solid

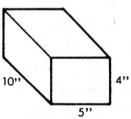

2. Cube

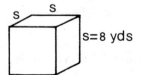

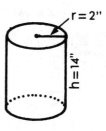

3. Cylinder

Answers: Volumes of Solid Figures Problems

1. $V = lwh = (10)(5)(4) = 200$ cu in

2. $V = s^3 = 8 \times 8 \times 8 = 512$ cu yd

3. $V = \pi r^2 h = \dfrac{22}{\cancel{14}} \times \dfrac{2}{1} \times \dfrac{2}{1} \times \dfrac{\overset{2}{\cancel{14}}}{1} = 22(8) = 176$ cu in

Surface Areas of Solid Figures

Surface Area of a Rectangular Solid

● To find the *surface area of a rectangular solid,* proceed as follows.

Area of side 1 = 3 × 4 = 12 sq in
Area of side 2 = 5 × 3 = 15 sq in
Area of side 3 = 5 × 4 = 20 sq in

Since there are two of each of these sides:

Surface Area = 2(12) + 2(15) + 2(20)
            = 24 + 30 + 40
            = 94 sq in

Surface Area of a Right Circular Cylinder

- To determine the *surface area of a right circular cylinder*, it is best envisioned "rolled out" onto a flat surface as below.

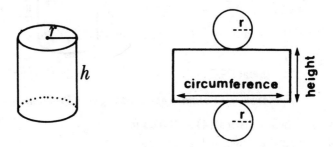

Now find the area of each individual piece. The area of each circle equals πr^2. Note that the length of the rectangle equals the circumference of the circle. The rectangle's area equals circumference times height. Adding the three parts gives the surface area of the cylinder: *For example:*

Find the surface area
of a cylinder with radius 5′
and height 12′.

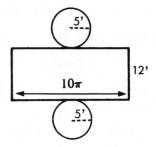

The area of the top circle $= \pi(r^2) = \pi(5^2) = 25\pi$.
The area of the bottom circle is the same, 25π.
The length of the rectangle is the circumference of the circle, or $2\pi r = 2\pi(5) = 10\pi$.
Therefore the area of the rectangle equals its height times $10\pi = 12 \times 10\pi = 120\pi$.
Totaling all the pieces gives $25\pi + 25\pi + 120\pi = 170\pi$.

Practice: Volumes and Surface Areas of Solids Problems

1. What is the volume of a cube whose side is $5\frac{1}{2}''$?

2. If a rectangular solid has a length of 4 inches, a width of 3 inches, and a height of 2 feet, find its volume.

3. Given that a cylinder's height is 42″ and its radius is 3″, determine its volume.

4. Find the surface area of a rectangular solid that measures 4″ by 7″ by 6″.

5. Find the surface area of a right regular cylinder that has a height of 20″ and a radius of 4″.

Answers: Volumes and Surface Areas of Solids Problems

1. $166\frac{3}{8}$ cu in

   $V = s^3 = 5\frac{1}{2} \times 5\frac{1}{2} \times 5\frac{1}{2} = \frac{11}{2} \times \frac{11}{2} \times \frac{11}{2} = \frac{1331}{8} = 166\frac{3}{8}$ cu in

2. 288 cu in

   $V = l \times w \times h = 4 \times 3 \times 24 = 288$ cu in

   Note: The 2 feet had to be converted to 24 inches so that all dimensions would be expressed in the same units.

3. 1,188 cu in.

   $V = \pi r^2 h = \dfrac{22}{\cancel{7}} \times \dfrac{3}{1} \times \dfrac{3}{1} \times \dfrac{\overset{6}{\cancel{42}}}{1} = 1,188$ cu in

4. 188 sq in.

   Area of side 1 = 4 × 6 = 24 sq in
   Area of side 2 = 6 × 7 = 42 sq in
   Area of side 3 = 4 × 7 = 28 sq in
   Surface area = 2(24) + 2(42) + 2(28)
   = 48 + 84 + 56
   = 188 sq in

5. $192\,\pi$ sq in.

Area of top circle $= \pi r^2 = 16\pi$ sq in
Area of bottom circle $= \pi r^2 = 16\pi$ sq in
Area of rectangle $= 20 \times$ circumference
$\qquad\qquad\quad = 20 \times 2\pi r$
$\qquad\qquad\quad = 20 \times 2\pi(4)$
$\qquad\qquad\quad = 20 \times 8\pi$ sq in
$\qquad\qquad\quad = 160\pi$ sq in

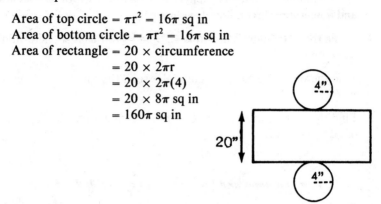

Adding all the pieces, total surface area is 192π sq in.

Geometry Formulas That You Should Be Familiar With

TRIANGLE
Perimeter $= s_1 + s_2 + s_3$
Area $= \frac{1}{2}bh$

SQUARE
Perimeter $= 4s$
Area $= s \cdot s$, or s^2

RECTANGLE
Perimeter $= 2(l + w)$, or $2l + 2w$
Area $= bh$, or lw

PARALLELOGRAM
Perimeter $= 2(l + w)$, or $2l + 2w$
Area $= bh$

TRAPEZOID
Perimeter $= b_1 + b_2 + s_1 + s_2$
Area $= \frac{1}{2}h(b_1 + b_2)$, or $h\left(\dfrac{b_1 + b_2}{2}\right)$

CIRCLE
Circumference $= 2\pi r$, or πd
Area $= \pi r^2$

PYTHAGOREAN THEOREM
(for right triangles)
$a^2 + b^2 = c^2$
The sum of the squares of the legs of a right triangle equals the square of the hypotenuse.

CUBE
Volume $= s \cdot s \cdot s$, or s^3
Surface area $= s \cdot s \cdot 6$

RECTANGULAR PRISM
Volume $= l \cdot w \cdot h$
Surface area $= 2(lw) + 2(lh) + 2(wh)$

RIGHT CIRCULAR CYLINDER
Volume $= \pi r^2 h$
Surface area $= 2(\pi r^2) + h(2\pi r)$

GEOMETRY REVIEW TEST

Questions

1. The study of shapes and figures in two dimensions is called _____ .

2. The study of shapes and figures in three dimensions is called _____ .

3. An angle is formed by two rays that have the same endpoint; that endpoint is called the _____ .

4. Which of the following name the same angle in the triangle? _____ .

    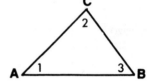

    (A) ∠A, ∠ACB, and ∠CAB
    (B) ∠ACB and ∠CAB
    (C) ∠A, ∠1, ∠B
    (D) ∠A, ∠CAB, and ∠1
    (E) ∠ACB, ∠1, and ∠B

5. A right angle measures _____ .

6. An acute angle measures _____ .

7. An obtuse angle measures _____ .

8. A straight angle measures _____ .

9. Two angles next to each other, sharing a common side and vertex, are called _____ .

10. In the diagram _____ .

    (A) ∠1 = ∠3
    (B) ∠1 = ∠2 and ∠3 = ∠4
    (C) ∠2 = ∠4 and ∠2 = ∠3
    (D) ∠1 = ∠2 and ∠3 = ∠2
    (E) ∠1 = ∠4 and ∠2 = ∠3

    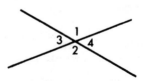

11. Two angles the sum of whose measures is 90° are said to be _____ to each other.

12. Two angles the sum of whose measures is 180° are said to be _____ to each other.

13. An angle bisector _____.

14. A _____ is often described as the shortest distance between two points; it continues forever in both directions.

15. A part of a line with two endpoints is called _____.

16. A part of a line that continues in one direction and has only one endpoint is called _____.

17. If two lines meet at a point they are called _____ lines.

18. Two lines that meet at right angles are _____ to each other.

19. Two or more lines that remain the same distance apart at all times are called _____.

20. In the diagram _____.

    I. $\angle 1 = \angle 2 = \angle 4 = \angle 5$
    II. $\angle 1 = \angle 4 = \angle 5 = \angle 8$
    III. $\angle 2 = \angle 3 = \angle 6 = \angle 7$
    IV. $\angle 5 = \angle 8$ only
    V. $\angle 5 = \angle 6 = \angle 8$

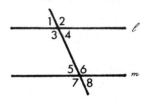

(A) I and V   (D) II and III
(B) II   (E) II and IV
(C) III

For questions 21 through 28, name the following.

21. A three-sided polygon. _____

22. A four-sided polygon. _____

23. A five-sided polygon. _____

24. A six-sided polygon. _____

25. A seven-sided polygon. _____

26. An eight-sided polygon. _____

27. A nine-sided polygon. _____

28. A ten-sided polygon. _____

29. If all sides and angles have the same measure, the polygon is called _____.

30. In a polygon, a line segment that connects one vertex to another but is not the side of the polygon is called a _____.

31. The polygon at the right is called a _____ polygon.

32. The sum of the measures of the angles of any triangle is _____.

33. If all sides of a triangle are equal, the triangle is _____.

34. A triangle that has two equal sides is called _____.

35. A triangle whose three sides are of different lengths is called _____.

36. A triangle having a 90° angle is called _____.

37. A triangle containing an angle greater than 90° is called _____.

38. If all angles in a triangle are less than 90°, then the triangle is called _____.

39. In a triangle, a line segment drawn from a vertex to the midpoint of the opposite side is called _____.

40. If two angles of a triangle measure 43° each, what is the measure of the third angle? _____.

41. The longest side of triangle ABC is _____.

42. A triangle can have sides of length 2, 2, and 5. True or false?

43. Find the measure of angle z in the triangle shown right.
    ∠z = _____

44. Find the length of side c
   in right triangle ABC.
   c = _____

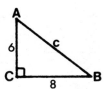

45. Find the length of side r
   in right triangle QRS.
   r = _____

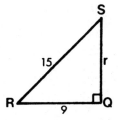

46. Find x, y, and z in
   the triangle shown right.
   x = _____
   y = _____
   z = _____

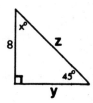

47. Find a, b, and c in the
   triangle shown right.
   a = _____
   b = _____
   c = _____

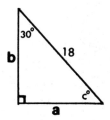

For questions 48 through 51, name the following figures.

48. _____

AB ∥ DC
AD ∥ BC

49. _____

AB = BC = DC = AD

50. _____

AB ∥ DC
AD ∥ BC

51. _____

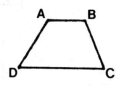

AB ∥ DC

52. What is the sum of the measures of the interior angles of a heptagon? _____

53. Find the area of triangle ABC.

    area = _____

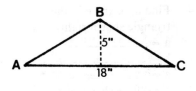

54. Find the area and perimeter of square ABCD.

    area = _____
    perimeter = _____

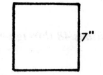

55. Find the area and perimeter of rectangle ABCD.

    area = _____
    perimeter = _____

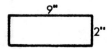

56. Find the area of
    parallelogram ABCD.
    area = _____

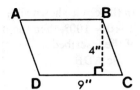

57. Find the area of
    trapezoid ABCD.
    area = _____

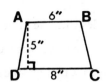

In the circle below

58. OA is called a
    _____ of circle O.

59. BC is called a
    _____ of circle O.

60. DC is called a
    _____ of circle O.

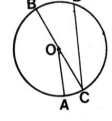

61. Find the area and
    circumference of
    circle A (in terms
    of π).
    area = _____
    circumference = _____

62. In the circle shown below,
    if $\overset{\frown}{AB} = 50°$, then the measure of the central
    angle AOB = _____.

63. In the circle shown right, if $\overset{\frown}{AB}$ = 100°, then the measure of the inscribed angle ADB = _____.

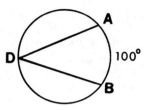

64. Circles with the same center are called _____.

65. A line that touches a circle at one point is called _____.

66. Polygons that are the same shape, but different in size are called _____.

67. Polygons that are exactly the same in shape and size are called _____.

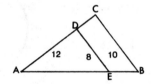

68. In the triangle shown above, DE ∥ CB. What is the length of AC?

For questions 69 through 71, find the volumes and surface areas of the figures below.

69. volume = _____
    surface area = _____

cube

70. volume = _____
    surface area = _____

rectangular solid

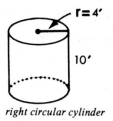

right circular cylinder

71. volume = _____
    surface area = _____

Answers

Page numbers following each answer refer to the review section applicable to this problem type.

1. plane geometry (p. 288)
2. solid geometry (p. 288)
3. vertex (p. 288)
4. (D) ∠A, ∠CAB, ∠1 (p. 288)
5. 90° (p. 289)
6. less than 90° (p. 289)
7. greater than 90° but less than 180° (p. 289)
8. 180° (p. 289)
9. adjacent angles (p. 290)
10. (B) ∠1 = ∠2 and ∠3 = ∠4 (p. 291)
11. complementary (p. 291)
12. supplementary (p. 291)
13. divides an angle into two angles of equal measure (p. 292)
14. a line (p. 293)
15. a line segment (p. 293)
16. a ray (p. 294)
17. intersecting (p. 294)
18. perpendicular (p. 295)
19. parallel lines (p. 295)
20. (D) II and III (p. 295)
21. triangle (p. 299)
22. quadrilateral (p. 299)
23. pentagon (p. 299)
24. hexagon (p. 299)
25. heptagon (p. 299)
26. ootagon (p. 299)
27. nonagon (p. 299)
28. decagon (p. 299)
29. regular (p. 299)
30. diagonal (p. 299)
31. concave (p. 299)
32. 180° (p. 299)

33. equilateral (p. 300)

34. isosceles (p. 300)

35. scalene (p. 300)

36. a right triangle (p. 300)

37. an obtuse triangle (p. 301)

38. an acute triangle (p. 301)

39. a median (p. 302)

40. 94° (p. 305)

41. AB (p. 303)

42. false (p. 303)

43. 120° (p. 304)

44. 10 (p. 308)

45. 12 (p. 308)

46. $x = 45°, y = 8, z = 8\sqrt{2}$
    (p. 308)

47. $a = 9, b = 9\sqrt{3}, c = 60°$
    (p. 309)

48. rectangle (p. 312)

49. square (p. 312)

50. parallelogram (p. 312)

51. trapezoid (p. 313)

52. 900° (p. 314)

53. 45 sq in (p. 315)

54. area = 49 sq in
    perimeter = 28 in (p. 315)

55. area = 18 sq in
    perimeter = 22 in (p. 315)

56. 36 sq in (p. 315)

57. 35 sq in (p. 315)

58. radius (p. 318)

59. diameter (could be called
    a chord) (p. 319)

60. chord (p. 319)

61. area = 25π sq in
    circumference = 10π in (p. 320)

62. 50° (p. 321)

63. 50° (p. 322)

64. concentric circles (p. 323)

65. a tangent line (p. 323)

66. similar (p. 324)

67. congruent (p. 324)

68. AC = 15 (p. 324)

69. volume = 216 cu ft (p. 324)
    surface area = 216 sq ft
    (p. 329)

70. volume = 60 cu ft (p. 328)
    surface area = 94 sq ft
    (p. 329)

71. volume = 160π cu ft (p. 328)
    surface area = 112π sq ft
    (p. 329)

GEOMETRY GLOSSARY OF TERMS

ACUTE ANGLE: An angle whose measure is less than 90°.

ACUTE TRIANGLE: A triangle containing all acute angles.

ADJACENT ANGLES: Angles that share a common side and a common vertex.

ANGLE: Formed by two rays with a common endpoint.

ARC: The set of points on a circle that lie in the interior of a central angle.

AREA: The space within a shape; measured in square units.

BISECTS: Divides into two equal parts.

CENTRAL ANGLE: An angle whose vertex is the center of the circle. The measure of a central angle is equal to the measure of its arc.

CHORD: A line segment joining any two points on a circle.

CIRCLE: In a plane, the set of points all equidistant from a given point.

CIRCUMFERENCE: The distance around a circle; equals two times π times the radius or π times the diameter ($C = 2\pi r$ or πd).

COMPLEMENTARY ANGLES: Two angles the sum of whose measures is 90°.

CONCAVE POLYGON: A polygon which contains at least one diagonal outside the figure.

CONCENTRIC CIRCLES: Circles with the same center.

CONGRUENT: Exactly alike. Identical in shape and size.

CONSECUTIVE: Next to each other.

CONVEX POLYGON: A polygon in which all diagonals lie within the figure.

CORRESPONDING: In the same position. Coinciding

CUBE: A six-sided solid. All sides are equal squares and all edges are equal.

DECAGON: A plane closed figure with ten sides and ten angles.

DEGREE: A unit of measurement of an angle.

DIAGONAL OF A POLYGON: A line segment connecting one vertex to another vertex, and not a side of the polygon.

DIAMETER: A line segment that contains the center and has its endpoints on the circle. Also, the length of this segment. (A chord through the center of the circle.)

EQUILATERAL TRIANGLE: A triangle in which all three angles are equal in measure and all three sides have the same length.

EXTERIOR ANGLE: An angle formed outside the polygon by extending one side. In a triangle, the measure of an exterior angle equals the sum of the measures of the two remote interior angles.

HEIGHT: Altitude. From the highest point, a perpendicular drawn to the base.

HEPTAGON: A plane closed figure with seven sides and seven angles.

HEXAGON: A plane closed figure with six sides and six angles.

HYPOTENUSE: In a right triangle, the side opposite the 90° angle.

INSCRIBED ANGLE: In a circle, an angle formed by two chords. Its vertex is on the circle. The measure of an inscribed angle equals one-half the measure of its arc.

INTERIOR ANGLES: Angles formed inside the shape or within two parallel lines.

INTERSECTING LINES: Lines that meet at a point.

ISOSCELES RIGHT TRIANGLE: A triangle having two equal sides, two equal angles, and one 90° angle. Its sides are always in the ratio 1, 1, $\sqrt{2}$.

ISOSCELES TRIANGLE: A triangle having two equal sides (and thus two equal angles across from those sides).

LEGS: In a right triangle, the two sides forming the 90° angle. In a trapezoid, the nonparallel sides.

LINE SEGMENT: A part of a line; has two endpoints.

MEDIAN: In a triangle, a line segment drawn from a vertex to the midpoint of the opposite side.

MEDIAN: In a trapezoid, a line segment parallel to the bases and bisecting the legs.

MIDPOINT: The halfway point of a line segment, equidistant from each endpoint.

MINUTE: A subdivision of an angle, one-sixtieth of a degree.:

NONAGON: A plane closed figure with nine sides and nine angles.

OBTUSE ANGLE: An angle greter than 90° but less than 180°.

OBTUSE TRIANGLE: A triangle containing an obtuse angle.

OCTAGON: A plane closed figure with eight sides and eight angles.

PARALLEL LINES: Two or more lines, always the same distance apart. Parallel lines never meet.

PARALLELOGRAM: A four-sided plane closed figure having opposite sides equal and parallel. (Opposite angles are equal, and consecutive angles are supplementary.)

PENTAGON: A five-sided plane closed figure. The sum of its five angles is 540°.

PERIMETER: The total distance around the outside of any polygon. The total length of all the sides.

PERPENDICULAR LINES: Two lines that intersect at right angles.

PI (π): A constant used in determining a circle's area or circumference. Equals approximately 3.14 or $^{22}/_7$.

PLANE: Often described as a flat surface.

PLANE FIGURE: Shape having only length and width (two dimensional).

PLANE GEOMETRY: The study of shapes and figures in two dimensions.

POINT: A basic element of geometry, a location. If two lines intersect, they do so at a point.

POLYGON: Many-sided plane closed figure. Triangle, quadrilateral, pentagon, etc.

PRISM: A three-dimensional shape bounded by congruent parallel faces and a set of parallelograms formed by joining the corresponding vertices of the bases.

PYTHAGOREAN THEOREM: A theorem which applies to right triangles. The sum of the squares of a right triangle's two legs equals the square of the hypotenuse ($a^2 + b^2 = c^2$).

QUADRILATERAL: A four-sided plane closed figure. The sum of its four angles equals 360°.

RADII: Plural of *radius*.

RADIUS: A line segment whose endpoints lie one at the center of a circle and one on the circle. Also, the length of this segment.

RAY: A half-line. Continues forever in one direction. Has one endpoint.

RECTANGLE: A four-sided plane closed figure having opposite sides equal and parallel and four right angles.

REGULAR POLYGON: A polygon in which sides and angles are all equal. For example, a regular pentagon has five equal angles and five equal sides.

RHOMBUS: A parallelogram with four equal sides.

RIGHT ANGLE: An angle whose measure is equal to 90°.

RIGHT CIRCULAR CYLINDER: A solid shaped like a can. Base meets side at a right angle.

RIGHT TRIANGLE: A triangle containing a 90° angle.

SCALENE TRIANGLE: A triangle having none of its sides equal (or angles equal).

SIMILAR: Having the same shape but not the same size, in proportion.

SOLID GEOMETRY: The study of shapes and figures in three dimensions: length, width, and thickness.

SQUARE: A four-sided plane closed figure having equal sides and four right angles. Its opposite sides are parallel.

STRAIGHT ANGLE: An angle equal to 180°. Often called a line.

STRAIGHT LINE: Often described as the shortest distance between two points. Continues forever in both directions. (*Line* means *straight line*.)

SUPPLEMENTARY ANGLES: Two angles the sum of whose measures is 180°.

SURFACE AREA: The total surface of all sides of a solid, or the total area of faces.

TANGENT TO A CIRCLE: A line, line segment, or ray that touches a circle at one point (cannot go within the circle).

TRANSVERSAL: A line crossing two or more parallel or nonparallel lines in a plane.

TRAPEZOID: A four-sided plane closed figure with only one pair of parallel sides, called bases.

TRIANGLE: A three-sided plane closed figure. Contains three angles the sum of whose measures is 180°.

VERTEX: The point at which two rays meet and form an angle, or the point at which two sides meet in a polygon.

VERTICAL ANGLES: The opposite angles formed by the intersection of two lines. Vertical angles are equal in measure.

VERTICES: Plural of *vertex*.

VOLUME: Capacity to hold, measured in cubic units. Volume of rectangular prism = length times width times height.

WORD PROBLEMS

WORD PROBLEMS DIAGNOSTIC TEST

Questions

1. If a plane travels 980 miles in four hours, what is its average speed in miles per hour?

2. In a senior class of 800, only 240 decide to attend the senior prom. What percentage of the senior class attend the senior prom?

3. A suit that originally sold for $120 is reduced 30%. What is the new sale price?

4. What is the simple interest on $2,500 invested at 8% annual rate over three years?

5. A map's key shows that $1'' = 25$ miles. How many inches apart on the map will two cities be if they are exactly 12 miles apart?

6. A plane flies from Los Angeles to Denver, a distance of 1,120 miles, at 280 miles per hour. A train from Denver to Los Angeles travels at a rate of 70 miles per hour. If a passenger took the plane to Denver and then returned to Los Angeles on the train, how long did the entire trip take?

7. In order to pass an examination, a student must answer exactly thirty questions correctly to obtain the minimum passing grade of 60%. How many questions are on the examination?

8. Last year, Tom's income was $18,000. This year, he was given a new position with the company with a salary of $24,000. What was the percent increase in Tom's salary?

9. If one number is four times as large as another number and the smaller number is decreased by two, the result is fourteen less than the larger number. What are the two numbers?

10. Fred is six years older than Sylvia. In two years, the sum of their ages will be eighteen. How old is Sylvia now?

11. The length of a rectangle is three more than the width. If the perimeter of the rectangle is twenty-six inches, what are the measures of length and width?

Answers

Page numbers following each answer refer to the review section applicable to this problem type.

1. 245 mph (p. 356)
2. 30% (p. 359)
3. $84 (p. 359)
4. $600 (p. 351)
5. .48 inches (p. 353)
6. 20 hours (p. 356)

7. 50 questions (p. 359)
8. 33⅓% (p. 364)
9. 4 and 16 (p. 366)
10. 4 years old (p. 369)
11. 8 inches and 5 inches (p. 373)

WORD PROBLEMS REVIEW

Word problems are often the nemesis of even the best math student. For many, the difficulty is not the computation. The problems stem from what is given and what is being asked.

Solving Technique

There are many types of word problems involving arithmetic, algebra, geometry, and combinations of each with various twists. It is most important to have a systematic technique for solving word problems. Here is such a technique.

1. First, *identify what is being asked.* What are you ultimately trying to find? How far a car has traveled? How fast a plane flies? How many items can be purchased? Whatever it is, find it and then *circle it.* This helps insure that you are solving for what is being asked.

2. Next, *underline and pull out information you are given* in the problem. Draw a picture if you can. This helps you know what you have and will point you to a relationship or equation. Note any key words in the problem (see "Key Words and Phrases" following).

3. If you can, *set up an equation or some straightforward system* with the given information.

4. *Is all the given information necessary to solve the problem?* Occasionally you may be given more than enough information to solve a problem. *Choose what you need* and don't spend needless energy on irrelevant information.

5. *Carefully solve the equation or work the necessary computation.* Be sure you are working in the same units (for example, you may have to change feet into inches, pounds into ounces, etc., in order to keep everything consistent).

6. *Did you answer the question?* One of the most common errors in answering word problems is the failure to answer what was actually being asked.

7. And finally, *is your answer reasonable?* Check to make sure that an error in computation or a mistake in setting up your equation did not give you a ridiculous answer.

Key Words and Phrases

In working with word problems, there are some words or phrases that give clues as to how the problem should be solved. The most common words or phrases are as follows.

Add

Sum—as in *the sum of 2, 4, and 6* . . .
Total—as in *the total of the first six payments* . . .
Addition—as in *a recipe calls for the addition of five pints* . . .
Plus—as in *three liters plus two liters* . . .
Increase—as in *her pay was increased by $15* . . .
More than—as in *this week the enrollment was eight more than last week*
Added to—as in *if you added $3 to the cost* . . .
Successive—as in *the total of six successive payments* . . .

Subtract

Difference—as in *what is the difference between* . . .
Fewer—as in *there were fifteen fewer men than women* . . .
Remainder—as in *how many are left* or *what quantity remains* . . .
Less—as in *a number is five less than another number* . . .
Reduced—as in *the budget was reduced by $5,000* . . .
Decreased—as in *if he decreased the speed of his car by ten miles per hour* . . .
Minus—as in *some number minus 9 is* . . .

Multiply

Product—as in *the product of 8 and 5 is* . . .
Of—as in *one-half of the group* . . .
Times—as in *five times as many girls as boys* . . .
At—as in *the cost of ten yards of material at 70¢ a yard is* . . .
Total—as in *if you spend $15 a week on gas, what is the total for a three week period* . . .
Twice—as in *twice the value of some number* . . .

Divide

Quotient—as in *the final quotient is* . . .
Divided by—as in *some number divided by 12 is* . . .

Divided into—as in *the group was divided into* . . .
Ratio—as in *what is the ratio of* . . .
Half—as in *half the profits are* . . . (dividing by 2)

As you work a variety of word problem types, you will discover more "clue" words.

A Final Reminder:

Be sensitive to what each of these questions is asking. What time? How many? How much? How far? How old? What length? What is the ratio?

Simple Interest

Example:

How much simple interest will an account earn in five years if $500 is invested at 8% interest per year?

First circle what you must find—*interest*. Now use the equation.

> *Interest* = *principal* times *rate* times *time*
> I = prt

Simply plug into the equation.

> I = $500(.08)5
> I = $200

Note that both rate and time are in yearly terms (annual rate; years).

Practice: Simple Interest Problems

1. What is the simple interest on $5,000 invested at 6% annual rate over four years.

2. What is the simple interest on a loan of $10,000 at a 6½% rate over five years?

3. What is the simple interest on $4,000 at a 4% semiannual rate over three years?

Answers: Simple Interest Problems

1. What is the simple interest on $5,000 invested at 6% annual rate over four years?

First circle what you must find—*simple interest*. Now using the information given in the problem, plug into the equation.

$$I = prt$$
$$I = \$5,000(.06)4$$
$$I = \$300(4)$$
$$I = \$1,200$$

Interest was therefore $1,200.

2. What is the simple interest on a loan of $10,000 at a 6½% rate over five years.

First circle what you must find—*simple interest*. Now using the information given in the problem, plug into the equation.

$$I = prt$$
$$I = \$10,000(.065)5$$
$$I = \$650(5) = \$3,250$$

Therefore simple interest is $3,250.

3. What is the simple interest on $4,000 at a 4% semiannual rate over three years?

First circle what you must find in the problem—*simple interest*. However, note that the 4% figure is a *semiannual* rate. Therefore, before plugging into the I = prt equation, you should change the rate to an annual rate. Since semiannual means every half year, the annual rate would be twice 4%, or 8%, annual rate. Thus,

$$I = prt$$
$$I = \$4,000(.08)3$$
$$I = \$320(3)$$
$$I = \$960$$

The simple interest is thus $960.

Ratio and Proportion

Examples:

1. If Arnold can type 600 pages of manuscript in twenty-one days, how many days will it take him to type 230 pages if he works at the same rate?

First circle what you're asked to find—*how many days.* One simple way to work this problem is to set up a "framework" (proportion) using the categories given in the equation. Here the categories are *pages* and *days.* Therefore a framework may be

$$\frac{\text{Pages}}{\text{Days}} = \frac{\text{Pages}}{\text{Days}}$$

Note that you also may have used

$$\frac{\text{Days}}{\text{Pages}} = \frac{\text{Days}}{\text{Pages}}$$

The answer will still be the same. Now simply plug into the equation for each instance.

$$\frac{600}{21} = \frac{230}{x}$$

Cross multiplying

$$600x = 21(230)$$
$$600x = 4,830$$

$$\frac{600x}{600} = \frac{4,830}{600}$$

$$x = 8\frac{1}{20}$$

Therefore it will take $8\frac{1}{20}$ days to type 230 pages. (Some of you may have simplified the original proportion before solving.)

2. Harmon's new sportscar averages 35 miles per each gallon of gasoline. Assuming Harmon is able to maintain his average miles per gallon, how far can he drive on 12 gallons of gas?

Sometimes you will be able to solve the problem intuitively. Since Harmon's sportscar averages 35 miles for each gallon of gas, on 12 gallons he'll be able to drive 12 × 35, or 420 miles. The proportion would look like this:

$$\frac{35 \text{ miles}}{1 \text{ gallon}} = \frac{x \text{ gallons}}{12 \text{ gallons}}$$

Cross multiplying

$$x = 420$$

Practice: Ratio and Proportion Problems

1. A map's key shows that 1″ = 35 miles. How many inches apart on the map will two cities be if they are exactly seven miles apart?

2. If eight pounds of apples cost 98¢, at the same rate, how much will twelve pounds of apples cost?

3. If a girl can run m miles in h hours, at the same rate, how fast will she run k miles?

4. In six years a man was able to build fifty-eight violins. Considering that he works at the same speed, how many complete violins can he build in eleven years?

Answers: Ratio and Proportion Problems

1. A map's key shows that 1″ = 35 miles. How many inches apart on the map will two cities be if they are exactly seven miles apart?

First circle what you must find in the problem—*how many inches apart.* Now using the information given in the problem, construct a framework for a proportion and plug into it.

$$\frac{\text{miles}}{\text{inches}} = \frac{\text{miles}}{\text{inches}}$$

$$\frac{35}{1} = \frac{7}{x}$$

Cross multiplying

$$35x = 7$$

$$\frac{35x}{35} = \frac{7}{35}$$

$$x = \tfrac{1}{5}$$

The two cities will be ⅕ of an inch apart.

2. If eight pounds of apples cost 98¢, at the same rate, how much will twelve pounds of apples cost?

First circle what you must find—*how much will twelve pounds of apples cost*. Now using the information given in the problem, set up a framework for a proportion and plug into it.

$$\frac{\text{pounds}}{\text{price}} = \frac{\text{pounds}}{\text{price}}$$

$$\frac{8}{98¢} = \frac{12}{x}$$

Cross multiplying

$$8x = 98(12)$$
$$8x = 1,176$$

$$\frac{8x}{8} = \frac{1,176}{8}$$

$$x = 147¢$$

The answer is 147¢ or $1.47.

3. If a girl can run m miles in h hours, at the same rate, how fast will she run k miles?

First circle what you must find—*how fast will she run k miles* (how many hours). Now using the information given in the problem, set up a framework for a proportion and plug into it.

$$\frac{\text{miles}}{\text{hours}} = \frac{\text{miles}}{\text{hours}}$$

$$\frac{m}{h} = \frac{k}{x}$$

Cross multiplying

$$mx = kh$$

$$\frac{mx}{m} = \frac{kh}{m}$$

$$x = \frac{kh}{m} \text{ or } \frac{hk}{m}$$

4. In six years a man was able to build fifty-eight violins. Considering that he works at the same speed, how many complete violins can he build in eleven years?

First circle what you must find in the problem—*how many complete violins* (note the word *complete*). Now using the information given in the problem, set up a proportion and plug in.

$$\frac{\text{violins}}{\text{years}} = \frac{\text{violins}}{\text{years}}$$

$$\frac{58}{6} = \frac{x}{11}$$

Cross multiplying

$$638 = 6x$$

$$\frac{638}{6} = \frac{6x}{6}$$

$$106.33 \simeq x$$

Therefore he can build 106 complete violins.

Motion

Example:

How long will it take a bus traveling 72 km/hr to go 36 kms? First circle what you're trying to find—*how long will it take* (time). Motion problems are solved by using the equation

$$\text{distance} = \text{rate times time}$$
$$d = rt$$

Therefore, simply plug in: 72 km/hr is the rate (or speed) of the bus, and 36 km is the distance.

$$d = rt$$
$$36 \text{ km} = (72 \text{ km/hr})(t)$$

$$\frac{36}{72} = \frac{72t}{72}$$

$$\frac{1}{2} = t$$

Therefore, it will take one-half hour for the bus to travel 36km at 72 km/hr.

Practice: Motion Problems

1. How many miles will a speedboat travel going 80 mph for 2½ hours?

2. How long will it take a car averaging 55 mph to travel a distance of 594 miles?

3. What is the average speed of a train if it takes three complete days to travel 3,600 miles?

4. A plane flies from New York to Chicago (a distance of 1,600 miles) at 400 mph. Returning from Chicago to New York it flies into a headwind and averages only 320 mph. How many hours total was the plane in the air for the entire trip?

5. Frank rows a boat at 5 mph but travels a distance of only 7 miles in two hours. How fast was the current moving against him?

Answers: Motion Problems

1. How many miles will a speedboat travel going 80 mph for 2½ hours?

First circle what you must find—*how many miles.* Now, using the information given in the problem, plug into the equation.

$$d = rt$$
$$d = (80)(2.5)$$
$$d = 200 \text{ miles}$$

Thus the speedboat will travel 200 miles.

2. How long will it take a car averaging 55 mph to travel a distance of 594 miles?

First circle what you must find—*how long will it take* (time). Now, using the information given in the problem, plug into the equation.

$$d = rt$$
$$594 = 55t$$

$$\frac{594}{55} = \frac{55t}{55}$$

$$10.8 = t$$

Therefore, it will take 10.8 hours.

3. What is the average speed of a train if it takes three complete days to travel 3,600 miles?

First circle what you must find—*average speed.* Now, using the information given in the problem, plug into the equation.

$$d = rt$$
$$3,600 = r(3 \text{ days})$$

Note that three days equals 3 times 24 hours, or 72 hours.

$$3,600 = r(72)$$

$$\frac{3,600}{72} = \frac{r(72)}{72}$$

$$50 = r$$

The average speed of the train is 50 mph.

4. A plane flies from New York to Chicago (a distance of 1,600 miles) at 400 mph. Returning from Chicago to New York it flies into a headwind and averages only 320 mph. How many hours total was the plane in the air for the entire trip?

First circle what you must find—*how many hours was the plane in the air* (time). Note that this is a two-part question, as the time each way will be different. First to find the time going to Chicago, plug into the equation.

$$d = rt$$
$$1,600 = 400t$$

$$\frac{1,600}{400} = \frac{400t}{400}$$

$$4 = t$$

Thus it took four hours to fly from New York to Chicago. Now, returning to New York:

$$d = rt$$
$$1,600 = 320t$$

$$\frac{1,600}{320} = \frac{320t}{320}$$

$$5 = t$$

Since returning took five hours of flying time, the total time in the air was 4 hours + 5 hours = 9 hours.

5. Frank rows a boat at 5 mph but travels a distance of only 7 miles in two hours. How fast was the current moving against him?

First circle what you must find—*how fast was the current moving against him.* Using the information given in the problem, plug into the equation. Note that Frank traveled 7 miles in two hours. Thus

$$d = rt$$
$$7 = r(2)$$
$$3.5 = r$$

Therefore, Frank's actual speed in the water was 3½ mph. If Frank rows at 5 mph, to find the current against him simply subtract.

Frank's speed − actual speed in water
5 mph − 3.5 mph = 1.5 mph

The current was going 1.5 mph against him.

Percent

Examples:

1. If an article that originally sells for $140 is reduced 30%, what is the new selling price?

First circle what you must find in the problem—*the new selling price.* Now simply take 30% of $140.

$$.30 \times 140 = 42$$

Then subtract $42 from the original price of $140.

$$140 - 42 = 98$$

Therefore, the new selling price is $98.

2. In a school of 280, only 35 students attend graduation. What percent of the school population attends graduation?

First circle what you are looking for; then set up the proper ratio.

$$\frac{part}{total} = \frac{students\ attending}{school\ population} = ?\%$$

To determine the percent of the school population that attends graduation

$$\frac{\text{part}}{\text{total}} = \frac{35}{280}$$

Dividing 35 by 280 gives .125, or 12.5%.

3. Thirty students are awarded doctoral degrees at the graduate school, and this number comprises 40% of the total graduate student body. How many graduate students were enrolled?

First circle what you must find in the problem—*how many graduate students*. Now, in order to plug into the percentage equation

$$\frac{\text{is}}{\text{of}} = \%$$

try rephrasing the question into a simple sentence. For example, in this case

30 is 40% of what total?

Note that the 30 sits next to the word *is;* therefore, 30 is the "is" number. 40 is the percent. Notice that *what total* sits next to the word *of*. Therefore, plugging into the equation,

$$\frac{\text{is}}{\text{of}} = \%$$

$$\frac{30}{x} = \frac{40}{100}$$

Cross multiplying $40x = 3,000$

$$\frac{40x}{40} = \frac{3,000}{40}$$

$$x = 75$$

Therefore, the total graduate enrollment was 75 students.

Practice: Percent Problems

1. An astronaut weighing 207 pounds on Earth would weigh 182 pounds on Venus. The weight of the astronaut on Venus would be approximately what percent of his weight on Earth?

2. In a school of three hundred students, sixty do not sign up for after-school sports. What percent of the school signs up for after-school sports?

3. In order to pass an examination, a student must answer exactly nine questions in order to receive the lowest passing grade, a 75%. How many questions are on the examination?

4. Seventy million Americans are registered voters. Sixty percent are registered Democrats, and the rest are either registered Republicans or uncommitted. If ten percent of the total registered voters are uncommitted, how many registered voters are registered Republicans?

5. A United States postage stamp collection was offered for sale at a stamp show for $800 but went unsold. Its owner resubmitted the collection for sale at the next stamp show but dropped his asking price 30%. The collection, however, still did not sell, so the owner offered an additional discount of 25% off the new asking price. What was the final price of the postage stamp collection?

Answers: Percent Problems

1. An astronaut weighing 207 pounds on Earth would weigh 182 pounds on Venus. The weight of the astronaut on Venus would be approximately what percent of his weight on Earth?

On this fairly simple problem type, circle what you must find, and then set up the ratio.

$$\frac{\text{weight on Venus}}{\text{weight on Earth}} = ?\%$$

$$\frac{\text{weight on Venus}}{\text{weight on Earth}} = \frac{182}{207} = 88\%, \text{ or approximately } 90\%$$

2. In a school of three hundred students, sixty do not sign up for after-school sports. What percent of the school signs up for after-school sports?

First circle what you must find in this problem—*what percent . . . signs up*. Now, using the information given in the problem, plug into the equation. Note that since sixty students do *not* sign up for after-school sports, the number that *does* sign up must be the total number of students minus sixty, or $300 - 60 = 240$ students. The problem may now be reworded as *240 students is what percent of 300.*

$$\frac{\text{is}}{\text{of}} = \%$$

$$\frac{240}{300} = \frac{x}{100}$$

Cross multiplying $24,000 = 300x$

$$\frac{24,000}{300} = \frac{300x}{300}$$

$$80 = x$$

Therefore, 80% of the school signs up for after-school sports.

3. In order to pass an examination, a student must answer exactly nine questions in order to receive the lowest passing grade, a 75%. How many questions are on the examination?

First circle what you are looking for—*how many questions are on the examination.* To plug into the equation, this problem may be reworded as *nine questions is 75% of how many questions.* Now plug in.

$$\frac{\text{is}}{\text{of}} = \%$$

$$\frac{9}{x} = \frac{75}{100}$$

Cross multiplying $900 = 75x$

$$\frac{900}{75} = \frac{75x}{75}$$

$$12 = x$$

Therefore, there are twelve questions on the test.

4. Seventy million Americans are registered voters. Sixty percent are registered Democrats, and the rest are either registered Republicans or uncommitted. If ten percent of the total registered voters are uncommitted, how many registered voters are registered Republicans?

First circle what you are asked to find—*how many . . . are registered Republicans.* Note that if 60% are Democrats and 10% are uncommitted, then 30% must be Republicans. Now you may restate the question as *how much is 30% of seventy million voters.* You may now plug into the equation.

$$\frac{is}{of} = \%$$

$$\frac{x}{70 \text{ million}} = \frac{30}{100}$$

Cross multiplying $100x = 2{,}100$ million

$$x = 21 \text{ million}$$

In this problem, since you are finding 30% of seventy million, you could simply multiply: .30 × 70 million = 21 million. Therefore, there are 21 million registered Republicans.

5. A United States postage stamp collection was offered for sale at a stamp show for $800 but went unsold. Its owner resubmitted the collection for sale at the next stamp show but dropped his asking price 30%. The collection, however, still did not sell, so the owner offered an additional discount of 25% off the new asking price. What was the final price of the postage stamp collection?

The original price was $800. Thirty percent drop in price is:

$$30\% \text{ of } 800 = .30 \times 800 = \$240 \text{ off}$$

The new price therefore is $800 − $240 = $560. Since the collection still did not sell (at $560), an additional 25% discount was offered:

$$25\% \text{ of } \$560 = .25 \times 560 = \$140 \text{ off}$$

Therefore the final asking price is $560 − $140 = $420.

Percent Change

Example:

Last year Harold earned $250 a month at his after-school job. This year his after-school earnings have increased to $300 per month. What is the percent increase in his monthly after-school earnings?

First circle what you're looking for—*percent increase.*
Percent change (percent increase, percentage rise, % difference, percent decrease, etc.) is always found by using the equation

$$\text{percent change} = \frac{\text{change}}{\text{starting point}}$$

$$\text{Therefore, percent change} = \frac{\$300 - \$250}{\$250}$$

$$= \frac{\$50}{\$250}$$

$$= \frac{1}{5} = .20 = 20\%$$

The percent increase in Harold's after-school salary was 20%.

Practice: Percent Change Problems

1. Last year Hank's income was $12,000. This year it rose to $15,000. What was the percent increase in Hank's salary?

2. A five-year study showed that the population of Hicksville, New York, fell from 65,000 in 1975 to 48,750 in 1980. What was the percent decrease in population over those five years?

3. Last year's Dow Jones averaged 900. This year's index averaged 1080. What was the percentage rise in the average Dow Jones index over those years?

Answers: Percent Change Problems

1. Last year Hank's income was $12,000. This year it rose to $15,000. What was the percent increase in Hank's salary?

First circle what you must find—*percent increase*. Now, using the information given in the problem, plug into the equation.

$$\text{percent increase} = \frac{\text{change}}{\text{starting point}}$$

$$= \frac{\$15,000 - \$12,000}{\$12,000}$$

$$= \frac{\$3,000}{\$12,000}$$

$$= .25, \text{ or } 25\%$$

The percent increase was 25%.

2. A five-year study showed that the population of Hicksville, New York, fell from 65,000 in 1975 to 48,750 in 1980. What was the percent decrease in population over those five years?

First circle what you must find—*percent decrease*. Now, using the information given in the problem, plug into the equation.

$$\text{percent decrease} = \frac{\text{change}}{\text{starting point}}$$

$$= \frac{65,000 - 48,750}{65,000}$$

$$= \frac{16,250}{65,000}$$

$$= .25, \text{ or } 25\%$$

The percent decrease was 25%. Note that the fact that the study was a five-year study had no bearing on the answer.

3. Last year's Dow Jones averaged 900. This year's index averaged 1080. What was the percentage rise in the average Dow Jones index over those years?

First circle what you must find—*percentage rise*. Now, using the information given in the problem, plug into the equation.

$$\text{percentage rise} = \frac{\text{change}}{\text{starting point}}$$

$$= \frac{1{,}080 - 900}{900}$$

$$= \frac{180}{900}$$

$$= .20, \text{ or } 20\%$$

The percentage rise in the average Dow Jones was 20%.

Number

Examples:

1. One number exceeds another number by 5. If the sum of the two numbers is 39, find the smaller number.

First circle what you are looking for—*the smaller number.* Now let the smaller number equal x. Therefore, the larger number equals x + 5. Now use the problem to set up an equation.

$$\underbrace{\text{If the sum of the two numbers}}\ \underbrace{\text{is 39}} \dots$$

$$x + (x + 5) \qquad\qquad = 39$$

$$2x + 5 = 39$$

$$2x + 5 - 5 = 39 - 5$$

$$2x = 34$$

$$\frac{2x}{2} = \frac{34}{2}$$

$$x = 17$$

Therefore, the smaller number is 17.

2. If one number is twice as large as another number and the smaller number is increased by 8, the result is 4 less than the larger number. What is the larger number?

First circle what you must find—*the larger number.* Now let x denote the smaller number. Therefore the larger number will be 2x, since it is twice as large as x. Now use the problem to set up an equation.

If the smaller number is increased by 8, the result is 4 less than the larger number.

$$x + 8 \qquad = \qquad 2x - 4$$

$$-x + x + 8 = 2x - x - 4$$
$$8 = x - 4$$
$$8 + 4 = x - 4 + 4$$
$$12 = x$$

Thus, the larger number, 2x, is 24.

3. The sum of three consecutive integers is 306. What is the largest integer?

First circle what you must find—*the largest integer.* Let the smallest integer equal x; let the next integer equal x + 1; let the largest integer equal x + 2. Now use the problem to set up an equation.

The sum of three consecutive integers is 306.

$$x + (x + 1) + (x + 2) \qquad = 306$$

$$3x + 3 = 306$$
$$3x + 3 - 3 = 306 - 3$$
$$3x = 303$$

$$\frac{3x}{3} = \frac{303}{3}$$

$$x = 101$$

Therefore, the largest integer, x + 2, will be 101 + 2, or 103.

Practice: Number Problems

1. The sum of three consecutive integers is 51. What is the largest integer?

2. Two integers total 35. One integer is 23 larger than the other. What are the two integers?

3. The difference between ½ of a number and ⅓ of the same number is 8. What is the number?

Answers: Number Problems

1. The sum of three consecutive integers is 51. What is the largest
   integer?

First circle what it is you must find—*the largest integer.* Let the
consecutive integers equal x, x + 1, and x + 2. Now use the problem
to set up an equation.

The sum of three consecutive integers is 51.

$$x + (x + 1) + (x + 2) = 51$$

$$3x + 3 = 51$$
$$3x + 3 - 3 = 51 - 3$$
$$3x = 48$$

$$\frac{3x}{3} = \frac{48}{3}$$

$$x = 16$$

Therefore, the largest integer, x + 2, will be 16 + 2 = 18.

2. Two integers total 35. One integer is 23 larger than the other.
   What are the two integers?

First circle what you must find—*the two integers.* Let the smaller
integer equal x. Therefore, the larger integer equals x + 23. Now use
the problem to set up an equation.

Two integers total 35.

$$x + (x + 23) = 35$$

$$2x + 23 = 35$$
$$2x + 23 - 23 = 35 - 23$$
$$2x = 12$$

$$\frac{2x}{2} = \frac{12}{2}$$

$$x = 6$$

Therefore, one integer, x, is 6 and the other integer, x + 23, is 29.

3. The difference between ½ of a number and ⅓ of the same number
   is 8. What is the number?

First circle what you must find—*the number*. Therefore, let the number equal x. Now use the problem to set up an equation.

The difference between ½ of a number and ⅓ of the same number is 8.

$$(\tfrac{1}{2})x - (\tfrac{1}{3})x = 8$$

$$\frac{x}{2} - \frac{x}{3} = 8$$

Using a common denominator
$$\frac{3x}{6} - \frac{2x}{6} = 8$$

$$\frac{x}{6} = 8$$

$$(6)\frac{x}{6} = (6)8$$

$$x = 48$$

The number is 48.

Age

Examples:

1. Tom and Phil are brothers. Phil is thirty-five years old. Three years ago Phil was four times as old as his brother was then. How old is Tom now?

First circle what it is you must ultimately find—*Tom now*. Therefore, let t be Tom's age now. Then three years ago Tom's age would be t − 3. Four times Tom's age three years ago would be 4(t − 3). Phil's age three years ago would be 35 − 3 = 32. A simple chart may also be helpful.

	NOW	3 YEARS AGO
Phil	35	32
Tom	t	t − 3

Now use the problem to set up an equation.

Three years ago Phil was four times as old as his brother was then.

$$32 = 4 \text{ times} \quad (t - 3)$$

$$\frac{32}{4} = \frac{4(t - 3)}{4}$$

$$8 = t - 3$$
$$8 + 3 = t - 3 + 3$$
$$11 = t$$

Therefore, Tom is now 11.

2. Lisa is 16 years younger than Kathy. If the sum of their ages is 30, how old is Lisa?

First circle what you must find—*Lisa.* Let Lisa equal x. Therefore, Kathy is x + 16. (Note that since Lisa is 16 years *younger* than Kathy, we must *add* 16 years to Lisa to denote Kathy's age.) Now use the problem to set up an equation.

If the sum of their ages is 30 . . .

$$\text{Lisa} + \text{Kathy} = 30$$
$$x + (x + 16) = 30$$
$$2x + 16 = 30$$
$$2x + 16 - 16 = 30 - 16$$
$$2x = 14$$
$$\frac{2x}{2} = \frac{14}{2}$$
$$x = 7$$

Therefore, Lisa is 7 years old.

Practice: Age Problems

1. Clyde is four times as old as John. If the difference between their ages is 39 years, how old is Clyde?

2. Sylvia is twenty years older than Jan. If the sum of their ages is 48 years, how old is Jan?

3. Sheila is three times as old as Kim. The sum of their ages is 24 years. How old is Sheila?

4. In eight years, Joy will be three times as old as she is now. How old is Joy now?

5. Matt is six years older than Hector. In two years Matt will be twice as old as Hector. How old is Hector now?

Answers: Age Problems

1. Clyde is four times as old as John. If the difference between their ages is 39 years, how old is Clyde?

First circle what you must find in this problem—*Clyde*. Let John (the smaller of the two ages) equal x. Therefore, Clyde equals 4x. Now use the problem to set up an equation.

$$\underbrace{\text{If the difference between their ages}}\ \underbrace{\text{is } 39} \ldots$$

$$\text{Clyde} - \text{John} = 39$$

$$4x - x = 39$$

$$3x = 39$$

$$\frac{3x}{3} = \frac{39}{3}$$

$$x = 13$$

Therefore, Clyde, 4x, will be 4(13), or 52 years old.

2. Sylvia is twenty years older than Jan. If the sum of their ages is 48 years, how old is Jan?

First circle what you must find in this problem—*Jan*. Let Jan (the younger of the two ages) equal x. Therefore, Sylvia equals x + 20. Now use the problem to set up an equation.

$$\underbrace{\text{If the sum of their ages}}\ \underbrace{\text{is } 48} \ldots$$

$$\text{Jan} + \text{Sylvia} = 48$$

$$x + (x + 20) = 48$$

$$2x + 20 = 48$$

$$2x + 20 - 20 = 48 - 20$$

$$2x = 28$$

$$\frac{2x}{2} = \frac{28}{2}$$

$$x = 14$$

Therefore, Jan is 14 years old.

3. Sheila is three times as old as Kim. The sum of their ages is 24 years. How old is Sheila?

First circle what you must find in the problem—*Sheila*. Now let Kim (the younger of the two ages) equal x. Therefore, Sheila equals 3x. Now use the problem to set up an equation.

$$\underbrace{\text{The sum of their ages}}\ \underbrace{\text{is}}\ \underbrace{24}\ldots$$

$$\text{Sheila} + \text{Kim} \quad = 24$$

$$3x + x \quad\quad = 24$$

$$4x = 24$$

$$\frac{4x}{4} = \frac{24}{4}$$

$$x = 6$$

Therefore, Sheila, 3x, is 3(6), or 18 years old.

4. In eight years, Joy will be three times as old as she is now. How old is Joy now?

First circle what you must find—*Joy now*. You may wish to set up a chart for this problem.

	NOW	IN 8 YEARS
Joy	x	x + 8

Let Joy's age now equal x. Therefore Joy's age eight years from now will be x + 8. Now use the problem to set up an equation.

$$\underbrace{\text{In eight years, Joy}}\ \underbrace{\text{will be}}\ \underbrace{\text{three}}\ \text{times as}\ \underbrace{\text{old as she is now.}}$$

$$x + 8 \quad\quad = \quad 3 \quad \text{times} \quad\quad x$$

$$x + 8 - x = 3x - x$$

$$8 = 2x$$

$$\frac{8}{2} = \frac{2x}{2}$$

$$4 = x$$

Therefore, Joy's age now is 4 years old.

5. Matt is six years older than Hector. In two years Matt will be twice as old as Hector. How old is Hector now?

First circle what you must find—*Hector now.* Let Hector now equal x. Therefore, Matt now equals x + 6. You may wish to set up a chart.

	NOW	IN 2 YEARS
Hector	x	x + 2
Matt	x + 6	x + 8

Now use the problem to set up an equation.

In two years Matt will be twice as old as Hector.

$$x + 8 \quad\quad = \quad 2 \quad times \quad (x + 2)$$

$$x + 8 = 2x + 4$$
$$x + 8 - x = 2x + 4 - x$$
$$8 = x + 4$$
$$8 - 4 = x + 4 - 4$$
$$4 = x$$

Therefore, Hector now is 4 years old.

Geometry

Examples:

1. The cross-sectional diagram of a downtown office building has dimensions as shown. What is the length along the roof?

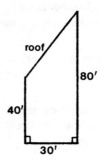

roof

80'

40'

30'

First circle what you must find—length along the roof. Next, mark in the diagram if possible. (If no diagram is given, you may wish to draw one.) By drawing a line which divides the diagram into two parts—a rectangle and a right triangle—the length of the roof can be determined.

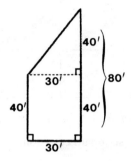

The upper triangular section has a base of 30′ and a height of 40′. Using the Pythagorean theorem for right triangles we get:

$$30^2 + 40^2 = (\text{length along roof})^2$$

$$900 + 1{,}600 = (\text{length along roof})^2$$

$$2{,}500 = (\text{length along roof})^2$$

Taking the square roots of both sides gives

$$50 = \text{length along roof}$$

(You may also recognize the sides of the right triangle as being in a 3–4–5 ratio, which is commonly found in right triangles.)

2. If a rectangle's length is twice its width and its area is 200 square inches, find its length and width.

First circle what you must find—*length and width.* Now let x denote the rectangle's width. Therefore, its length will be twice the width, or 2x. Now set up an equation.

$$\underbrace{\text{Width}}\ \text{times}\ \underbrace{\text{length}}\ \text{equals}\ \underbrace{\text{area.}}$$

$$(x) \qquad (2x) \quad = \quad 200$$

$$2x^2 = 200$$

$$\frac{2x^2}{2} = \frac{200}{2}$$

$$x^2 = 100$$
$$x = 10 \text{ then } 2x = 20$$

Therefore, the width is 10 inches and the length is 20 inches.
(*Note: Drawing diagrams in geometry problems is often helpful*)

Practice: Geometry Problems

1. In a triangle, the smallest angle is 20° less than the largest angle. The third angle is 10° more than the smallest angle. What is the measure of each angle?

2. In the diagram, circle O inscribed in square ABCD has an area of 36π square inches. Find the perimeter of square ABCD.

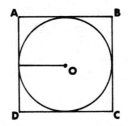

3. A regular cylindrical tank is to be ⅔ filled with water. If its height is 9 feet and its diameter is 12 feet, how many cubic feet of water will be needed?

4. Find the measure of the sides of a rectangle if the length is 5 inches longer than the width and the perimeter is 50 inches.

Answers: Geometry Problems

1. In a triangle, the smallest angle is 20° less than the largest angle. The third angle is 10° more than the smallest angle. What is the measure of each angle?

First circle what you must find—*the measure of each angle.* Now let the largest angle be known as x. Therefore, the smallest angle, since it is 20° less than the largest, will be x − 20°. The third angle is 10°

more than the smallest, or x − 20° + 10°, which equals x − 10°. Now set up the equation.

<u>The sum of the degrees in each angle of a triangle</u> <u>equals</u> <u>180°</u>.

$$x + (x - 20) + (x - 10) \qquad = \qquad 180$$

$$3x - 30 = 180$$
$$3x - 30 + 30 = 180 + 30$$
$$3x = 210$$

$$\frac{3x}{3} = \frac{210}{3}$$

$$x = 70$$

The largest angle is 70°; the smallest angle is 70 − 20, or 50°; the third angle is 70 − 10, or 60°.

2. In the diagram, circle O inscribed in square ABCD has an area of 36π square inches. Find the perimeter of square ABCD.

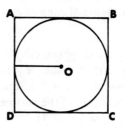

First circle what you must find—perimeter. Then fill in the diagram if possible. Since we know the area of circle O, we may find its radius.

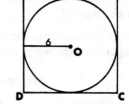

$A = \pi r^2$
$36\pi = \pi r^2$
$36\cancel{\pi} = \cancel{\pi} r^2$
$6 = r$

Now that we know the radius of the circle is 6, we can see that each side will be twice 6, or 12. Thus, its perimeter is 4(12), or 48

3. A regular cylindrical tank is to be ⅔ filled with water. If its height is 9 feet and its diameter is 12 feet, how many cubic feet of water will be needed?

First circle what you must find—cubic feet of water. A diagram is not needed here, but a formula is. The volume of the cylindrical tank is

$$V = \pi r^2 h$$

$$V = \pi(6)^2(9)$$

$$V = \pi 36(9)$$

$$V = 324\pi$$

However, the tank must be filled only 2/3. Therefore,

$$\frac{2}{3}(324\pi) = 216\pi$$

4. Find the measure of the sides of a rectangle if the length is 5 inches longer than the width and the perimeter is 50 inches.

First circle what you must find in the problem—*the measure of the sides*. Now let the width be denoted as x. Therefore, the length will be x + 5. Now set up the equation.

$$\underbrace{2 \text{ widths}}_{2x} \underbrace{\text{plus}}_{+} \underbrace{2 \text{ lengths}}_{2(x + 5)} \underbrace{\text{equal}}_{=} \underbrace{\text{the perimeter.}}_{50}$$

$$2x + 2x + 10 = 50$$

$$4x + 10 = 50$$

$$4x + 10 - 10 = 50 - 10$$

$$4x = 40$$

$$\frac{4x}{4} = \frac{40}{4}$$

$$x = 10$$

Therefore, the width is 10 and the length is x + 5, or 15.

WORD PROBLEMS REVIEW TEST

Questions

1. An automobile averages from 22 to 26 miles per gallon. What is its maximum driving range on 22 gallons?

2. If 20 pounds of grass seed cost $5.00, how much do 30 pounds of gress seed cost?

3. If 16 out of 400 dentists polled recommended Popsodint toothpaste, what percent recommended Popsodint?

4. What is the simple interest on a loan of $5,000 for eight years at an annual interest rate of 14%?

5. If Jim can bake twenty-seven pies in twelve days, how many pies can he bake in twenty days?

6. If p pencils cost k cents, at the same price how much will q pencils cost?

7. How long will it take a train traveling at an average speed of 80 miles per hour to travel a distance of 5,600 miles?

8. Two automobiles, A and B, leave at the same time and travel the same route. Automobile A goes at a rate of 55 miles per hour. Automobile B travels at a rate of 40 miles per hour. How many hours after they begin their trip will automobile A be 60 miles ahead of automobile B?

9. Mrs. Baum won $5,600 on a television quiz show. If she has to pay 20% of her winnings to the Internal Revenue Service, how much of her winnings will she have left?

10. A prized Amazon yellow nape parrot is placed on sale at a bird show for $900. It doesn't sell immediately, so its owner discounts the bird 30%. When the parrot still does not interest any buyers, the owner offers another 20% discount off the new price. What is the final price of the bird?

11. If Arnold's 1985 salary reflects a percent drop of 15% from the previous year, what was his 1985 salary if in 1984 he earned $30,000?

12. Three consecutive odd integers add up to total 33. What is the smallest of the three integers?

13. Judith is exactly 18 years older than Brad. If today the sum of their ages is 52, how old will Brad be in 1 year?

14. One angle of a triangle is twice as big as the smallest angle, and the third angle is three times as big as the smallest angle. What are the three angles of the triangle?

15. The figure shown represents the end of a garage. Find, in feet, the length of one of the equal rafters AB or CB if each extends 12 inches beyond the eaves.

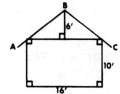

Answers

Page numbers following each answer refer to the review section applicable to this problem type.

1. 572 miles (p. 353)
2. $7.50 (p. 353)
3. 4% (p. 351)
4. $5,600 (p. 351)
5. 45 pies (p. 353)
6. qk/p or kq/p (p. 353)
7. 70 hours (p. 356)
8. 4 hours (p. 356)
9. $4,480 (p. 356)
10. $504 (p. 359)
11. $25,500 (p. 364)
12. 9 (p. 366)
13. 18 years old (p. 369)
14. 30°, 60°, 90° (p. 373)
15. 11 feet (p. 373)

WORD PROBLEMS GLOSSARY OF TERMS

ANNUAL: Once per year.

BALANCE: Beginning balance is the principal in interest problems. Ending balance is the principal plus interest acquired.

BIANNUAL: Twice per year, or every six months.

COMPOUNDED: In interest problems, means the interest is to be added to the principal at specific intervals.

CONSECUTIVE: What comes immediately after. For example, consecutive numbers are 1, 2, 3, 4, etc. Consecutive odd numbers are 1, 3, 5, 7, 9, etc.

DIFFERENCE: The result obtained by subtracting.

DIVIDEND: In interest problems, signifies the amount of interest paid.

EQUATION: A number sentence *with a balance relationship between numbers or symbols.*

EVALUATE: To determine the value or numerical amount.

EXCEEDS: Is more than.

INEQUALITY: A number sentence in which the *relationships between numbers or symbols are not equal.*

INTEGER: Whole number. For example, 6, 109, 0, −52.

PERCENTAGE CHANGE: Expressed also as percent rise, percent difference, percentage increase, % decrease, percent drop, etc. Found by dividing the actual amount of change by the numerical starting point.

PRINCIPAL: The amount of money invested or loaned upon which interest is paid.

PRODUCT: The result obtained by multiplying.

QUARTERLY: Four times per year, or every three months.

QUOTIENT: The result obtained by dividing.

RATE: How fast an object moves (speed).

RATIO: A comparison between items. For example, the ratio of 2 to 3 may be written as 2:3 or $\frac{2}{3}$.

SEMIANNUAL: Twice per year, or every six months.

SIMPLE INTEREST: Compounded at intervals determined by the rate. For interest, annual rate compounds every year. Quarterly rate compounds at each quarter, etc.

SIMPLIFY: To combine several terms into fewer terms.
SPEED: The rate at which an object moves.
SUM: The result obtained by adding.
VALUE: The numerical amount.
VELOCITY: The speed, or rate, at which an object moves.

INTRODUCTION TO GRAPHS

Certain problems will be based on graphs that are included in the test. You will need to be able to read and interpret the data on each graph as well as do some arithmetic with this data.

In working with graphs, spend a few moments to understand the title of each graph, as well as what the numbers on the graph are representing.

- Ask yourself if you can (1) read numbers and facts given on the graph and (2) understand what amount those numbers represent.

- There are three main types of graphs. They are (1) circle graphs, (2) bar graphs, and (3) line graphs.

- The amounts in decimal or fractional form on a cicle graph will always total one whole. The amounts in percentage form on a circle graph will always total 100%.

- The amounts written as money, or in numerical form, on a circle graph will always add up to the total amount being referred to.

- Be sure to thoroughly read the paragraph under a graph if there is one and to interpret a legend if one is included.

- On bar or line graphs it is sometimes helpful to use the edge of your answer sheet as a straightedge. This will help you line up points on the graph with their numerical value on the graph scale. Also, look for trends such as increases, decreases, sudden low points, or sudden high points.

Questions 1, 2, and 3 refer to the following circle graph (pie chart).

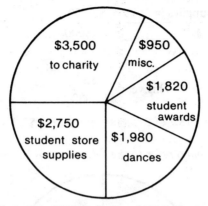

**How the Kettle School Distributed
Its Fund-Raising Earnings in 1979
(1979 fund-raising earnings totaled $11,000)**

1. The amount of money given to charity in 1979 was approximately what percent of the total amount earned?
   (A) 18%   (B) 34%   (C) 45%   (D) 50%   (E) 82%

2. Last year, 1978, the Kettle School spent 40% of its earnings on student store supplies. This percent exceeds the 1979 figure by how much?
   (A) 0%   (B) 10%   (C) 15%   (D) 30%   (E) 85%

3. If the Kettle School spends the same percentage on dances every year, how much will they spend in 1980 if their earnings are $13,000?
   (A) $15,000   (B) $11,000   (C) $4,000   (D) $2,700
   (E) $270

Answers to questions 1, 2, and 3

1. The answer is (B). Set up a simple ratio:

$$\frac{\text{money to charity}}{\text{total}} = \frac{\$3,500}{\$11,000} \cong \frac{1}{3} = 33\tfrac{1}{3}\%$$

2. The answer is (C).

$$\frac{\text{student store supplies in 1979}}{\text{total}} = \frac{\$2,750}{\$11,000} = 25\% \quad 40\% - 25\% = 15\%$$

3. The answer is (D).

$$\text{This year } \frac{\$1,980}{\$11,000} = 18\%$$

So 18% of $15,000 next year = $2,700

Questions 4, 5, and 6 refer to the following circle graph (pie chart).

How John Spends His Monthly Paycheck

4. If John receives $100 per paycheck, how much money does he put in the bank?
   (A) $2   (B) $20   (C) $35   (D) $80   (E) $100

5. John spends more than twice as much on _____ as he does on school supplies.
   (A) car and bike repair   (D) miscellaneous items
   (B) his hobby   (E) cannot be determined
   (C) entertainment

6. The ratio of the amount of money John spends on his hobby to the amount he puts in the bank is
   (A) ¾   (B) ⅔   (C) ⅝   (D) ½   (E) ⅙

Answers to questions 4, 5, and 6

4. The answer is (B). 20% of $100 = .2(100) = $20.00.

5. The answer is (C). School supplies are 10%. The only amount more than twice 10% (or 20%) is 25% (entertainment).

6. The answer is (A). Set up the ratio:

$$\frac{\text{amount to hobby}}{\text{amount to bank}} = \frac{15}{20} = \frac{3}{4}$$

Questions 7, 8, and 9 refer to the following bar graph.

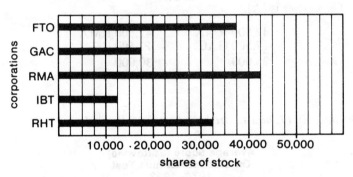

Shares of Stock X Owned by Five Major Corporations

7. The number of shares owned by RHT exceeds the number of shares owned by GAC by
   (A) 10,000   (D) 20,000
   (B) 15,000   (E) 32,500
   (C) 17,500

8. The number of shares of stock owned by IBT is approximately what percent of that owned by FTO?
   (A) 18%   (B) 25%   (C) 33%   (D) 42%   (E) 50%

9. The number of shares of stock owned by RMA exceeds which other corporations' by more than 20,000?
   (A) GAC and IBT   (D) IBT and FTO
   (B) FTO and RHT   (E) IBT and RHT
   (C) GAC and FTO

Answers to questions 7, 8, and 9

7. The answer is (B).

$$\begin{array}{r} 32{,}500 \text{ RHT} \\ - \underline{17{,}500 \text{ GAC}} \\ 15{,}000 \end{array}$$

8. The answer is (C). 12,500 is what percent of 37,500?

$$\frac{12{,}500}{37{,}500} = \frac{1}{3} \simeq 33\%$$

9. The answer is (A).

$$\begin{array}{r} 42{,}500 \text{ RMA} \\ - \underline{17{,}500 \text{ GAC}} \\ 25{,}000 \end{array} \qquad \begin{array}{r} 42{,}500 \text{ RMA} \\ - \underline{12{,}500 \text{ IBT}} \\ 30{,}000 \end{array}$$

Questions 10, 11, and 12 are based on the following graph.

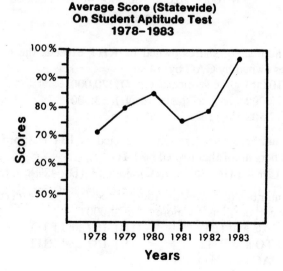

**Average Score (Statewide)
On Student Aptitude Test
1978–1983**

10. Between which two years was the greatest rise in average test scores?

(A) 1978 and 1979 (D) 1981 and 1982
(B) 1979 and 1980 (E) 1982 and 1983
(C) 1980 and 1981

11. In which year was the average score approximately 85%?

(A) 1978 (B) 1979 (C) 1980 (D) 1981 (E) 1982

12. Approximately what was the highest score achieved statewide on the test?

(A) 80% (D) 97%
(B) 85% (E) cannot be determined
(C) 90%

Answers to questions 10, 11, and 12

10. (E) The most efficient way to compute greatest rise is to locate the *steepest* upward slope on the chart. Note that the steepest climb is between 1982 and 1983. Therefore choice (E) indicates the greatest rise in average test scores.

11. (C) According to the graph, the average test score was approximately 85% in 1980 (C). In such cases when you must read the graph for a precise measurement, it may be helpful to use your answer sheet as a straightedge to more accurately compare points with the grid marks along the side.

12. (E) The first thing you should do when confronted with a graph or chart is read its title to understand what the graph is telling you. In this case the graph is relating information about *average scores*. It tells you nothing about the *highest* score achieved. Thus (E) is the correct answer.

PRACTICE GRAPH PROBLEMS

Questions 1 and 2 are based on the following graph.

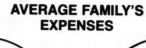

1970
Average Income $12,000

1975
Average Income $16,000

1. How much more money did the average family spend on medical expenses in 1975 than in 1970?

   (A) $500–$600   (D) $800–$900
   (B) $600–$700   (E) $900–$1,000
   (C) $700–$800

2. What was the approximate increase from 1970 to 1975 in the percentage spent on food and drink?

   (A) 4%   (B) 18%   (C) 22%   (D) 40%   (E) 50%

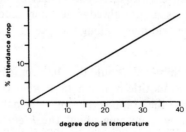

3. According to the graph above, if temperature falls 35 degrees, what percentage will school attendance drop?

   (A) 10   (B) 20   (C) 30   (D) 40   (E) 50

Questions 4 and 5 refer to the following graph.

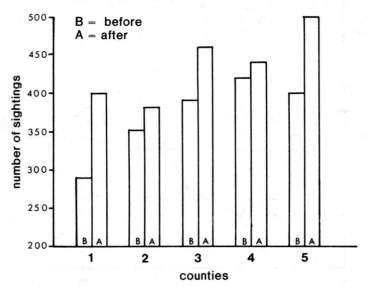

4. According to the graph, which county had the most bear sightings before the conservation measures?
   (A) 1   (B) 2   (C) 3   (D) 4   (E) 5

5. To determine in which county the sightings increased by approximately 25%, one would
   (A) find the county which had 250 more sightings after the conservation measures
   (B) find the county which had 25 more sightings after the conservation measures
   (C) find the county in which the "B" bar is ¼ taller than the "A" bar
   (D) find the county in which the number of sightings indicated by the "A" bar is 250 more than those indicated by the "B" bar
   (E) find the county in which the number of sightings indicated by the "A" bar is ¼ more than those indicated by the "B" bar

Questions 6 and 7 refer to the following graph.

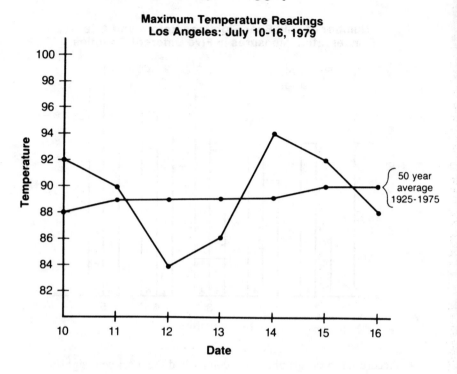

6. Of the seven days shown, about what percent of the days did the maximum temperature exceed the average temperature?
   (A) 3%   (B) 4%   (C) 43%   (D) 57%   (E) 93%

7. Between which two dates shown was the greatest increase in maximum temperature?
   (A) July 11–12   (D) July 14–15
   (B) July 12–13   (E) July 15–16
   (C) July 13–14

ANSWERS: GRAPH PROBLEMS

1. (C) In 1970, 10% of $12,000, or $1,200, was spent on medical. In 1975, 12% of $16,000, or $1,920, was spent on medical. Thus, there was an increase of $720.

2. (A) There was an increase from 18% to 22%, or 4%.

3. (B) Note that on the graph a 35 degree drop in temperature on the line correlates with a 20% attendance drop (the fourth slash up the graph).

4. (D) According to the graph, the tallest "B" (before) bar is county 4.

5. (E) To determine a 25% increase, find the county in which the increase in number of sightings equals ¼ of the original number of sightings.

$$\text{percent change} = \frac{\text{increase or change}}{\text{original number}}$$

$$25\% \ (\text{or } \tfrac{1}{4}) = \frac{A - B}{B}$$

Note that merely approximating the size of the bars will not work, as the bars do not begin at 0 (they begin at 200).

6. (D) There were 4 days (July 10, 11, 14, and 15) on which the maximum temperature exceeded the average; thus, 4/7 is approximately 57%.

7. (C) The maximum temperature rose from 86° to 94° from July 13 to July 14. This was the greatest increase.

Part III: Strategies

This section is designed to introduce you to some important test-taking strategies. These strategies will help you eliminate common mistakes and give you additional methods for attacking the more difficult problems.

Your most effective plan of attack to best prepare for the ELM test is to first ensure that you have a firm grasp of the "basics," which will enable you to answer the easy or average-in-difficulty problems correctly. Only then should you move on to the more difficult problems.

TWO SUCCESSFUL OVERALL APPROACHES

I. The "Plus-Minus" System

Many who take the ELM test don't get their best possible score because they spend too much time on difficult questions, leaving insufficient time to answer the easy questions. Don't let this happen to you. Since every question is worth the same amount, use the following system.

1. Answer easy questions immediately.

2. When you come to a question that seems "impossible" to answer, mark a large minus sign ("−") next to it on your test booklet.

3. Then mark a "guess" answer on your answer sheet and move on to the next question.

4. If you start a problem and realize that it is becoming too time consuming, or if you get stuck within a problem, mark a large plus sign ("+") next to that question in your test booklet and register a guess answer on your answer sheet. Then move on to the next question.

Since your time allotment is just a little more than one minute per question, a "time-consuming" question is a question that you estimate will take you more than several minutes to answer. But don't waste time deciding whether a question is a "+" or a "−." Act quickly, as the intent of this strategy is, in fact, to save you valuable time.

After working all the easy questions, your booklet should look something like this:

$$
\begin{aligned}
&1.\\
+&2.\\
&3.\\
-&4.\\
+&5.\\
&\text{etc.}
\end{aligned}
$$

5. After working all the problems you can do immediately (the easy ones), go back and work your "+" problems. Change your "guess" on your answer sheet, if necessary, for those problems you are able to work.

6. If you finish working your "+" problems and still have time left, you can either

(A) Attempt those "−" questions—the ones that you considered "impossible." Sometimes a problem later in that section will "trigger" your memory and you'll be able to go back and answer one of the earlier "impossible" problems.

or

(B) don't bother with those "impossible" questions. Rather, spend your time reviewing your work to be sure you didn't make any careless mistakes on the questions you thought were easy to answer.

REMEMBER: You do not have to erase the pluses and minuses you made on your *question booklet*. And be sure to fill in all your answer spaces—if necessary, with a guess. As there is no penalty for wrong answers, it makes no sense to leave an answer space blank.

II. The Elimination Strategy

Take advantage of being allowed to mark in your testing booklet. As you eliminate an answer choice from consideration, make sure to *mark it out in your question booklet* as follows:

(A)
?(B)
(C)
(D)
?(E)

Notice that some choices are marked with question marks, signifying that they may be possible answers. This technique will help you avoid reconsidering those choices you have already eliminated. It will also help you narrow down your possible answers.

Again, these marks you make on your testing booklet do not need to be erased.

MATHEMATICAL ABILITY STRATEGIES

Mathematical ability problems are a standard question type appearing on many different examinations. Typically you must answer a question or solve an equation using the information given in the problem and your knowledge of mathematics. Complex computation is usually not required. Five answer choices are given and you must choose the correct answer from the five. Some problems will require you to derive information from graphs and charts.

Suggested Approach with Examples

Here are a number of approaches that can be helpful in attacking many types of mathematics problems. Of course, these strategies will not work on *all* problems, but if you become familiar with them, you'll find they'll be helpful in answering quite a few questions.

Mark Key Words

Circling and/or underlining key words in each question is an effective test-taking technique. Many times you may be misled because you may overlook a key word in a problem. By circling or underlining these key words, you'll help yourself focus on what you are being asked to find. Remember, you are allowed to mark and write on your testing booklet. Take advantage of this opportunity.

Examples:

1. In the following number, which digit is in the ten-thousandths place?

$$56,874.12398$$

(A) 5   (B) 7   (C) 2   (D) 3   (E) 9

The key word here is *ten-thousandths*. By circling it you will be paying closer attention to it. This is the kind of question which, under time pressure and testing pressure, may often be misread. It may be easily misread as *ten-thousands* place. Your circling the important words will minimize the possibility of misreading. Your completed question may look like this after you mark the important words or terms.

1. Which(digit)is in the(ten-thousandths)place?

$$56,874.123\textcircled{9}8$$

   (A) 5   (B) 7   (C) 2   (D) 3   (E) 9

2. If six yards of ribbon cost $3.96, what is the price per foot?
   (A) $.22   (B) $.66   (C) $1.32   (D) $1.96   (E) $3.96

The key word here is *foot*. Dividing $3.96 by six will tell you only the price per *yard*. Notice that $.66 is one of the choices, (B). You must still divide by three (since there are three feet per yard) to find the cost per foot. $.66 ÷ 3 = $.22, which is choice (A). Therefore, it would be very helpful to circle the words *price per foot* in the problem.

3. If $3x + 1 = 16$, what is the value of $x - 4$?
   (A) -1 (B) 1   (C) 5   (D) 16   (E) 19

The key here is find the value of $x - 4$. Therefore, circle $x - 4$. Note that solving the original equation will tell only the value of x.

$$3x + 1 = 16$$
$$3x = 15$$
$$x = 5$$

Here again notice that 5 is one of the choices, (C). But the question asks for the value of $x - 4$, not just x. To continue, replace x with 5 and solve.

$$x - 4 =$$
$$5 - 4 = 1$$

The correct answer choice is (B).

4. Together a hat and coat cost $125. The coat costs $25 more than the hat. What is the cost of the coat?
   (A) $25   (B) $50   (C) $75   (D) $100   (E) $125

The key words here are *cost of the coat,* so circle those words. If we solve this algebraically

$$x = \text{hat}$$
$$x + 25 = \text{coat (cost \$25 more than the hat)}$$

Together they cost \$125.

$$(x + 25) + x = 125$$
$$2x + 25 = 125$$
$$2x = 100$$
$$x = 50$$

But this is the cost of the *hat.* Notice that \$50 is one of the answer choices, (B). Since x = 50, then x + 25 = 75. Therefore, the coat costs \$75, which is choice (C). *Always answer the question that is being asked.* Circling the key word or words will help you do that.

Pull out Information

Pulling information out of the wording of a word problem can make the problem more workable for you. Pull out the given facts and identify which of those facts will help you to work the problem. Not all facts will always be needed to work out the problem.

Examples:

1. Bill is ten years older than his sister. If Bill was twenty-five years of age in 1983, in what year could he have been born?
    (A) 1948   (B) 1953   (C) 1958   (D) 1963   (E) 1968

The key words here are *in what year* and *could he have been born.* Thus the solution is simple: 1983 − 25 = 1958, answer (C). Notice that you pulled out the information *twenty-five years of age* and *in 1983.* The fact about Bill's age in comparison to his sister's age was not needed, however, and was not pulled out.

2. Bob is twenty years old. He works for his father for ¾ of the year, and he works for his brother for the rest of the year. What is the ratio of the time Bob spends working for his brother to the time he spends working for his father per year?
    (A) ¼   (B) ⅓   (C) ¾   (D) ⁴⁄₃   (E) ⁴⁄₁

The key word *rest* points to the answer:

$1 - \frac{3}{4} =$

$\frac{4}{4} - \frac{3}{4} = \frac{1}{4}$ (the part of the year Bob works for his brother)

Also, a key is the way in which the ratio is to be written. The problem becomes that of finding the ratio of $\frac{1}{4}$ to $\frac{3}{4}$.

$$\frac{\frac{1}{4}}{\frac{3}{4}} = \frac{1}{4} \div \frac{3}{4} = \frac{1}{\cancel{4}_1} \times \frac{\cancel{4}^1}{3} = \frac{1}{3}$$

Therefore the answer is choice (B). Note that here Bob's age is not needed to solve the problem.

3. If gasohol is $\frac{2}{9}$ alcohol by volume and $\frac{7}{9}$ gasoline by volume, what is the ratio of the volume of gasoline to the volume of alcohol?
    (A) $\frac{2}{9}$ (B) $\frac{2}{7}$ (C) $\frac{7}{9}$ (D) $\frac{7}{2}$ (E) $\frac{9}{2}$

The first bit of information that you should pull out should be what you are looking for, *ratio of the volume of gasoline to the volume of alcohol*. Rewrite it as G:A and then into its mathematical working form G/A. Next you should pull out the volumes of each. G = $\frac{7}{9}$ and A = $\frac{2}{9}$ Now the answer can be easily figured by inspection or substitution. Using

$$\frac{\left(\frac{7}{9}\right)}{\left(\frac{2}{9}\right)} = ?$$

which is the same as $\frac{7}{9} \div \frac{2}{9} = ?$

invert the second fraction and multiply to get

$$\frac{7}{9} \times \frac{9}{2} = ?$$

The answer is $\frac{7}{2}$ (the ratio of gasoline to alcohol). The correct answer is (D). When pulling out information, actually write out the numbers and/or letters to the side of the problem, putting them into some form and eliminating some of the wording.

Plug in Numbers

When a problem involving variables (unknowns, or letters) seems difficult and confusing, simply *replace those variables with numbers*. Simple numbers will make the arithmetic easier for you to do.

Usually problems using numbers are easier to understand. Be sure to make logical substitutions. Use a positive number, a negative number, or zero when applicable to get the full picture.

Examples:

1. If x is a positive integer in the equation $12x = q$, then q must be
   - (A) a positive even integer
   - (B) a negative even integer
   - (C) zero
   - (D) a positive odd integer
   - (E) a negative odd integer

At first glance, this problem appears quite complex. But let's plug in some numbers and see what happens. For instance, first plug in 1 (the simplest positive integer) for x.

$$12x = q$$
$$12(1) = q$$
$$12 = q$$

Now try 2.

$$12x = q$$
$$12(2) = q$$
$$24 = q$$

Try it again. No matter what positive integer is plugged in for x, q will always be positive and even. Therefore, the answer is (A).

2. If a, b, and c are all positive integers greater than 1 such that $a < b < c$, which of the following is the largest quantity

   - (A) $a(b + c)$
   - (B) $ab + c$
   - (C) $ac + b$
   - (D) they are all equal
   - (E) cannot be determined

Substitute 2, 3, and 4 for a, b, and c, respectively.

$a(b + c) =$	$ab + c =$	$ac + b =$
$2(3 + 4) =$	$2(3) + 4 =$	$2(4) + 3 =$
$2(7) = 14$	$6 + 4 = 10$	$8 + 3 = 11$

Since 2, 3, and 4 meet the conditions stated in the problem and choice (A) produces the largest numerical value, it will consistently be the largest quantity. Therefore, $a(b + c)$ is the correct answer, (A).

Remember to substitute simple numbers, since *you* have to do the work.

3. If $x > 1$, which of the following decreases as x decreases?

$$\text{I.} \quad x + x^2$$

$$\text{II.} \quad 2x^2 - x$$

$$\text{III.} \quad \frac{1}{x + 1}$$

    (A) I   (B) II   (C) III   (D) I and II   (E) II and III

This problem is most easily solved by taking each situation and substituting simple numbers. However, in the first situation, I, $x + x^2$, you should recognize that this expression will decrease as x decreases. Trying $x = 2$, gives $2 + (2)^2$, which equals 6. Now trying $x = 3$, gives $3 + (3)^2 = 12$. Notice that choices (B), (C), and (E) are already eliminated because they do not contain I. You should also realize that now you only need to try the values in II; since III is not paired with I as a possible choice, III cannot be one of the answers. Trying $x = 2$ in the expression $2x^2 - x$, gives $2(2)^2 - 2$, or $2(4) - 2$, which leaves 6. Now trying $x = 3$ gives $2(3)^2 - 3$, or $2(9) - 3 = 18 - 3 = 15$. This expression also decreases as x decreases. Therefore the correct answer is choice (D). Once again notice that III was not even attempted, because it was not one of the possible choices.

Work from the Answers

At times, the solution to a problem will be obvious to you. At other times it may be helpful to *work from the answers*. This technique is even more efficient when some of the answer choices are easily eliminated.

Examples:

1. Approximate $\sqrt{1,596}$
    (A) 10   (B) 20   (C) 30   (D) 40   (E) 50

Without the answer choices this would be a very difficult problem, requiring knowledge of a special procedure to calculate square roots. With the answer choices, however, the problem is easily solvable.

How? By working up from the answer choices. Since $\sqrt{1,596}$ means *what number times itself equals 1,596,* you can take any answer choice and multiply it by itself. As soon as you find the answer choice that when multiplied by itself approximates 1,596, you've got the correct answer.

But here's another strategy. Start to work up from the *middle answer choice*. Why? Watch.

1. Approximate $\sqrt{1,596}$
   (A) 10   (B) 20   (C) 30   (D) 40   (E) 50

First try choice (C), 30. Multiplying it by itself, you get 30 × 30 = 900. Since 900 is too small (you are looking for approximately 1,596), you may eliminate choice (C). But notice that you may *also eliminate choices (A) and (B),* since they are also too small.

Working up from the middle choice will often allow you to eliminate more than one answer choice, since the answers are usually in increasing or decreasing order. This should save you valuable time.

2. If $(x/4) + 2 = 22$, find x.
   (A) 40   (B) 80   (C) 100   (D) 120   (E) 160

If you cannot solve this algebraically, you may use the *work up from your choices* strategy. But start with (C), 100. What if x = 100?

$$(x/4) + 2 = 22$$
$$(100/4) + 2 \overset{?}{=} 22$$
$$25 + 2 \overset{?}{=} 22$$
$$27 \neq 22$$

Note that since 27 is too large, choices (D) and (E) will also be too large. Therefore, try (A). If (A) is too small, then you know the answer is (B). If (A) works, the answer is (A).

$$(x/4) + 2 = 22$$
$$(40/4) + 2 \overset{?}{=} 22$$
$$10 + 2 \overset{?}{=} 22$$
$$12 \neq 22$$

Since (A) is too small, the answer must be (B).

Approximate

If a problem involves calculations with numbers that seem tedious and time consuming, scan your answer choices to see if you can *round off or approximate* those numbers. If so, replace those numbers with numbers easier to work with. Find the answer choice closest to your approximated answer.

Examples:

1. The value for $(.889 \times 55)/9.97$ to the nearest tenth is
    (A) .5   (B) 4.63   (C) 4.9   (D) 17.7   (E) 49.1

Before starting any computations, take a glance at the answers to see how far apart they are. Notice that the only close answers are (B) and (C), but (B) is not a possible choice, since it is to the nearest hundredth, not tenth. Now, making some quick approximations, $.889 \approx 1$ and $9.97 \approx 10$, leaving the problem in this form.

$$\frac{1 \times 55}{10} = \frac{55}{10} = 5.5$$

The closest answer is (C); therefore it is the correct answer. Notice that choices (A) and (E) are not reasonable.

2. The value of $\sqrt{\dfrac{9,986}{194}}$ is approximately

    (A) 7   (B) 18   (C) 35   (D) 40   (E) 50

Round off both numbers to the hundreds place. The problem then becomes

$$\sqrt{\frac{10,000}{200}}$$

This is much easier to work. By dividing, the problem now becomes

$$\sqrt{50} = \text{slightly more than 7}$$

The closest answer choice is choice (A).

Make Comparisons

At times, questions will require you to *compare* the sizes of several decimals, or of several fractions. If decimals are being compared, make sure that the numbers being compared have the same number of digits. (Remember: Zeros to the far right of a decimal point can be inserted or eliminated without changing the value of the number.)

Examples:

1. Put these in order from smallest to largest: .6, .16, .66⅔, .58
   (A) .6, .16, .66⅔, .58   (D) .66⅔, .6, .58, .16
   (B) .58, .16, .6, .66⅔   (E) .58, .6, .66⅔, .16
   (C) .16, .58, .6, .66⅔

Rewrite .6 as .60; therefore all of the decimals now have the same number of digits: .60, .16, .66⅔, .58. Treating these as though the decimal point were not there (this can be done only when all the numbers have the same number of digits to the right of the decimal), the order is as follows: .16, .58, .60, .66⅔. The correct answer is (C). Remember to circle *smallest to largest* in the question.

2. Put these in order from smallest to largest: 75%, ⅔, ⅝
   (A) ⅔, 75%, ⅝   (D) 75%, ⅝, ⅔
   (B) ⅔, ⅝, 75%   (E) 75%, ⅔, ⅝
   (C) ⅝, ⅔, 75%

Using common denominators, we find

$$\frac{2}{3} = \frac{16}{24}$$
$$\frac{5}{8} = \frac{15}{24}$$
$$75\% = \frac{3}{4} = \frac{18}{24}$$

Therefore the order becomes ⅝, ⅔, 75%. Using decimal equivalents

$$\frac{5}{8} = .625$$
$$\frac{2}{3} = .666\frac{2}{3}$$
$$75\% = .750$$

The order again is ⅝, ⅔, 75%. The answer is (C).

Mark Diagrams

When a figure is included with the problem, *mark the given facts on the diagram.* This will help you visualize all the facts that have been given.

Examples:

1. If each square in the figure
   has a side of length 3,
   what is the perimeter?
   (A) 12
   (B) 14
   (C) 21
   (D) 30
   (E) 36

Mark the known facts.

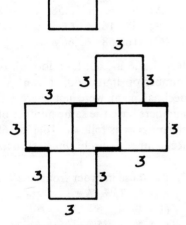

We now have a calculation for the perimeter: 30 *plus* the darkened parts. Now look carefully at the top two darkened parts. They will add up to 3. (Notice how the top square may slide over to illustrate that fact.)

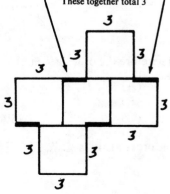

These together total 3

The same is true for the bottom darkened parts. They will add to 3.

Thus, the total perimeter is
30 + 6 = 36, choice (E).

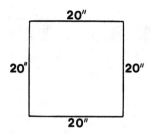

2. What is the maximum number of pieces of birthday cake of size 4″ × 4″ that can be cut from the cake above?

(A) 5   (B) 10   (C) 16   (D) 20   (E) 25

Marking in as follows makes this a fairly simple problem.

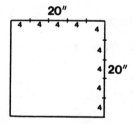

Notice that five pieces of cake will fit along each side; therefore 5 × 5 = 25. The correct answer is (E). Finding the total area of the cake and dividing it by the area of one of the 4 × 4 pieces would have also given you the correct answer, but beware of this method because it may not work if the pieces do not fit evenly into the original area.

3. The perimeter of the isosceles triangle is 44″. The two equal sides are each five times as long as the third side. What are the lengths of each side?

(A) 21, 21, 21
(B) 6, 6, 18
(C) 18, 21, 3
(D) 20, 20, 4
(E) 4, 4, 36

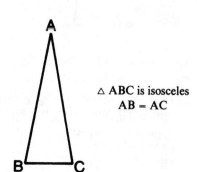

△ ABC is isosceles
AB = AC

Mark the equal sides on the diagram.

AB and AC are each five times as long as BC.

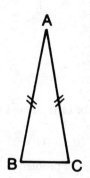

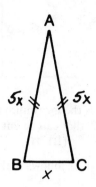

The equation for perimeter is

$$5x + 5x + x = 44$$
$$11x = 44$$
$$x = 4$$

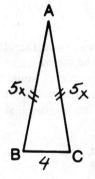

becomes

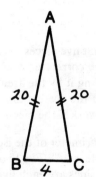

The answer is (D). Note: This problem could have been solved by working from the answers given.

4. In the following triangle, CD is an angle bisector, angle ACD is 30°, and angle ABC is a right angle. What is the measurement of angle x in degrees?
   (A) 30°   (D) 75°
   (B) 45°   (E) 180°
   (C) 60°

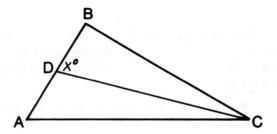

You should have read the problem and marked as follows:

In the triangle above, CD is an angle bisector (STOP AND MARK IN THE DRAWING), angle ACD is 30° (STOP AND MARK IN THE DRAW-ING), and angle ABC is a right angle (STOP AND MARK IN THE DRAWING). What is the measurement of angle x in degrees? (STOP AND MARK IN OR CIRCLE WHAT YOU ARE LOOKING FOR IN THE DRAW-ING.)

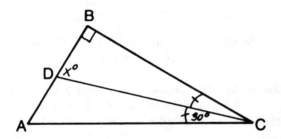

Now with the drawing marked in, it is evident that, since angle ACD is 30°, then angle BCD is also 30° because they are formed by an angle bisector (divides an angle into two equal parts). Since angle ADC is 90° (right angle) and BCD is 30°, then angle x is 60° because there are 180° in a triangle, $180 - (90 + 30) = 60$. The correct answer is (C). ALWAYS MARK IN DIAGRAMS AS YOU READ DESCRIP-TIONS AND INFORMATION ABOUT THEM. THIS INCLUDES WHAT YOU ARE LOOKING FOR.

Draw Diagrams

Drawing diagrams to meet the conditions set by the word problem can often make the problem easier for you to work. Being able to "see" the facts is more helpful than just reading the words.

Examples:

1. If all sides of a square are halved, the area of that square
   (A) is halved
   (B) is divided by 3
   (C) is divided by 4
   (D) remains the same
   (E) not enough information to tell

One way to solve this problem is to draw a square and then halve all its sides. Then compare the two areas.

Your first diagram

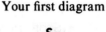
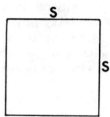

Halving every side

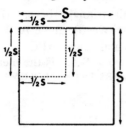

Notice that the total area of the new square will now be one-fourth the original square. The correct answer is (C).

2. A hiking team begins at camp and hikes 5 miles north, then 8 miles west, then 6 miles south, then 9 miles east. In what direction must they now travel in order to return to camp?
   (A) north
   (B) northeast
   (C) northwest
   (D) west
   (E) They already are at camp.

For this question, your diagram would look something like this:

Thus, they must travel northwest (C) to return to camp. Note that in this case it is important to draw your diagram very accurately.

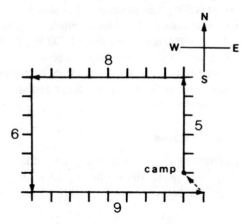

Multiple-Multiple-Choice

Some mathematical ability questions use a *"multiple-multiple-choice"* format. At first glance, these appear more confusing and more difficult than normal five-choice (A, B, C, D, E) multiple-choice problems. Actually, once you understand "multiple-multiple-choice" problem types and technique, they are often easier than a comparable standard multiple-choice question.

Example:

If X is a positive integer, then which of the following *must* be true?

  I. $X > 0$
 II. $X = 0$
III. $X < 1$

(A) I only (B) II only (C) III only (D) I and II (E) I and III

Since X is a positive integer, it must be a counting number. Note that possible values of X could be 1, or 2, or 3, or 4, and so on. Therefore, statement I, $X > 0$, is always true. So next to I on your question booklet place a *T* for *true*.

$$T \quad \text{I. } X > 0$$
$$\text{II. } X = 0$$
$$\text{III. } X < 1$$

Now realize that the correct final answer choice (either A, B, C, D, or E) *must* contain *true statement I*. This eliminates (B) and (C) as possible correct answer choices, as they do *not* contain true statement I. You should cross out (B) and (C) on your question booklet.

Statement II is *incorrect*. If X is positive, X cannot equal zero. Thus, next to II, you should place an *F* for false.

$$T \quad \text{I. } X > 0$$
$$F \quad \text{II. } X = 0$$
$$\text{III. } X < 1$$

Knowing that II is false allows you to eliminate any answer choices that contain *false statement II*. Therefore, you should cross out (D), as it contains a false statement II. Only (A) and (E) are left as possible correct answers. Finally you realize that statement III is also false, as X must be 1 or greater. So you place an F next to III, thus eliminating choice (E) and leaving (A), I only.

This technique often saves some precious time and allows you to take a better educated guess should you not be able to complete all parts (I, II, III, IV, etc.) of a multiple-multiple-choice question.

Tips for Working Math Problems

1. Read the question carefully, circling what you are looking for.
2. Pull out important information.
3. Draw, sketch, or mark in diagrams.
4. If you know a simple method, or formula, work the problem out as simply and quickly as possible.
5. If you do not know a simple method, or formula,
   (a) try eliminating some unreasonable choices.
   (b) work from the answers or substitute in numbers if appropriate.
   (c) try approximating to clarify thinking and simplify work.
6. Always make sure that your answer is reasonable.